Otto Christian Näf

A conversational grammar of the German language; with comprehensive reference-pages

For use in translation and composition

Otto Christian Näf

A conversational grammar of the German language; with comprehensive reference-pages
For use in translation and composition

ISBN/EAN: 9783337085643

Printed in Europe, USA, Canada, Australia, Japan

Cover: Foto ©Paul-Georg Meister /pixelio.de

More available books at **www.hansebooks.com**

A Conversational Grammar

of the

German Language

WITH COMPREHENSIVE

REFERENCE-PAGES

FOR USE IN TRANSLATION AND COMPOSITION

AND

NOTES ON THE HISTORY AND ETYMOLOGY OF GERMAN

BY

OTTO CHRISTIAN NAF

B.A. LOND. UNIV.

LATE GERMAN MASTER AT GIGGLESWICK SCHOOL

RIVINGTONS

WATERLOO PLACE, LONDON

MDCCCLXXXVII

PREFACE

During a long experience in teaching German in English schools and preparing pupils for various Examinations, I have often felt the want of a sufficiently complete Grammar *of small bulk*, and especially of comprehensive Reference-Pages, for constant use in Translation and Composition. I have here tried to supply this want, and I hope this effort will meet with some favour, and be granted a trial.

I wish to draw special attention to the "*Reference-Pages*" interspersed throughout the book. I have used them with success for some years in my own classes, and have found them much appreciated by the more thoughtful students. They ought first to be gone through in portions in the Grammar lessons, and the Examples attached to each portion learnt, and the Exercises written out and learnt after correction by the teacher. Then, in the Translation and Composition lessons, these Reference-Pages should be constantly by the side of the student, to be again and again referred to until thoroughly familiar; for it is only thus that they will become of real advantage.

The whole Grammar will be found divided into *Six Terms*, every one complete in itself. Each of the first four has appended to it *Additional Exercises*, to be written out when revising the work of the Term, and a *Dictionary* of the words to be used in the Exercises for writing during the Term, besides a page of *Conversational Sentences*, and a *Poem* or two for Repetition. I have found it a good plan to set a few sentences, words, and verses for every lesson, to be heard by the teacher *viva voce*, before beginning the regular work of the lesson. The same sentences or words, repeated over and over again, must at last become fixed in the memory, and accustom the pupil to the sound and genius of a language.

In the Exercises for writing during the first two Terms, I have purposely confined myself to very few words, so as not to hamper the ready understanding of the grammatical rules and their application, and also because it is important that some common words, though they may be few, should be firmly fixed in the memory during the first few months of learning a new language.

After the Second Term an easy translation-book should be at once begun, and every new word should be shortly parsed in writing. I have, at the commencement of the Third Term, inserted a page containing a short easy piece for translation, and shown how the words ought to be parsed. The number of words to be parsed will of course very rapidly decrease. It is now that the Reference-Pages will become specially useful, and indeed necessary, and they should always be at hand.

A German Dictionary may at this stage be put with advantage into the hands of the student.

The *First Three Terms* treat of the Simple Principal Sentence, and the rules as to the sequence of words in it will be found to go hand in hand with the treatment of the Parts of Speech *per se*.

The *Fourth Term* treats of the Accessory Sentences, and finally the Compound Sentence, with some hints on the Complex Sentence.

The *Fifth Term* introduces the student, now practically acquainted with all rules in Accidence and Syntax, to the idiomatic peculiarities of the various parts of speech, and many differences between the English and German idioms.

The *Sixth Term* contains hints on the Formation of Words, the meaning of Prefixes and Affixes, and the Etymology of many German words; for the more advanced examinations now-a-days require some little knowledge of all these.

This little work does not claim to be a complete guide to all the intricacies of the German language; indeed, any one attempting to write a Grammar of a rich living language must soon become convinced that he has undertaken a task practically interminable, and necessarily incomplete; for though he pile rule upon rule, and *Nota bene* upon *Nota bene*, until the fear arises that the very multiplicity of instructions and hints may hopelessly confuse and discourage the average student, yet there will loom behind, in the recesses of a living, and therefore progressing, language, whole hosts of idiomatic uses of words or phrases which nothing but a long life in the country itself can teach. The following pages are, then, only compiled with the modest aim of introducing the pupil, in a rational manner, to the broad facts of the German idiom, and thus to lay a safe foundation, upon which an ultimate sound knowledge may be built up by means of diligent study of the German authors, and, if possible, actual intercourse with the people itself.

I shall be thankful for any friendly suggestions as to shortcomings in this work, and I hope that, combining, as it does, the synthetical with the analytical methods of teaching living languages, it may be found to supply a want which I, in company with many of my colleagues, have long felt, namely, that of a handy, yet tolerably complete, companion to the study of German literature and the composition of German themes or letters.

OTTO C. NÄF.

LONDON, *December* 1886.

CONTENTS

REFERENCE-PAGE **A**. The German Alphabet—German Handwriting, . . . xiii

FIRST TERM.

REFERENCE-PAGE **B**. On Pronunciation, ... 2
Lessons 1 and 2. Introductory Rules (1-7); **Present Indicative**; **Imperfect Indicative** of Regular Verbs, ... 3
REFERENCE-PAGE **C**. "Definite" and "Indefinite Article groups" (with Exercises), . 5
Lessons 3, 4, 5, and 6. Introductory Rules continued (8-20); Tenses of Verbs and Auxiliaries continued, ... 7
Additional Exercises on the First Term's Grammar, ... 11
Dictionary of Words, to be used for the Exercises in the First and Second Terms, . . 12
Conversational Sentences, to be learnt during the First Term, . . . 13
Poem ("Lurline"), to be learnt by heart during the First Term, . . . 14

SECOND TERM.

Lesson 7. General Rules continued (21, 22); **Imperative**, . . . 16
General Scheme of the Declensions, and Formation of Plural, of the Noun, . 17
REFERENCE-PAGE **D**. Detailed Formation of **Plural of Nouns** (with Exercises), 18
Lesson 8. General Rules continued (23-26); **Present Subjunctive**, . . 21
REFERENCE-PAGE **E**. Detailed Declension of Nouns (with Exercises), . 22
Lesson 9. **General Rules** continued (27-29); Imperfect Subjunctive, . . 24
REFERENCE-PAGE **F**. Rules for recognising the Gender of Nouns (with **Exercises**), . 25
Lesson 10. General Rules continued (30-32); Compound Tenses; Conditional, . 27
REFERENCE-PAGE **G**. On the Declension of the Adjective (with Exercises), . 28
Lesson 11. General Rules continued (33-36); Compound Tenses, . . 31
Lesson 12. General Rules continued (37-40); Compound Tenses (continued), . 32
Additional Exercises on the Second Term's Grammar, . . . 33
REFERENCE-PAGE **H**. **Scheme** of Conjugation of Regular Verbs (*to say*), . 34
REFERENCE-PAGE **I**. **Scheme** of Conjugation of: *to have, to be, to become*, . 35
Conversational Sentences to **be** learnt during the Second **Term**, . . 36
Poems (Two), to be learnt by heart during the Second Term, . . 37
REFERENCE-PAGE **J**. Scheme of Sequence of Words in a Primary Sentence, . 38

THIRD TERM.

Example of Parsing, ... 40
REFERENCE-PAGE **K**. The Auxiliaries of Mood (with Exercises), . . 41
    ,,   ,,   **L**. Hints on recognising Regular Verbs; Notes on Auxiliary, 44
    ,,   ,,   **M**. General hints on the Irregular Verb (Exercises), . 46
    ,,   ,,   **N**. Alphabetical List of Irregular Verbs, . . 49
    ,,   ,,   **O**. On the Prepositions (with Exercises), . . 52
    ,,   ,,   **P**. Separable and Inseparable Verbs (with Exercises), 54
    ,,   ,,   **Q**. Personal Pronouns; Reflexive **Pronouns**, . 56

				PAGE
Dictionary of Words for the Exercises in the Third Term,				58
Additional Exercises on the Third Term's Grammar,			.	60
Conversational Sentences, to be learnt during the Third Term,				61
Poem ("The Thunderstorm"), to be learnt by heart during the Third Term,				62

FOURTH TERM.

REFERENCE-PAGE	**R.**	The Numerals (with Exercises),				64
,,	,, **S.**	Possessive, Demonstrative, Interrogative Pronouns (Exercises),				66
,,	,, **T.**	Comparison of Adjectives (with Exercises),				68
,,	,, **U.**	Indefinite Pronouns; Adverbs (with Exercises),				70
,,	,, **V.**	Relative, Correlative Pronouns (with Exercises),				72
,,	,, **W.**	Conjunctions; **Alphabetical List,**				74
		Exercises on the above,				76
,,	,, **X.**	Oratio Obliqua (Indirect statements, **questions, commands**), .				78
,,	,, **Y.**	Interjections; **Impersonal V**erbs (Exercises),				80
		On the Assertion and Predicate,				82
,,	,, **Z.**	Complete Rules on the Sequence of Words (Exercises),				83
General Sentences (Recapitulatory),						85
Dictionary of Words for the Exercises in the Fourth Term,						86
Conversational Sentences, to be learnt during the Fourth Term,						88
Poems (Two), to be learnt by heart during the Fourth Term,						89

FIFTH TERM.

NOTES ON IDIOMATIC USES OF THE PARTS OF SPEECH.

REFERENCE-PAGE	**AA.**	Noun and Article (Exercises),		92
,,	,, **BB.**	Gender of Nouns,		94
,,	,, **CC.**	Number of Nouns,		95
,,	,, **DD.**	Adjective (Exercises),		96
,,	,, **EE.**	Prepositions (with Exercises),		98
,,	,, **FF.**	**Pronouns** (Personal, **Possessive, Relative**),		106
		Indefinite Pronouns,		108
,,	,, **GG.**	On the Government of Verbs,		110
,,	,, **HH.**	On the Translation of the English Infinitive,		114
,,	,, **KK.**	On the Translation of the English Verbal in -*ing*,		116
,,	,, **LL.**	On the Past Participle and some Tenses,		118
Idioms and Proverbs, to be learnt during the Fifth Term,				120
Poems, to be learnt by heart during the Fifth Term,				121
Example of German Composition,				124

SIXTH TERM.

HISTORICAL OUTLINE, ETYMOLOGY, AND WORD-FORMATION.

HISTORICAL OUTLINE,		128
ETYMOLOGY. Vowel and Consonant Changes—		
I. Vowels:		
A. Ablaut,		133
B. Umlaut,		134
C. Brechung [with Schwächung and Dehnung],		134

	PAGE
II. Consonants:	
A. Spirantes,	135
B. Liquidae,	135
C. Mutae,	136
Word-Formation. General Remarks,	137
I. Inner or Root-vowel changes (List),	137
II. Derivation of Words—	
A. By *Suffixes*:	
(a) *Verbs* [-en, -ein, -iren, -ern, -zen],	139
(b) *Substantives* [-er, -ner, -in, -el, -sal, -ling, -lein, -chen, -ung, -ei, -niß, -heit, -tum, -schaft],	139
(c) *Adjectives* [-en, -ern, -ig, -icht, -isch, -lich, -sam, -bar, -haft],	140
B. By *Prefixes*:	
(a) *Verbs* [ge-, be-, er-, ver-, zer-, ent-, miß-],	140
(b) *Substantives* [Ge-, Un-, Miß-],	141
(c) *Adjectives* [un-],	141
III. Composition of Words—	
(a) **Verbs (with Prepositions and** Adverbs),	**141**
(b) *Substantives*:	
(i.) with Prepositions or Adverbs,	142
(ii.) with Verbs,	142
(iii.) with Substantives,	142
(iv.) **with Adjectives,**	142
(c) *Adjectives*:	
(i.) with Prepositions or Adverbs,	142
(ii.) **with** Verbs,	142
(iii.) with Substantives,	142
(iv.) with Adjectives,	142

APPENDIX.

A. SHORT ETYMOLOGICAL DICTIONARY (about 300 words),	143
B. LISTS OF WORDS QUITE OR NEARLY ALIKE IN ENGLISH AND **GERMAN**,	150

ERRATA

Page 19. Feminine Nouns. *After* GENERAL RULE: *Plural:* ——en (*or* -n);
Insert (-n *after* e *or* l *or* r); as: . . .

,, 25. In B, Feminine, No. 3, *for* e<s>ch</s>t *read* acht.

,, 26. Under heading: *Using Reference-Pages* D. *and* E. *with* F., alter the 3d column as follows:
der Frau, E. II.
des Bruders, E. I. B.
der Straße, E. II.
des Tages, E. I. n.
des Fräuleins, E. III.

,, 54. II. Separable Verbs (1)—
for: (See Rules 10 and 11 on page 38)
read: (See 5, pages 38 and 83, *and also page* 82, B. (c.)).

GERMAN HANDWRITING

REFERENCE-PAGE **A.**

The German Alphabet.

ALTHOUGH there is a tendency in Germany now both to print books and write letters, etc., in English characters, yet it is still absolutely necessary to be acquainted with the peculiar characters used in printing and writing German, and it is very desirable that students should use such in translating the Exercises given here, in writing.

Capitals.			Small letters.				Examples.		
A	𝔄		a	a			Alexander	Alexander	
B	𝔅		b	b			Belfast	**Belfast**	
C	ℭ		c	c			Columbus	Columbus	
D	𝔇		d	d			Dublin	Dublin	
E	𝔈		e	e			England	England	
F	𝔉		f	f			Fingal	Fingal	
G	𝔊		g	g			Gladstone	Gladstone	
H	ℌ		h	h			Himalaya	Himalaya	
I	ℑ		i	i			Ignatius	**Ignatius**	
J	ℑ		j	j			Juno	Juno	
K	𝔎		k	k			Kingston	**Kingston**	
L	𝔏		l	l			London	London	
M	𝔐		m	m			Mexico	**Mexico**	
N	𝔑		n	n			November	**November**	
O	𝔒		o	o			Odessa	**Odessa**	
P	𝔓		p	p			Pesth	Pesth	
Q	𝔔		q	q			Queensland	Queensland	
R	𝔑		r	r			Russland (Russia)	Rußland	
S	𝔖		s ſ				St. James	St. James	
T	𝔗		t	t			Tiber	Tiber	
U	𝔘		u	u			Uhlan	Uhlan	
V	𝔙		v	v			Venus	**Venus**	
W	𝔚		w	w			Warwick	**Warwick**	
X	𝔛		x	x			Xerxes	**Xerxes**	
Y	𝔜		y	y			Yacht	**Yacht**	
Z	ℨ		z	z			Zululand	**Zululand**	

Notes.—ſ at the beginning or in the middle of a word or syllable is ſ ; but s at the end of a word or syllable is s . Distinguish ſ = s from f = f. ss at the end of a word or syllable is always ß. Distinguish ß = ss from b. St is sometimes written St instead of St. Distinguish N = St from N = N. i loses the little mark when in combination with ch, sch.

Examples in German Writing.

Albert	hat	einen	Bruder	in	Calais	oder	Dover
Albert	has	a	brother	in	Calais	or	Dover

England	und	Frankreich	sind	zwei	Großmächte
England	and	France	are	two	great-powers

Heinrich	war	in	Irland;	Johann	in	Kalifornien
Henry	was	in	Ireland;	John	in	California

London	ist	die	Metropole	Europas;	Neu-York,	Amerikas
London	is	the	metropolis	of Europe;	New-York,	of America

Ofen	und	Pest	sind	Zwillings-Städte	in	Ungarn
Ofen (Buda)	and	Pest	are	twin-towns	in	Hungary

Das	Quecksilber	ist	wie	flüssiges	Silber	anzusehen
Quicksilver		is	like	liquid	silver	to look at

Rom	war	das	Zentrum	der	alten	Welt
Rome	was	the	centre	of the	old	world

Der	Titicaca	See	liegt	in	Süd-Amerika
The	Titicaca	lake	lies	in	South-America

Die	Uhlanen	sind	die	Leichte-Infanterie	der	Preußen
The	Uhlans	are	the	Light Infantry	of the	Prussians

Von	den	Knaben	ist	Wilhelm	nach	Yokohama	gegangen
Of	the	boys	is	William	to	Yokohama	gone

Der	Xylograph	ist	eine	neue	Schreibmaschine
The	Xylograph	is	a	new	writing-machine

Notice.—Capital initials *must* be used in German for all nouns and words used as nouns, and also for the Pronouns of the 3d person plural, if used instead of the 2d person, in addressing persons.—ich, *I*, has no capital initial, except, like all other words, when at the beginning of a sentence.

NOTICE

The student will find that in this Grammar the useless $\mathfrak{h}$ after a **t** is regularly omitted; thus: tun, *to do;* Türe (f.), *door.* As this return to the more correct old spelling may however be too thorough for many, attention is here drawn to the fact that the etymologically doubtful or incorrect **th** is still retained in most modern books, etc., in the following words, and of course all their derivatives or compounds:

but:
- Thal (n.), *valley, dale*
- Thon (m.), *clay*
- Ton (m.), *sound*
- Thor (m.), *fool*

- Thor (n.), *gate*
- Thräne (f.), *tear*
- Thron (m.), *throne*
- thun (irreg.), *to do*

- [That (f.), *deed*]
- [Unterthan (m.), *subject*]
- Thüre (f.), *door*

as also in the foreign words which have an original **th**, as:

- Theater (n.), *theatre*
- Thee (m.), *tea*

- Thema (n.), *theme*
- These (f.), *thesis*

- Katheder (n.), *professor's chair*
- Kathedrale (f.), *cathedral*

and also in Proper Names of persons, towns, or countries, as: Agathe, Bertha, Mathilde, Theodor, Athen, etc.

In the following words and their derivatives, on the other hand, the $\mathfrak{h}$ after the **t** is universally omitted in modern spelling:

- Abenteuer (n.), *adventure*
- Tau (m.), *dew*
- Tau (n.), *rope, hawser*

- Teil (m.), *part*
- [teils, *partly*]
- teuer, *dear*

- Turm (m.), *tower*
- verteidigen, *to defend*

thus also in the suffix *-tum*, as: Kaisertum (n.), *empire;* and in *final* **th** the $\mathfrak{h}$ is regularly omitted now:

- Armut (f.), *poverty*
- Atem (m.), *breath*
- Blüte (f.), *blossom*
- Flut (f.), *flood*

- Glut (f.), *glow*
- Heirat (f.), *marriage*
- Lot (n.), *ounce*
- Miete (f.), *rent*

- Mut (m.), *courage*
- Not (f.), *need*
- Pate (m.), *godfather*
- raten, *to advise*

- rot, *red*
- Rute (f.), *rod*
- Wert (m.), *worth*
- Wut (f.), *fury*.

FIRST TERM

As soon as the pupil can read and write German a little, the Lessons should be begun; and also a very short portion of the Conversational Sentences on page 13, of the Dictionary on page 12, and of the Poem on page 14, should be set for each lesson, after being two or three times read over (and explained) by the teacher.

REFERENCE-PAGE B.
On Pronunciation.

The most important **rules only** are given here. Pronunciation in its nicer shades must be learnt orally from a well-educated German.

Vowels.

a　a　always like *a* in *art*.　　　　　　u　u　always like *u* in *rule*.
o　o　always like *o* in *tone*.　　　　　au　au　always like *ou* in *thou*.

e　e　$\begin{cases}(1)\text{ open}\begin{cases}(i.)\text{ long, as in }there;\ \mathfrak{d}er,\ er,\ wer,\text{ etc.}\\(ii.)\text{ short, almost like }a\text{ in }hat;\ \mathfrak{H}err,\ \mathfrak{W}erf,\text{ etc.}\end{cases}\\(2)\text{ close}\begin{cases}(i.)\text{ long, like }a\text{ in }sane;\ \mathfrak{geht},\ \mathfrak{Weg},\text{ etc.}\\(ii.)\text{ short, as in }then;\ \mathfrak{wenn},\ \mathfrak{Held},\text{ etc.}\end{cases}\end{cases}$ [NEVER like *e* in *he*.]

N.B.—ee, eh is always close and long, as *a* in *sane*; except only in ſeer and Scheere, where it is **open** and long, as *e* in *there*.

i　i　$\begin{cases}(1)\text{ short, as in }this;\ \mathfrak{wild},\ \mathfrak{Hirt},\text{ etc.}\\(2)\text{ long, like }e\text{ in }these;\ \mathfrak{wir},\ \mathfrak{ihn},\text{ etc.}\end{cases}$ [NEVER like *i* in *high*.]

ü　ü　always like *u* in *sûr* (*safe*) in French; für, müde.

ö　ö　$\begin{cases}(1)\text{ open, short, almost like }e\text{ in }her;\ \mathfrak{Hölle},\ \mathfrak{können}.\\(2)\text{ close, long, like }eu\text{ in }deux\text{ in French};\ \mathfrak{Söhne},\ \mathfrak{schön}.\end{cases}$

ä　ä　$\begin{cases}(1)\text{ open, long, like }e\text{ in }there;\ \mathfrak{Bär},\ \mathfrak{gähren}.\\(2)\text{ close, long, like }a\text{ in }sane;\ \mathfrak{Träne},\ \mathfrak{gähnen}.\end{cases}$

N.B.—Vowels followed by a *doubled* consonant are, as a rule, pronounced short.

eu, äu ⎫ have a short sound made up of that of *e* in *her* and that of the *u* in the French *une*;
(eu), (äu) ⎭ Freund, Häuſer. This sound somewhat approaches that of *oy* in *boy*.

N.B.—ie sounds like *e* in *he*; ei sounds like *i* in *high*.

Consonants.

The consonants in German have the same sound as in English, except:

c before *ä, e, i* sounds like *-ts* in *gets*.

ch is guttural after *a, o, u, au*, as *ch* in *loch* (Scotch); it is soft in all other cases at the end of a syllable, (but like *k* in *king* when at the beginning of a word.)

c before *a, **o, u**,* or any consonant (except *h*), is like *k* in *king*.

g at the beginning of a syllable is hard, like *g* in *gone*.

g after *e, i, ä, ö, ü, äu*, or a consonant, is sounded like a soft ch.

h always aspirated at the beginning of a syllable, as *h* in *horse*; when **not initial**, it is scarcely sounded at all.

j　always like *y* in *young*.　　　　　*v* always like *f* in *feel*.
w　always **like *v* in *real*.**　　　　*z* always like *-ts* in *gets*.

　　　　　qu always like *kv* as in *buck-venison*.

ph like *ph* in **Philip**.　　　　　　　*sch* always like *sh* in *shoot*.

Most German words have one strongly accented syllable, which must be carefully noted by the pupil. In words alike in English and German, the accented syllable often differs, and in most cases the German accent is nearer the end of the word than in English, as: Konzert, Paris, Berlin, Muſik, etc.

Lesson I.

1. The Noun or Pronoun expressing the doer of the action indicated by the verb is in the Nominative, that expressing the object of the action, generally in the Accusative Case.

2. The Accusative and Nominative of all Feminine and Neuter words in the Singular, as well as of all Plural words, are the same in form.

3. The Verb expressing the action of a Substantive must always be in the Third Person and agree with it as to Number.

4. All Infinitives end in —en (or —n); if this ending is cut off, the *root* of the Verb remains; this root never changes in the Regular Verbs.

PRESENT INDICATIVE OF REGULAR VERBS.

Subject.	Assertion.	Object.	Subject.	Assertion.	Object.
ich	lobe	die Birne	I	fetch	the pear
du	lobst	das Dorf	thou	praisest	the village
er (sie, es)	lauft	das Huhn	he (she, it)	buys	the fowl
wir	suchen	das Ei	we	seek	the egg
ihr	verkaufet	die Frucht	ye	sell	the fruit
sie (Sie)	hören	das Lied	they (you)	hear	the song

WORDS.

die (f. s.), das (n. s.), the	und, and	eine (f. s.), ein (n. s.), a, an
die Mutter, the mother	loben, to praise	das Kind, the child
die Blume, the flower	sagen, to say	das Dorf, the village
die Feder, the pen	kaufen, to buy	das Buch, the book
die Rose, the rose	suchen, to seek	das Glas, the glass
die Stadt, the town	holen, to fetch	das Mädchen, the girl
die Schule, the school	verkaufen, to sell	das Ei, the egg

Exercise for Translation into German.

1. We seek the child.
2. The girl buys a pen and a rose.
3. The mother praises the school. [3.]
4. Ye sell the flower.
5. The child seeks the book.
6. The mother seeks the child.
7. They praise the town.
8. You praise the rose.
9. You sell the flower and a glass.
10. A child fetches an egg.

Lesson 2.

5. Almost all verbs **with o**, u, eu or å, ö, ü, äu in the Root are regular, *i.e.* the Root never changes throughout the Conjugation.

6. In Simple Statements the order of words in German is the same **as in** English, *i.e.* Subject, Assertion (Verb), Object.

7. In Questions the order is: **Assertion** (Verb), Subject, Object; hence the English *do, does, did,* etc., are never translated.

AFFIRMATIVE: Der Vater lobt das Kind. *The father praises the child.*
INTERROGATIVE: Lobt der Vater das Kind? *Does the father praise the child?*

IMPERFECT INDICATIVE OF REGULAR VERBS.

SUBJECT.	ASSERTION.	OBJECT.	SUBJECT.	ASSERTION.	OBJECT.
ich	hol-te	die Dame	I	fetched	the lady
du	hör-test	das Horn	thou	didst hear	the horn
er (sie, es)	lieb-te	das Thier	he (she, it)	loved	the animal
wir	such-ten	die Pfeife	we	sought	the pipe
ihr	sag-tet	das Wort	ye	said	the word
sie (Sie)	kauf-ten	das Gemälde	they (you)	bought	the picture

WORDS.

der (m. s.), *the*
der König, *the king*
der Vater, *the father*
die Tochter, *the daughter*
die Straße, *the street*
die Frau, *the woman*
das Wort, *the word*

ein (m. s.), *a, an*
hör-en, *to hear*
lieb-en, *to love*
glaub-en, *to believe*
nein, *no* (in answers)
kein, *no* (before a noun)
aber, *but* (conjunction)

einige, *some*
das Pferd, *the horse*
das Bild, *the picture*
ja, *yes* (in answers)
sehr, *very, much* (intensity)
viel, *much* (quantity)
sehr viel, *very much* (quantity)

Exercise.

1. The daughter loved the picture much.
2. Did the father buy (7) the horse? Yes.
3. Did you seek (7) the street? Yes.
4. The king heard the lady.
5. Do they fetch (7) the child? No.
6. We bought no horse, but a picture.
7. Does the father praise (7) the daughter?
8. Did the king praise (7) the woman?
9. The mother praises the child.
10. She loved the picture and bought it.

Reference-Page C.

(a) The 'DEFINITE ARTICLE GROUP' of Determinative Adjectives.

	M. S.	F. S.	N. S.	PLURAL	ENGLISH
Nom.	der	die	das	die	the
Acc.	den	die	das	die	the
Gen.	des	der	des	der	of the
Dat.	dem	der	dem	den	to the

1. All the members of this group are declined like **der** and are pure adjectives, *i.e.* they belong to some noun, with which they must strictly agree in Gender, Number, and Case.

The Only Members of this group are:

Nom. M. S.	F. S.	N. S.	PLURAL	ENGLISH
der	die	das	die	the
dieser	diese	dieses	diese	this, these
jener	jene	jenes	jene	that, those

Nom. M. S.	F. S.	N. S.	PLURAL	ENGLISH
welcher?	welche?	welches?	welche?	which?
jeder	jede	jedes		every, each
mancher	manche	manches	(manche)	many-a

NOTICE: *es* (n. s.) of **das** becomes *es* in the other members of the group.

2. Sometimes *this, that, which?* are separated from their nouns by a 3d person of some tense of the verb *to be*, as, *This is my father;* when used thus, the neuter singular **das** or **dieses, jenes, welches?** are employed, and no agreement with the noun takes place, as, **das ist mein Vater**.

(b) The 'INDEFINITE ARTICLE GROUP' of Determinative Adjectives.

	M. S.	F. S.	N. S.	PLURAL	ENGLISH
Nom.	ein	eine	ein	keine	no
Acc.	einen	eine	ein	keine	no
Gen.	eines	einer	eines	keiner	of no
Dat.	einem	einer	einem	keinen	to no

1. All the members of this group are declined like **ein**, and are pure adjectives, and must be followed by a noun, with which they agree strictly in Gender, Number, and Case.

The Only Members of this group are:

Nom.	M. S.	F. S.	N. S.	PLURAL	ENGLISH
	ein	eine	ein	(einige)	a, an (some)
	kein	keine	kein	keine	no (before a substantive)
	was für ein...?	was für eine...?	was für ein...?	was für...?	What sort of..?

and all the Possessive Adjectives

Nom. M. S.	F. S.	N. S.	PLURAL	ENGLISH
mein	meine	mein	meine	my
dein	deine	dein	deine	thy
sein	seine	sein	seine	his
ihr	ihre	ihr	ihre	her
sein	seine	sein	seine	its

Nom. M. S.	F. S.	N. S.	PLURAL	ENGLISH
unser	unsere	unser	unsere	our
euer	euere	euer	euere	your
ihr	ihre	ihr	ihre	their
[Ihr	Ihre	Ihr	Ihre	your]

(The latter used in polite address.)

2. When the noun to which these adjectives belong is not expressed after them, they change like the members of the "Definite Article" group (see *a* above), as: **meiner, meine, meines, meine,** *mine*. **Was für eines?** *What sort?* (neuter).

Examples and Exercises on Reference-Page C.

WORDS.

er (sie, es), ist, *he (she, it) is*
der Bleistift, *the pencil*
der Brief, *the letter*
der Hund, *the dog*
der Hut, *the hat*

belohnen *to reward*
sagen (with Dative) *to say* (*to*)
der Lehrer, *the teacher*
der Schüler, *the pupil*
der Mann, *the man*

strafen, *to punish*
fragen, *to ask*
der Ring, *the ring*
der Rock, *the coat*
der Wein, *the wine*

(a.)

1. *This teacher punished this pupil.*
2. *This child said it to the father.*
3. *Which man praises that school?*
4. *That man seeks this letter.*
5. *This is the ring of that woman.*

Dieser Lehrer strafte diesen Schüler.
Dieses Kind sagte es dem Vater.
Welcher Mann lobt jene Schule?
Jener Mann sucht diesen Brief.
Dieses ist der Ring jener Frau.

Exercise on (a.)

1. That pupil asks this teacher.
2. This teacher seeks this pencil.
3. Which [C. a. 2.] is the pen of the daughter?
4. He rewarded many-a pupil.
5. Which book did you buy, this or that?
6. Did the king (Nom.) seek this letter?
7. No, he sought that letter.
8. This [C. a. 2.] is the hat of that woman.
9. Many-a man praises that child.
10. Which coat did he buy? This.

(b.)

1. *My father sold his wine.*
2. *Her mother said it to her daughter.*
3. *Their teacher seeks his pupil.*
4. *This is my ring, it is mine.*
5. *What sort of dog did he buy?*

Mein Vater verkaufte seinen Wein.
Ihre Mutter sagte es ihrer Tochter.
Ihr Lehrer sucht seinen Schüler.
Dieses ist mein Ring, es ist meiner.
Was für einen Hund kaufte er?

Exercise on (b.)

1. We reward his pupil.
2. I said it to my teacher.
3. Thy dog loves its teacher.
4. This man bought our wine.
5. Do they hear our dog? Yes or no?
6. Our mother loves her ring.
7. He bought his coat and mine. [C. b. 2.]
8. He punished my dog and my child.
9. I heard your father and your mother.
10. What sort of pencil did he seek?

Lesson 3.

8. In German one person is familiarly addressed by du, *thou*, several persons by ihr, *you, ye*. In addressing any one politely, strangers especially, the third person Plural must be used, both in the Singular, and the Plural. In writing, the pronouns of the third person Plural have in this case a capital letter always. Thus:

du liebst, *thou lovest;* ihr liebt, *ye love;* Sie lieben, *you love.*

9. Be very careful to make the Possessive Adjectives agree in person with the Personal Pronouns, if they refer to the same person, thus:

du liebst deine Mutter	thou lovest thy mother.
ihr liebt eure Mutter	ye love your mother.
Sie lieben Ihre Mutter	you love your mother.
sie lieben ihre Mutter	they love their mother.

PRESENT AND IMPERFECT OF INDICATIVE OF haben, *to have.*

SUBJECT.	ASSERTION (Verb).	OBJECT.	SUBJECT.	ASSERTION (Verb).	OBJECT.
ich	habe, hatte	den Tisch	I	have, had	the table
du	hast, hattest	diese Uhr	thou	hast, hadst	this watch
er (sie, es)	hat, hatte	dieses Geld	he (she, it)	has, had	this money
wir	haben, hatten	manche Frucht	we	have, had	many-a fruit
ihr	habt, hattet	jenes Messer	ye	have, had	that knife
sie (Sie)	haben, hatten	jede Blume	they (you)	have, had	every flower

WORDS.

der Kaiser, *the emperor*	belohn-en, *to reward*	die Stadt, *the town*
der Jüngling, *the young-man*	gehorch-en (with dativo), *to obey*	die Uhr, *the watch*
der Teppich, *the carpet*	oder, *or*	die Frucht, *the fruit*
der Tisch, *the table*	auch, *also (even)*	das Geld, *the money*
der Stuhl, *the chair*	wer? *who?*	das Papier, *the paper*
der Oheim, *the uncle*	brav, *well-behaved*	das Messer, *the knife*
die Stunde, *the hour*	unartig, *naughty*	das Leben, (*the*) *life*

Exercise.

1. Which paper have you, this or that?
2. I have no paper, but I have a pen.
3. Had I the money? No.
4. Has the emperor a watch? He has this.
5. The girl had a picture, but which?
6. We have very much money.
7. Who had this horse? He had that.
8. Has he this knife or that? That.
9. They obey (to) the young man. (*Dative.*)
10. She does reward her daughter.

LESSON 4.

10. The verbs ſein (*to be*) and werden (*to become*) are generally accompanied by a noun or adjective as Predicate. **This** Predicate, if a noun, is always Nominative, and if an adjective, is invariable; it stands after the assertion.

11. Place of the negation nicht, *not*: [*do, did, does* are *not* translated].

    (*a*) After the object or Accusative: Er liebt das Kind nicht. *He does not love the child.*
    (*b*) Before the predicate or **Nominative**: Es ist nicht das Kind. *It is not the child.*

Note.—nicht often precedes the object, **if it negatives it emphatically**:
    Er liebt nicht den Vater, er liebt den Bruder.
Kein, *no*, is preferred to nicht ein, *not a*; as, er ist kein König, *he is not a king*.

Present Indicative of ſein, *to be*, and werden, *to become*.

SUBJECT.	ASSERTION (Verb).	PREDICATE.	SUBJECT.	ASSERTION (Verb).	PREDICATE.
ich	bin, werde	ein König	*I*	*am, become*	*a king*
du	biſt, wirſt	alt	*thou*	*art, becomest*	*old*
er (ſie, es)	iſt, wird	brav	*he (she, it)*	*is, becomes*	*well-behaved*
wir	ſind, werden	jung	*we*	*are, become*	*young*
ihr	ſeid, werdet	reich	*ye*	*are, become*	*rich*
ſie (Sie)	ſind, werden	arm	*they (you)*	*are, become*	*poor*

WORDS.

der Bruder, **the brother**
der Sohn, *the son*
der Neffe, *the nephew*
die Schweſter, *the sister*
die Nichte, *the niece*
die Tante, *the aunt*
die Liebe, *(the) love*

machen, *to make*
lachen, *to laugh*
gut, *good*
ſchön, *beautiful*
groß, *great, tall*
klein, *small*
ſchmutzig, *dirty*

das Haus, *the house*
das Silber, *(the) silver*
das Gold, *(the) gold*
das Zimmer, *the room*
das Tal, *the valley*
das Blatt, *the leaf*
rein, *clean*

Exercise.

1. Am I tall? No, thou art not tall.
2. Are the rooms beautiful? Yes, they are clean.
3. Do we become very poor? Yes, very.
4. The king is not good, but he is rich.
5. They become rich, but we are poor.
6. What sort of [C. *b.*] man is he? He is good.
7. You are not well-behaved, my child.
8. Which is my son? This is he. [C. *a.* 2.]
9. This [C. *a.* 2] is not my pen. No.
10. Does she buy his table? She buys this.

Lesson 5.

12. Throughout the verbs, regular and irregular, the third person is the same in form as the first, with the one exception of the third person Singular Present Indicative.

13. The Imperfect Indicative has the following invariable rules: The 2d person Singular adds —ſt to the first, the third person is the same in form exactly as the first, and the Plurals are always in: 1. —en; 2. —et; 3. —en.

14. The Future Simple of all Verbs, without one exception, is formed by adding the Infinitive of any verb to the Present Indicative of werden, (to become) [see Lesson 4.] as, du wirſt lachen, thou wilt laugh.

15. In Primary Sentences, whether affirmative, negative, or interrogative, always place the Infinitive last in the sentence.

IMPERFECT INDICATIVE of ſein (to be) and werden (to become).

SUBJECT.	ASSERTION.	PREDICATE.	SUBJECT.	ASSERTION.	PREDICATE.
ich	war, wurde	ein König	I	was, became	a king
du	warſt, wurdeſt	reich	thou	wast, becamest	rich
er (ſie, es)	war, wurde	wohl	he (she, it)	was, became	well
wir	waren, wurden	fleißig	we	were, became	diligent
ihr	waret, wurdet	nicht gut	ye	were, became	not good
ſie (Sie)	waren, wurden	glücklich	they (you)	were, became	happy

WORDS.

der Menſch, the human being
der Mann, the man, male
der Wald, the forest
der Fürſt, the prince
der Knabe, the boy
die Sonne, the sun
die Erde, the earth

wählen, to choose
zählen, to count
zeigen, to show
reiſen, to travel
wie? how?
lange, long
wann? when?

die Liebe, the love
das Kleid, the dress
das Hemd, the shirt
das Eiſen, the iron
das Heft, the copy-book
das Kindlein, the little child
das Eſſen, the dinner

Future: Er wird den Mann nicht holen. He will not fetch the man.

Exercise.

1. His father became an emperor. (*Nom.*)
2. You choose your dress.
3. Their mother was very beautiful.
4. She will become my daughter.
5. Where will you buy this copy-book?
6. How long was he well-behaved?
7. Which [C. a. 2.] is her pen?
8. Will they not choose a king? (*Acc.*)
9. Was he not your father? (*Nom.*)
10. How happy he was!

Lesson 6.

16. The "Compound Tenses" are formed in German, as in English, by means of auxiliaries and the Past Participle of the Verb. This Past Participle is however (unless there be an Infinitive also in the sentence) always placed last in the sentence.

17. Regular verbs form their Past Participle thus: Put ge.. before the Verb, and replace the final —en by —t, as: loben, *to praise*; gelobt, *praised*.

18. If the Infinitive of a verb begins with an unaccented inseparable prefix (see 19) no ge.. is placed before it for the Past Participle.

19. All prefixes are capable of being separated from their root, except only: be.., ge.., emp.., ent.., er.., ver..., zer.., hinter.., miß.., voll.., wider... (These ought to be learnt by heart.)

20. In speaking of completed actions of recent date, the Germans, like the French, use the Perfect in preference to the English Imperfect.

EXAMPLES ON THE COMPOUND TENSES.

1. Werden Sie das Geld brauchen?
2. Nein, ich werde es nicht brauchen.
3. Wer hat dieses Land entdeckt?
4. Dieser Mann hat es nicht entdeckt.
5. Hat er Strafe verdient? Nein.
6. Wer ist König? Wo ist der Graf?
7. Der Graf wird nicht hier sein.
8. Wird der Sohn fleißig werden?
9. Nein, er ist sehr unartig.
10. Hatte er Geld? Er hat keines gehabt.

1. *Will you want the money?*
2. *No, I (will) shall not want it.*
3. *Who discovered this land?*
4. *This man has not discovered it.*
5. *Did he deserve punishment? No.*
6. *Who is king? Where is the count?*
7. *The count will not be here.*
8. *Will the son become diligent?*
9. *No, he is very naughty.*
10. *Had he money? He had none.*

WORDS.

der Graf, *the count*
die Belohnung, *the reward*
die Strafe, *the punishment*
das Leben, *the life*
das Land, *the land*
das Schaf, *the sheep*

verdienen, *to deserve*
entdecken, *to discover*
brauchen, *to use, to want*
noch nicht (inseparable) *not yet*
wer? *who?*
wo? *where?*

oder, *or*
hier, *here*
dort, *there*
das Geld, *the money*
das Fräulein, *the young lady*
das Feuer, *the fire*

Exercise.

1. Who has deserved (a) **punishment**?
2. This child deserved a reward.
3. **Where** is the count? He is not yet here.
4. Had our father used the money?
5. No, he had not used it yet.
6. Have you discovered the land?
7. **Who** is king? He is not yet king.
8. **Where** will you use the money?
9. Has the man sought his sheep?
10. He will seek it here and there.

ADDITIONAL EXERCISES.

(On revising the work of the First Term.)

On Lesson 1.

1. He says, they fetch the flower.
2. We say, she buys the pen.
3. The mother seeks a rose.
4. They fetch a glass and a flower.
5. The child says, they buy a pen.
6. The mother and the child say it.
7. The girl and the mother say it.
8. We praise the school and the town.
9. We buy the pen and a flower.
10. The mother says, they seek the girl.

On Lesson 2.

1. We hear, you love the horse.
2. Do you hear the child? Yes, father.
3. Did the child seek the pen? Yes.
4. Did he praise the pupil? No.
5. The king loved the town.
6. The teacher bought the paper.
7. Did the daughter seek the child? No.
8. We loved the town much.
9. He said very much.
10. Did you buy the picture? No, mother.

On Lesson 3, and Reference-Page C.

1. Thou hast thy pen there.
2. Had you your dog? Yes.
3. We have our pencil here.
4. Many a town has much money.
5. Have ye your money? No.
6. That king had no son.
7. We had no watch.
8. Has this young man no father?
9. The man loved his child much.
10. Which emperor has this? This.

On Lesson 4.

1. My son is not very tall.
2. My teacher is very good.
3. Our street was not clean.
4. Are these rooms beautiful?
5. What sort of king is this king?
6. He is very small, but is very well-behaved.
7. I have a dress. What sort? (C. b. 2.)
8. Does she become poor?
9. He is becoming a man. (*Nom.*)
10. They are becoming rich and not poor.

On Lesson 5.

1. Will the king buy this horse?
2. The daughter was very well-behaved.
3. He became very rich.
4. My son was my teacher.
5. Did you become his scholar?
6. It was here or there.
7. The man will become poor.
8. Will the father become a teacher?
9. When will they fetch this book?
10. What sort of man was this king?

On Lesson 6.

1. The pupil has deserved a reward.
2. We shall punish this man.
3. Who has fetched my son? This man.
4. Here was the count, and not there.
5. Had they discovered their money.
6. Where will the emperor be? Here.
7. You will believe this or not.
8. The king has not yet used his money.
9. Will they use their money, there?
10. Will he deserve punishment?

DICTIONARY of Words.

(For the Exercises in the First and Second Terms.)

a, an, ein (C. b.)
and, und
to ask, fragen
to be, sein
beautiful, schön
to become, werden
the book, das Buch
but, aber
to buy, kaufen
the child, das Kind
to choose, wählen
clean, rein
the coat, der Rock
the copy-book, das Heft
the count, der Graf
the daughter, die Tochter
to deserve, verdienen
to discover, entdecken
do, does, did (not translated)
the dog, der Hund
the dress, das Kleid
the egg, das Ei
the emperor, der Kaiser
the father, der Vater
to fetch, holen
the flower, die Blume
the girl, das Mädchen
the glass, das Glas
good, gut
happy, glücklich
the hat, der Hut
to hear, hören
her, ihr (C. b. 1)
here, hier
hers, ihrer (C. b. 2)
his, sein (C. b.)
the horse, das Pferd

how? Wie?
its, sein (C. b. 1, 2)
the king, der König
the knife, das Messer
the lady, die Dame
the land, das Land
the letter, der Brief
long, lange
to love, lieben
the man, der Mann
many-a, mancher (C. a.)
mine, meiner (C. b. 2)
the money, das Geld
the mother, die Mutter
much (intensity), sehr
much (quantity), viel
my, mein (C. b. 1)
no (before Noun), kein (C. b. 1)
no (answers), nein
not, nicht (Rule 11)
to obey, gehorchen (Dative)
old, alt
or, oder
our, unser (C. b. 1)
ours, unserer (C. b. 2)
the paper, das Papier
the pen, die Feder
the pencil, der Bleistift
the picture, das Bild
poor, arm
to praise, loben
to punish, strafen
the punishment, die Strafe
the pupil, der Schüler
to reward, belohnen
the reward, die Belohnung
rich, reich

the ring, der Ring
the room, das Zimmer
the rose, die Rose
to say, sagen (Dative)
the school, die Schule
to seek, suchen
to sell, verkaufen
the sheep, das Schaf
the son, der Sohn
what sort of? Was für ein... (C. b.)
the street, die Straße
the table, der Tisch
tall, groß
the teacher, der Lehrer
that, jener (C. a.)
the, der (C. a.)
their, ihr (C. b. 1)
theirs, ihrer (C. b. 2)
there, dort
thine, deiner (C. b. 2)
this, dieser (C. a.)
thy, dein (C. b. 1)
the town, die Stadt
to use, brauchen
very, sehr
the watch, die Uhr
well-behaved, brav
where? Wo?
which? Welcher?
who? Wer?
the wine, der Wein
the woman, die Frau
yes, ja
not yet, noch nicht
the young man, der Jüngling
your, euer, Ihr (C. b. 1)
yours, euerer, Ihrer (C. b. 2)

CONVERSATIONAL SENTENCES.—First Term.

(To be learnt in small portions over and over again.)

1. Guten Morgen, mein Herr. — Good morning, Sir.
2. Ich wünsche Ihnen guten Tag. — I wish you good day.
3. Befinden Sie sich recht wohl? — Are you very well?
4. Ja, ich danke, ich bin immer wohl. — Yes, I thank you, I am always well.
5. Und wie geht es Ihrer Frau Mutter? — And how is your mother?
6. Danke, sie ist etwas besser heute. — Thank you, she is a little better to-day.
7. Werden Sie in die Stadt gehen? — Will you be going to town?
8. Ja, ich komme heute in die Stadt. — Yes, I am coming to town to-day.
9. Wir wollen in das Theater gehen. — We will go to the theatre.
10. Diesen Abend gehen wir in das Conzert. — This evening we are going to the concert.
11. Wird Ihre Schwester mit uns kommen? — Will your sister come with us?
12. Nein, sie muß zu Hause bleiben. — No, she must remain at home.
13. Ich bitte Sie, geben Sie ihr ein Billet. — I beg you, give her a ticket.
14. Vielen Dank, ich werde es gern thun. — Many thanks, I will gladly do so.
15. Haben Sie meinen Bruder gesehen? — Have you seen my brother?
16. Ja, aber er war sehr unwohl. — Yes, but he was very unwell.
17. Ich bitte Sie, geben Sie mir das Buch. — Pray give me the book.
18. Was wird er morgen machen? — What will he do to-morrow?
19. Er geht nach Berlin morgen früh. — He is going to Berlin early to-morrow.
20. Wann wird er zurückkommen? — When will he return?
21. Ich weiß es nicht; vielleicht bald. — I do not know, perhaps soon.
22. Haben Sie dieses Geld gebraucht? — Have you used this money?
23. Nein, ich habe es immer noch. — No, I have it still.
24. Werden Sie es nicht brauchen? — Will you not use it?
25. Ich hoffe, ich werde nicht Alles brauchen. — I hope, I shall not use all of it.
26. Hat er keinen Regenschirm? — Has he no umbrella?
27. Nein, und es regnet sehr stark. — No, and it is raining very hard.
28. Wird dieser Knabe Deutsch lernen? — Will this boy learn German?
29. Ja, und auch Französisch. — Yes, and French also.
30. Ich hoffe, er wird recht fleißig sein. — I hope he will be very diligent.

POEM.

(To be learnt by heart in small portions.)

Die Lorelei (von Heine).

1. Ich weiß nicht, was soll es bedeuten,
   Daß ich so traurig bin;
   Ein Märchen aus alten Zeiten
   Das kommt mir nicht aus dem Sinn.

2. Die Luft ist kühl und es dunkelt,
   Und ruhig fließt der Rhein;
   Der Gipfel des Berges funkelt
   Im Abendsonnenschein.

3. Die schönste Jungfrau sitzet
   Dort oben wunderbar;
   Ihr goldnes Geschmeide blitzet;
   Sie kämmt ihr goldenes Haar.

4. Sie kämmt es mit goldenem Kamme,
   Und singt ein Lied dabei;
   Das hat eine wundersame
   Gewaltige Melodei.

5. Den Schiffer im kleinen Schiffe
   Ergreift es mit wildem Weh;
   Er schaut nicht die Felsenriffe.
   Er schaut nur hinauf in die Höh'.

6. Ich glaube, die Wellen verschlingen
   Am Ende Schiffer und Kahn;
   Und das hat mit ihrem Singen
   Die Lorelei gethan.

Lurline (Literal Translation).

1. *I know not, what it can mean,*
   That I am so sad;
   A legend of olden times
   Will not leave my mind (keeps haunting).

2. *The air is cool and it is getting dark,*
   And quietly the Rhine is flowing;
   The summit of the mountain sparkles
   In the evening sunshine.

3. *The most beauteous maiden is sitting*
   Up there wonderful (to behold);
   Her golden ornaments glisten;
   She is combing her golden hair.

4. *She is combing it with (a) golden comb;*
   And is singing a song withal,
   Which has a wondrous
   Powerful melody.

5. *The boatman in the little boat,*
   It seizes with a wild woe;
   He looks not at the rocky reefs,
   He looks only up on high.

6. *I believe the waves will swallow*
   In the end the boatman and (his) boat;
   And this has with her singing
   The Lurline (naiad) done.

Note.—The above is one of **the** best-known German poems, and one of the most favourite popular songs. The *Lurline* rock, near Bingen and Mayence on the Rhine, overlooks some rather dangerous rapids in the stream, and **the** many accidents there formerly were ascribed popularly to a naiad, sitting on that **rock** combing her hair, and drawing the attention of boatmen from their boats by her singing.

SECOND TERM

A FEW of the Conversational Sentences on pages 13 and 34, as well as a few of the words in the Dictionary on page 12, should form an integral part of the work set for every lesson during this term. The little poems on page 35 should also gradually be learnt by heart. It is only by constant repetition of the same few words or sentences, that they become thoroughly fixed in the memory, and in Modern languages such viva voce practice is absolutely indispensable.

For the order of words in the Exercises for translation consult Reference Page J at the end of this term (page 38).

Lesson 7.

21. Sentences beginning with Interrogative Pronouns, as: Wer? *who?* Was? *what?* etc., invert the order of Subject and Assertion; so also do sentences beginning with adverbs, as, Hier ist er, *Here he is.*

22. The Imperative has no third person, properly speaking; if a third person is commanded (indirectly), we have, as in English, to use auxiliaries, lassen, *to let*, with Accusative of the person commanded, or sollen, *shall*—Infinitive at end of sentence. In addressing a command to a person or persons politely, use invariably the verb (Infinitive) itself, with Sie, *you*, added, as, Wählen Sie! *Choose!*

Imperative.

All regular Verbs.
- 2d. Hole! *Fetch (thou)!*
- 3d. { Er soll suchen! *He shall seek!*
  Laßt ihn tanzen! *Let him dance!*
- 1st. Gehorchen wir! *Let us obey!*
- 2d. { Suchet! *Seek (ye)!*
  Suchen Sie! *Seek!*
- 3d. { Sie sollen lachen! *They shall laugh!*
  Laßt sie lachen! *Let them laugh!*

sein, *to be.*
- 2d. Sei! *Be (thou)!*
- 3d. { Er soll sein! *He shall be!*
  Laßt ihn sein! *Let him be!*
- 1st. Seien wir! *Let us be!*
- 2d. { Seid! *Be (ye)!*
  Seien Sie! *Be!*
- 3d. { Sie sollen sein! *They shall be!*
  Laßt sie sein! *Let them be!*

Examples on the Imperative.

1. Mein Kind, frage den Lehrer!
2. Dort ist es; sagen Sie es der Frau!
3. Der König soll sein Land lieben!
4. Laßt den Vater wählen!
5. Hören Sie den Hund!

1. *My child, ask (thou) the teacher!*
2. *There it is; tell it to the woman!*
3. *The king shall love his land!*
4. *Let the father choose!*
5. *Hear (listen to) the dog.*

Exercise.

[*Notice.*—For the words to be used in these Exercises see page 12 in the First Term.]

1. Let us obey the teacher. (*Dative.*)
2. Punish that dog!
3. Be (ye) well-behaved!
4. Let the woman choose the dress!
5. Seek the child! Here is the book.
6. What did he say? Let him say!
7. Let them be happy! They are good.
8. Use your money! Where is it?
9. Where is my son? Let him be here.
10. Do not use this book, my son.

[*Notice.*—Put the Infinitive last in the sentence, except in the Imperative with Sie.]

GENERAL RULES
about the Declension of German Substantives.

German nouns may be said to be either *weak* or *strong* as to their declension: *weak*, if the Genitive Singular ends in ·n or does not alter from the Nominative; *strong*, if the Genitive Singular ends in ·ß. Grammarians differ as to the number of Declensions; here, the Nouns are treated simply according to *gender, number of syllables*, and *termination*.

CHANGES IN THE SINGULAR. [See Ref.-Page E.]

I. MASCULINE NOUNS:
   (a) { Nominatives in ·e (and ten monosyllables) } take ·n (or ·en) for Accusative, Genitive, and
       { Foreign words *not* in ·al, ·an, ·aft, ·r } Dative.
   (b) All other masculine Nouns take ·ß for Genitive, and do *not* change for Accusative and Dative.

II. FEMININE NOUNS never change at all in the Singular.

III. NEUTER NOUNS, all (except das Herz) take ·ß for Genitive, and do *not* change for Accusative and Dative.

CHANGES IN THE PLURAL. [See Ref.-Page D.]

Notice carefully: Accusative, Genitive, and Dative Plural are always like the Nominative Plural, but the Dative Plural *must* in every noun end in ·n. (This ·n has to be added, if the other cases have not already the termination ·n.)

I. MASCULINE NOUNS:
   A. *Monosyllables* have *Plural:* modify root-vowel and take ·e.
   B. *Dissyllables and Polysyllables:*
      (a) Nominative Singular ending in ·el, ·en, ·er have *Plural:* modify root-vowel without other change.
      (b) { Nominative Singular ending in ·ig, ·ich, ·at, ·ing
          { Foreign words ending in ·al, ·an, ·aft, ·r (not ·or) } *Plural:* modify root-vowel and add ·e.
          { Monosyllables with prefix Be·, Ge·
      (c) { Nominative Singular ending in ·e [see Singular (a)]
          { Foreign words not ending in ·al, ·an, ·aft, ·r } *Plural:* do *not* modify root-vowel, but take ·(e)n.
          { Foreign words ending in ·or

II. FEMININE NOUNS have *Plural:* do *not* modify root-vowel, but take ·(e)n.

III. NEUTER NOUNS:
   A. Monosyllables have *Plural:* modify root-vowel and take ·er.
   B. Dissyllables and Polysyllables:
      (a) Nominative Singular ending in ·er, ·el, ·en, ·chen, ·lein have no change for Plural.
      (b) Nominative Singular not ending in ·er, ·el, ·en, ·chen, ·lein have *Plural:* do not modify root-vowel, but take ·e.

Notes.

1. Compound nouns change only their last component, according to its own rule.
2. All nouns which take ·er for Plural modify their vowel.
3. The only vowels which can modify are: a (into ä), o (into ö), u (into ü), au (into äu).

Reference-Page **D.** (*a*).

Formation of Nominative PLURAL OF NOUNS from the Nominative Singular.

GENERAL RULES:

1. When seeking to **form the** Plural of any Noun, answer these three questions: *a.* What gender is the Noun? *b.* How many syllables has it? *c.* What termination has it? Then, if the noun is not given among the exceptions in its class, to which it belongs in virtue of the answers to the above questions, it will follow the Rule.

2. By "⸺" is meant, a, o, u, au of the singular become ä, ö, ü, äu in the plural.

3. **A vowel already** modified in the Singular remains so for the Plural; e, i, ei, ie, eu, **cannot modify.**

4. In compound nouns, the last component only changes for the Plural according to its own class.

MASCULINE NOUNS.

A. Monosyllables. RULE: **Plural:** ⸺e; as: der Sohn, *the son*, die Söhne.

EXCEPTIONS: 1. **Plural:** ⸺e; as: der Hund, *the dog*, die Hunde.

der Aal, *the eel*	der Grad, *the degree*	der Pfad, *the path*	der Stoff, *the stuff*
der Arm, *the arm*	der Hund, *the dog*	der Punkt, *the point*	der Tag, *the day*
der Dachs, *the badger*	der Huf, *the hoof*	der Schuh, *the shoe*	der Thron, *the throne*

2. **Plural:** ⸺en; as: der Dorn, *the thorn*, **die Dornen.**

der Bär, *the bear*	der Held, *the hero*	der Pfau, *the peacock*	der Staat, *the state*
der Christ, *the Christian*	der Herr, *the gentleman*	der Prinz, *the prince*	der Strahl, *the beam*
der Dorn, *the thorn*	der Mast, *the mast*	der See, *the lake*	der Tor, *the fool*
der Fürst, *the prince*	der Mensch, *the human being*	der Sporn, *the spur*	
der Graf, *the count*	der Narr, *the fool*	der Schmerz, *the pain*	

3. **Plural:** ⸺"⸺er; as: der Mann, *the man*, die Männer.

der Geist, *the spirit*	der Leib, *the body*	der Ort, *the place*	der Wald, *the forest*
der Gott, *the god*	der Mann, *the man*	der Rand, *the edge*	der Wurm, *the worm*

B. Dissyllables and Polysyllables.

(*a.*) Singular in -el, -en, -er, -ar. RULE Plural " as: der Vater, *the father*, die Väter.

EXCEPTIONS: 1. **Plural:** ⸺ [no change]; as: der Adler, *the eagle*, die Adler.

der Adler, *the eagle*	der Gulden, *the florin*	der Maler, *the painter*	der Sommer, *the summer*
der Amerikaner, *the American*	der Kanzler, *the chancellor*	der Morgen, *the morning*	der Taler, *the dollar*
der Bewohner, *the inhabitant*	der Knochen, *the bone*	der Panzer, *the armour*	der Tropfen, *the drop*
der Bogen, *the bow, arc*	der Kuchen, *the cake*	der Rahmen, *the frame*	der Wagen, *the carriage*

2. **Plural:** ⸺n; as: der Bauer, *the peasant*, die Bauern.

der Baier, *the Bavarian*	der Gevatter, *the godfather*	der Nachbar, *the neighbour*	der Stachel, *the sting*
der Bauer, *the peasant*	der Muskel, *the muscle*	der Pantoffel, *the slipper*	der Vetter, *the cousin*

(*b.*) { Singulars in -ig, -ich, -al, -ing.
Foreign words in -al, -an, -ast, -on, -r (not -er).
Monosyllables with prefix Ge-, Ges-. } **RULE: Plural:** ⸺e; as: der Palast, *the palace*, die Paläste.

EXCEPTIONS: Plural: ⸺e; as: der Monat, *the month*, die Monate.

der Charakter, *the character*	der Monat, *the month*	der Postillon, *the postilion*	der Spion, *the spy*; also,
der Baron, *the baron*	der Pokal, *the goblet*	der Roman, *the novel*	der Abend, *the evening*

(*c.*) { Singulars in -e; also
Foreign words not ending in -al, -an, -ast, -r; and
Foreign words ending in -or; except, der Major, die Majore } RULE: Plural: ⸺(e)n; as:
der Knabe, *the boy*, die Knaben;
der Doktor, *the doctor*, die Doktoren.

To class (*c.*) belong also—

The following ten in -e (sometimes spelt with -en in the Nominative Singular); in the Plural they must end in -en, as: der Gedanke (or Gedanken), *the thought*, die Gedanken.

der Buchstabe, *the letter*	der Funke, *the spark*	der Haufe, *the heap*	der Same, *the seed*; and
der Fels, *the rock*	der Gedanke, *the thought*	der Name, *the name*	der Wille, *the will*
der Friede, (*the*) *peace*	der Glaube, *the faith*		

Reference-Page **D.** (*b*).
Formation of Nominative **PLURAL OF NOUNS** from the Nominative Singular.
FEMININE NOUNS.

GENERAL RULE: *Plural*: ——en (or -n); as: die Schlacht, *the battle*, die Schlachten.
　　EXCEPTIONS: 1. *Plural*: ——¨e; as: die Braut, *the bride*, die Bräute.

die Axt, *the* axe	die Gans, *the goose*	die Laus, *the louse*	die Not, *the need*
die Angst, *the anxiety*	die Gruft, *the tomb, vault*	die Luft, *the air*	die Nuß, *the nut*
die Bank, *the bench*	die Haut, *the skin*	die Lust, *the pleasure*	die Sau, *the sow*
die Braut, *the bride*	die Kluft, *the cleft, abyss*	die Magd, *the servant*	die Stadt, *the town*
die Brust, *the breast*	die Kraft, *the force*	die Macht, (*the*) *might*	die Schnur, *the string*
die Faust, *the fist*	die Kuh, *the cow*	die Maus, *the mouse*	die Wand, *the wall*
die Frucht, *the fruit*	die Kunst, (*the*) *art*	die Nacht, *the night*	die Wurst, *the sausage*

　　　　2. *Plural*: ——e; as: die Kenntniß, *knowledge*, die Kenntnisse (*attainments*).

die Drangsal, *need*	die Trübsal, *sorrow*	die Kenntniß, *knowledge*	die Besorgniß, *apprehension*

　　　　3. *Plural*: ——¨ ; die Mutter, *the mother*; die Tochter, *the daughter*.

NEUTER NOUNS.

A. Monosyllables. RULE: *Plural*: ——¨er; as: das Haus, *the house*, die Häuser.
　　EXCEPTIONS: 1. *Plural*: ——e; as: das Jahr, *the year*, die Jahre.

das Bein, *the leg*	das Heft, *the copy-book*	das Pfund, *the pound*	das Seil, *the rope*
das Beil, *the hatchet*	das Jahr, *the year*	das Recht, *the right*	das Spiel, *the game, play*
das Brod, *the bread*	das Knie, *the knee*	das Reh, *the roe*	das Stück, *the piece*
das Boot, *the boat*	das Loos, *the lot; ticket*	das Reich, *the empire*	das Tier, *the animal*
das Ding, *the thing*	das Maaß, *the measure*	das Roß, *the horse*	das Tor, *the gate*
das Fell, *the skin, hide*	das Meer, *the sea*	das Salz, *the salt*	das Werk, *the work*
das Gift, *the poison*	das Netz, *the net*	das Schaf, *the sheep*	das Zelt, *the tent*
das Haar, *the hair*	das Paar, *the couple, pair*	das Schiff, *the ship*	das Zeug, *the stuff*
das Heer, *the army*	das Pferd, *the horse*	das Schwein, *the pig*	das Ziel, *the aim, goal*

　　　　2. *Plural*: ——en; as: das Ohr, *the ear*, die Ohren.

das Bett, *the bed*	das Hemd, *the shirt*	das Herz, *the heart*	das Ohr, *the ear*

B. Dissyllables and Polysyllables.

(*a*.) Singulars ending in the derivative suffixes, -er, -el, { RULE: *Plural*: —— [no change], as:
　　　-en, -chen, -lein.　　　　　　　　　　　　　　　　　das Ufer, *the shore*, die Ufer.
　　　　Except: das Kloster, *the convent*, die Klöster.

(*b*.) Singulars not ending in the derivative suffixes, -er, { RULE: *Plural*: ——e; as:
　　　-el, -en, -chen, -lein.　　　　　　　　　　　　　　　das Metall, *the metal*, die Metalle.
　　EXCEPTIONS: 1. *Plural*: ——¨er; as: das Spital, *the hospital*, die Spitäler.

das Gemach, *the apartment*	das Gesicht, *the face*	das Regiment, *the regiment*
das Gemüt, *the temper*	das Gespenst, *the ghost*	das Spital (Hospital), *the hospital*
das Geschlecht, *the race, sex*	das Gewand, *the garment*	

　　　　2. *Plural*: ——n (or en): as: das Juwel, *the jewel*, die Juwelen.

das Auge, *the eye*	das Ende, *the end*	das Insekt, *the insect*	das Juwel, *the jewel*

　　　　3. *Altogether irregular*.

das Kapital, *the capital*, die Kapitalien　　　　das Drama, *the Drama*, die Dramen
das Mineral, *the mineral*, die Mineralien　　　das Thema, *the theme*, die Themata
das Studium, *the study* (*abstract*), die Studien　　(and a few others, foreign words).

N.B.—Foreign words in -o take -s for Plural, as: das Casino, *the Casino*, die Casinos, etc.

DOUBLE PLURALS.

die Bank, *the bench, bank*; die Bänke, *the benches*; die Banken, *the banks* (for money).
das Band, *the bond, ribbon*; die Bande, *the bonds*; die Bänder, *the ribbons*.
das Wort, *the word, expression*; die Wörter, *separate, disconnected words*; die Worte, *expressions, sentences*.

N.B.—Some words have to manufacture a plural, not having one naturally, as: der Tod, *death*, die Todesfälle, *deaths*; der Rat, *advice*, die Ratschläge, *counsels*, and a few others.

Examples and Practice on Reference-Page D.

Masculine Nouns. Form the Nom. Plural of der Bruder, *the brother*.

   Ask yourself: 1st. What gender is it? *Answer*: Masculine, therefore look among the Masculines.

          2d. How many syllables? *Answer*: Two, **therefore look** among the Dissyllables (**B.**).

          3d. What termination? *Answer*: er, therefore look among B. a.

          4th. Is it among the exceptions in B. a.? *Answer*: No, therefore its Plural is according to the Rule, given **for B. a.**; that is, the Plural is die Brüder.

Form the Plural of der Graf, *the count*.

   Ask yourself: 1st. What gender **is it?** *Answer*: Masculine, therefore look among the Masculines.

          2d. How many syllables? *Answer*: One, therefore look among the Monosyllables (**A.**).

          3d. Is it among the exceptions in **A.**? *Answer*: Yes, in **2**, therefore its Plural is according to the headline of the exceptions in **A. 2**; that is, the Plural is die Grafen.

Exercise.

Write out the Nominative Plural, according to the answers in each case, **of**:—

der Tisch, **the table**	der Altar, *the altar*	der Abend, *the evening*	der Herr, *the gentleman*
der Stuhl, *the chair*	der Kuchen, *the cake*	der Haufe, *the heap*	der Ast, *the branch*
der Hahn, *the cock*	der Morgen, *the morning*	der Bauer, *the peasant*	der Professor, *the professor*
der Nachbar, *the neighbour*	der Tag, *the day*	der Käfig, *the cage*	der Prinz, *the prince*
der Name, *the name*	der Affe, *the monkey*	der Hund, *the dog*	der Wald, *the* **forest**

Feminine Nouns. Form the Plural of die Uhr, *the watch*.

   In **answer to the above** questions, we **find it is among the Feminine Nouns**, and *not* among **the** exceptions, therefore the **Plural is according to the General Rule there**: die Uhren.

Exercise.

Write out the Nominative Plural, according to the answers in each case, of—

die Maus, *the mouse*	die Schwester, *the sister*	die Tante, *the aunt*	die Sache, *the thing*
die Nacht, *the night*	die Stadt, *the town*	die Trübsal, *the sorrow*	die Unruhe, *uneasiness*
die Burg, *the castle*	die Erzählung, *the relation*	die Feder, *the pen*	die Mutter, *the mother*

Neuter Nouns. Form the Plural of das Dorf, *the village*.

   In answer to the above questions, we find it is among the Neuter **Nouns**, a Monosyllable, **and** *not* **among** the exceptions, therefore the Plural is, according to the Rule in **A.**, die Dörfer.

Exercise.

Write out the Nominative Plural, **according to** the answers in each case, of—

das Mädchen, *the girl*	das Juwel, *the jewel*	das Theater, *the theatre*	das Buch, *the book*
das Auge, *the eye*	das Opfer, *the victim*	das Haus, *the house*	das Kloster, *the convent*
das Band, **the ribbon**	das Studium, *the study*	das Pfund, *the pound*	das Pferd, *the horse*
das Feuer, *the fire*	das Gewand, *the garment*	das Laster, *the vice*	das Gewehr, *the gun*
das Knäblein, *the little boy*	das Ohr, *the ear*	**das** Jahr, *the year*	das Gemach, *the apartment*

Lesson 8.

23. Notice carefully, that by "Assertion" in a sentence is meant the conjugated verb, i.e. in simple tenses the verb itself, as liebt in der Mann liebt die Frau; but in compound tenses the conjugated auxiliary and NEVER the Infinitive or Past Participle, as hat in er hat mir dieses geholt, and wird in er wird es holen.

24. The order of words is not altered in the Subjunctive, if the latter is not introduced by a conjunction, as: er sagt, er hoffe es, he says, he hopes so.

25. Verbs like sagen, to say; glauben, to believe, require the Subjunctive in German, though they are followed by Indicative in English, as: ich glaube, er sei hier, I believe, he is here.

26. The Present Subjunctive of all verbs, regular or irregular, is formed in the same way; but sein, to be, does not add e for 1st and 3d person Singular.

PRESENT SUBJUNCTIVE.

(man sagt,) ich lob-e den Schüler, (they say,) *I praise the pupil*   ich sei reich, *I am rich*
(er hofft,) du hab-est die Feder, (he hopes,) *thou hast the pen*   du sei-est hier, *thou art here*
(wir sagen,) er lieb-e den Hund, (we say,) *he loves the dog*   er sei dort, *he is there*
(ihr glaubt,) wir kauf-en das Haus, (you believe,) *we buy the house*   wir sei-en gut, *we are good*
(sie hoffen,) ihr hol-et den Mann, (they hope,) *ye fetch the man*   ihr sei-et arm, *ye are poor*
(man glaubt,) sie (Sie) such-en das Kind, (they believe,) *they (you) seek the child*   sie sei-en brav, *they are good*

Examples on the Present Subjunctive.

1. Sagt man, ich habe das Haus gekauft?
2. Nein, man sagt, Sie werden es kaufen.
3. Glauben Sie, der Graf sei dort?
4. Ja, ich hoffe, er werde dort sein.
5. Hoffst du, du werdest das Buch haben?
6. Ich glaube, ich werde es nicht brauchen.
7. Wirst du sagen, er sei nicht reich?
8. Ja, ich sage, er sei arm aber brav.
9. Er sagt, du liebest diesen Mann.
10. Ja, und ich werde dem Mann glauben.

1. *Do they say, I have bought the house?*
2. *No, they say, you will buy it.*
3. *Do you believe, the count is there?*
4. *Yes, I hope, he will be there.*
5. *Dost thou hope, thou wilt have the book?*
6. *I believe, I shall not want it.*
7. *Will you say, he is not rich?*
8. *Yes, I say, he is poor but well-behaved.*
9. *He says, you love this man.*
10. *Yes, and I shall believe the man (Dat.).*

Exercise.

1. They say, you believe this man.
2. Will he say, they are very poor?
3. No, he believes, they are not poor.
4. Where will the count be?
5. They hope, he will be here or there.
6. Do you hope, you will be rich? Yes.
7. They will say, I am not well-behaved.
8. Do not believe the king will be here.
9. Which wine have they bought?
10. I believe, they have bought no wine.

REFERENCE-PAGE E.

The Declension of German Nouns.

I. SINGULAR.

I. Masculine Nouns:

(A.) The following take *en* (or *n*) for Accusative, Genitive and Dative (see D. B. c.)

    1. All Masculine Nominatives in *-e*, as: der Knabe, *the boy*: den, des, dem Knaben.

    2. The following ten monosyllables, which were once dissyllables, **and ended in** *-e*:

der Bär, *the bear*	der Graf, *the count*	der Narr, *the fool*	
der Christ, *the Christian*	der Held, *the hero*	der Mensch, *the human being*	der Tor, *the fool*
der Fürst, *the duke, earl*	der Herr, *the gentleman*	der Prinz, *the prince*	

    3. Foreign words, **not ending in** *-al, -an, -aß, -r* (not *-or*), as: der Student, *the student*.

(B.) All other Masculine Nouns take *-s* for Genitive **Singular** and may remain unchanged for Accusative and Dative. To these **belong the following ten in** *-en*, which sometimes are written without the *-n* in the Nominative Singular, as: der Frieden or Friede, *peace* (see D. B. c.)

der Buchstaben, *the letter, type*	der Gedanken, *the thought*	der Namen, *the name*
der Frieden, *peace*	der Glauben, *the belief, faith*	der Samen, *the seed*
der Funken, *the spark*	der Haufen, *the heap*	der Willen, *the will*

der Felsen or Fels, *the rock*

N.B.—For the **sake of euphony**, masculine monosyllables sometimes take *-es* for Genitive Singular and *-e* for Dative Singular, as: der Fisch, *the fish*; des Fisches, dem Fische.

II. Feminine Nouns:

    Never change at **all in the Singular.**

III. Neuter Nouns: (Only exception: das Herz, *the heart*, declined as if it had Nominative das Herzen.) All these take *-s* for Genitive Singular and may remain unchanged for Accusative and Dative.

N.B.—For the sake of euphony neuter monosyllables sometimes take *-es* for Genitive Singular and *-e* **for Dative Singular, as:** das Dorf, *the village*; des Dorfes, dem Dorfe.

II. PLURAL.

Form the Nominative Plural from the Nominative Singular according to Reference-Page D. **Then remember: All cases are** the same as the Nominative, but the Dative Plural always must **end in** *-n*; this *-n* must therefore be added in every word which has not an *-n* at the end **already** in the other cases. This rule is without any exceptions.

Declension of Proper Nouns.

    1. Proper **Names, preceded** by an article, preposition, adjective or noun with article, do not change at all.

    2. If used without these before them, **they take** *-s* in Genitive **Singular**, but do not change for the other cases.

    3. Personal names, ending in sch, *-ß, -z,* -x, and feminine names in *-e*, take *-(e)ns* for Genitive **Singular and** *-(e)n* for Dative **Singular.**

N.B.—**Of** before Names is often translated by **von with** the Name unchanged. Before **names of Countries** or Towns translate **in** by **in**; from by **von** or **aus**; to by **nach**; and leave **the name of the country or town** unchanged.

Examples and Exercises on Reference-Page E.
(With the Plural according to Reference-Page D.)

Decline in Singular and Plural:

der Vater, *the father*	der Name, *the name*	der Graf, *the count*	der Sohn, *the son*
die Mutter, *the mother*	die Stadt, *the town*	das Ufer, *the bank*	das Dorf, *the village*

SINGULAR.

Nom.	der Vater	der Name(n)	der Graf	der Sohn	*the father, the name, etc.* (Subject)
Acc.	den Vater	den Namen	den Grafen	den Sohn	*the father, the name, etc.* (Object)
Gen.	des Vaters	des Namens	des Grafen	des Sohn(e)s	*of the father or the father's, etc.*
Dat.	dem Vater	dem Namen	dem Grafen	dem Sohn(e)	*to the father, to the name, etc.*

PLURAL.

Nom. Acc.	die Väter	die Namen	die Grafen	die Söhne	*the fathers, the names, etc.*
Gen.	der Väter	der Namen	der Grafen	der Söhne	*of the fathers, the fathers', etc.*
Dat.	den Vätern	den Namen	den Grafen	den Söhnen	*to the fathers, to the names, etc.*

SINGULAR.

Nom. Acc.	die Stadt	die Mutter	*the town, the mother*	das Ufer	das Dorf	*the shore, the village*
Gen.	der Stadt	der Mutter	*of the town (the town's)*	des Ufers	des Dorfes	*of the shore (the shore's)*
Dat.	der Stadt	der Mutter	*to the town, etc.*	dem Ufer	dem Dorfe	*to the shore, etc.*

PLURAL.

Nom. Acc.	die Städte	die Mütter	*the towns, the mothers*	die Ufer	die Dörfer	*the shores, the villages*
Gen.	der Städte	der Mütter	*of the towns (the towns')*	der Ufer	der Dörfer	*of the shores (the shores')*
Dat.	den Städten	den Müttern	*to the towns, etc.*	den Ufern	den Dörfern	*to the shores, etc.*

Exercise.

Decline in full, Singular and Plural (using Reference Tables E: and for the Plural D (*a*) and (*b*)):

der Hahn, *the cock*	der Mann, *the man*	das Gewehr, *the gun*	der Bauer, *the peasant*
die Uhr, *the watch, clock*	die Schlacht, *the battle*	der Same(n), *the seed*	das Haus, *the house*
das Buch, *the book*	der Palast, *the palace*	das Mädchen, *the girl*	der Mensch, *the human being*
der Bruder, *the brother*	das Jahr, *the year*	die Welt, *the world*	die Tante, *the aunt*
die Nacht, *the night*	der Prinz, *the prince*	das Gesetz, *the law*	der Wald, *the forest*

Examples of Proper Names.

Nom. Acc.	Karl, Charles	Fritz, Fred	Maria, Marie, Mary	der den } Mar	der Herr Schmidt, *Mr. Smith* / den Herrn Schmidt, *Mr. Smith*
Gen.	Karls, *of Charles*	Fritzens, *Fred's*	Marias, Mariens, *Mary's*	des Mar	des Herrn Schmidt, *Mr. Smith*
Dat.	Karl, *to Charles*	Fritzen, *to Fred*	Maria, Marien, *to Mary*	dem Mar	dem Herrn Schmidt, *to Mr. Smith*

Exercise.

Decline (Singular only of course): Luise, *Louise*; Bertha, *Bertha*; Ludwig, *Lewis*; die Frau Gold, *Mrs. Gold*; Friedrich, *Frederick*; Otto, *Otto*; der Doktor Braun, *Dr. Brown*; Schulz, *Schulz*; mein Vetter Gottlieb, *my cousin Gottlieb*; Heinrich, *Henry*.

Lesson 9.

27. In indirect speech, or indirect questions, we must use the Subjunctive in German, though in English the Indicative be used, unless an absolute **fact is stated** emphatically as a fact: *He says, he has heard it,* er sagt, er habe es gehört (Subjunctive).

28. It is generally optional, to use either **Present Subjunctive or Imperfect** Subjunctive in the dependent clause; in the 3d person **Singular,** however, the **Present** Subjunctive is generally preferred, as:

    wir hofften, sie seien (or wären) reich, *we hoped they were rich.*
    ich glaubte, er sei (not wäre) hier, *I thought he was here.*

29. But if an action is referred to as distinctly completed and past, the German idiom requires the Perfect Subjunctive in the oblique clause (see Rule 20, lesson 6):

    wir hörten, er habe das Pferd verkauft, *we heard, he sold the horse.*

IMPERFECT SUBJUNCTIVE.

In all regular verbs, the Imperfect Subjunctive is the same in form as the Imperfect Indicative, but the two tenses differ in all irregular Verbs, and in all auxiliaries.

Man sagte, *they said:* (one said:)

ich kaufte es, *I bought it*	ich hätte, *I had*	ich wäre, *I was*	ich würde, *I became*
du lobtest sie, *thou praisedst her*	du hättest, *thou hadst*	du wärest, *thou wast*	du würdest, *thou becamest*
er hörte das, *he heard that*	er hätte, *he had*	er wäre, *he was*	er würde, *he became*
wir liebten jenes, *we loved that*	wir hätten, *we had*	wir wären, *we were*	wir würden, *we became*
ihr wähltet dieses, *ye chose this*	ihr hättet, *ye had*	ihr wäret, *ye were*	ihr würdet, *ye became*
sie (Sie) suchten es, *they (you) sought it*	sie hätten, *they had*	sie wären, *they were*	sie würden, *they became*

Examples.

1. *We said, he did not fetch the book.*
2. *Do you believe, we (were or are) not happy?*
3. *The child says, it is not yet chosen.*
4. *We hoped, you would become well-behaved.*
5. *Does the boy believe he is in London?*
6. *They say, we are rich.*
7. *Do they say, you would become happy?*
8. *He hoped, you had it (would have had it).*

1. Wir sagten, er habe das Buch nicht geholt.
2. Glauben Sie, wir wären nicht glücklich?
3. Das Kind sagt, es sei noch nicht gewählt.
4. Wir hofften, Sie würden brav.
5. Glaubt der Knabe, er sei in London?
6. Man sagt, wir wären reich.
7. Sagt man, du würdest glücklich?
8. Er hoffte, Sie hätten es gehabt.

Exercise.

1. He hoped, you loved your teacher.
2. He said he was a man and no child.
3. Did you hear, they were rich or poor?
4. I heard, they had a horse there.
5. They said, we bought these books. [29.]
6. Have you heard, they are not yet here?
7. The lady said, she wanted [28] money.
8. We thought (believed), the king was not rich.
9. We believed, he became rich.
10. They heard, you chose this horse.

REFERENCE-PAGE F.

Some Rules for recognising the Gender of some Nouns.

As we have seen, in order to decline a Noun in the Singular or form its Plural, the first thing we must know, is its Gender, and although German Nouns are proverbially erratic in this respect, yet some rules for recognising Gender may with great advantage be learnt. Remember, however: In all cases learn the Definite Article with every new Noun.

A. Masculine are: [subject to the "absolute" rules in the neuter below.]
1. All male beings, and most larger wild animals, as: der Lehrer, *the teacher*; der Löwe, *the lion*.
2. All stones, seasons, months, and days, as: der Rubin, *the ruby*; der Juli, *July*.
3. Nouns ending in -en, as: der Garten, *the garden*.
   Except: das Kissen, *the cushion*; das Becken, *the basin*; das Wappen, *the coat of arms*.
4. Nouns ending in -ig, -ich, -ing, and -ee, as: der Käfig, *the cage*; der Tee, *tea*.

B. Feminine are: [subject to the "absolute" rules in the neuter below.]
1. Female beings, as: die Königin, *the queen*; die Tochter, *the daughter*.
   Except: das Weib, *the woman, wife*; das Frauenzimmer, *the female*.
2. Dissyllables denoting inanimate beings, ending in -e, as: die Rose, *the rose*.
   Except: das Auge, *the eye*; das Ende, *the end*; das Erbe, *the inheritance*; and the ten masculine substantives in -e or -en, beginning with der Buchstabe (see D. B. c.)
3. Nouns ending in -acht, -icht, -ulb, -unft, as: die Nacht, *the night*.
   Except: der Bedacht, *consideration*; der Schacht, *the mine*; der Verdacht, *suspicion*.
4. Derivatives in -ei, -heit, -keit, -schaft, -ung, as: die Freiheit, *liberty*.
   Except: das Petschaft, *the seal*.
5. Foreign words in -ie, -ion, -it, -tät, as: die Universität, *the university*.

Neuter are: [1 and 2 are "absolute" rules.]
1. All parts of speech not nouns or adjectival nouns, when used substantively, as: das „Wenn" und das „Aber," the "*if*" and the "*but*"; das Essen, *the eating (meal)*.
2. All diminutives; these all have if possible a modified root-vowel, and end in -chen, or -lein, as: das Mädchen, *the little girl*; das Knäblein, *the little boy*.
3. Metals, as: das Gold, *the gold*; except only der Stahl, *the steel*.
4. Countries, as: (das) England, *(the) England*; (das) Frankreich, *(the) France*.
   Except: die Schweiz, *Switzerland*; die Türkei, *Turkey*; die Pfalz, *the Palatinate*, and a few other provinces.

Note.—*Compound Nouns* are of the Gender of their last component, which also alone is declined, as: der Nußbaum, *the nut-tree* (though *nut* = die Nuß.) But compounds of der Mut, *courage*, are mostly feminine, as: die Anmut, *beauty*; die Armut, *poverty*; die Demut, *humility*; die Großmut, *generosity*; die Sanftmut, *gentleness*; die Langmut, *patience*; die Wemut, *melancholy*. [All other compounds of Mut are masculine.]

Other exceptions: die Antwort, *the answer* (Plural: die Antworten) (das Wort, *the word*); das Gegenteil, *the contrary* (der Teil, *the part*); der Mittwoch, *Wednesday* (die Woche, *the week*); der Abscheu, *horror* (die Scheu, *shyness*).

D

Examples and Exercises on Reference-Page F.

Give Gender and Reason for Gender, of—

Schneider, *tailor*	masc. (der)	male being	. . .	A. 1.
Blume, *flower*	fem. (die)	Dissyllable, inanimate, in -e		B. 2.
Herbst, *autumn*	masc. (der)	a season	. . .	A. 2.
Abend, *evening*	masc. (der)	part of a day	. .	A. 2.
Gleichheit, *equality*	fem. (die)	Derivative in -heit	.	B. 4.
Gold, *gold*	neut. (das)	a metal	. .	C. 3.
Mittwoch, *Wednesday*	masc. (der)	a day of the week	.	A. 2.
Stahl, *steel*	masc. (der)	exception to metals	.	C. 3.
Sonne, *sun*	fem. (die)	Dissyllable, inanimate, in -e	B. 2.
Nation, *nation*	fem. (die)	Foreign word, in -ion	.	B. 5.
Fräulein, *young lady*	neut. (das)	diminutive	. .	C. 2.
Winter, *winter*	masc. (der)	a season	. .	A. 2.

Exercise.

Give Gender and Reasons for Gender, of—

Graben, *ditch*	Schlacht, *battle*	Schweiz, *Switzerland*	Spielerei, *plaything*
Sonntag, *Sunday*	Väterchen, *little father*	Eroberung, *conquest*	Garten, *garden*
Schönheit, *beauty*	Ankunft, *arrival*	Sperling, *sparrow*	Rhetorik, *rhetoric*
Tiger, *tiger*	Tanzen, *dancing*	Nacht, *night*	Diamant, *diamond*
Häring, *herring*	Eisen, *iron*	Philosophie, *philosophy*	Blau, *blue*
Wenn, *if*	Klee, *clover*	Rußland, *Russia*	Geduld, *patience*

Using Reference-Pages D. and E. with F.

Give Gender, Genitive Singular, and Nominative Plural of—

	Gender.	Genitive Singular.	Nominative Plural.
Frau, *woman*	die, F. B. 1.	der Frau, E. D.	die Frauen, D. (b) Femin. General Rule.
Bruder, *brother*	der, F. A. 1.	des Bruders, E. A. b.	die Brüder, D. (a) B. (a) Rule.
Straße, *street*	die, F. B. 2.	der Straße, E. D.	die Straßen, D. (b) Femin. General Rule.
Tag, *day*	der, F. A. 2.	des Tages, E. A. b.	die Tage, D. (a) A. exception 1.
Fräulein, *young lady*	das, F. C. 2.	des Fräuleins, E. c.	die Fräulein, D. (b) Neuter, B. (a) Rule.

Exercise (using Reference-Pages D., E. and F.).

Give Gender, Genitive Singular and Nominative Plural, as above, of—

Blume, *flower*	Diamant (*foreign*) *diamond*	Mädchen, *girl*	Monat, *month*
Käfig, *cage*	Sonne, *sun*	Schlacht, *battle*	Rose, *rose*
Winter, *winter*	Garten, *garden*	Weib, *woman*	Knabe, *boy*
Auge, *eye*	Nacht, *night*	Vater, *father*	Dörfchen, *little village*

Lesson 10.

30. Many Verbs are conjugated in their Compound Tenses with ſein, *to be*, instead of haben, *to have*. Past Participles, when used as adjectives, take ſein as their auxiliary, as: es iſt gekauft, *it is bought*.

31. The Past Participle of ſein, *to be*, is **geweſen**, *been*, and of werden, *to become*, geworden [or worden, when used in connection with another Verb], as: er iſt gut geweſen, *he has been good*; er iſt ein Graf geworden, *he has become a count*; es iſt gekauft worden, *it has been (become) bought.* Remember to place the Past Participle last.

32. The English *"to be"* must be rendered by **werden**, *to become*, in the Passive voice; *i.e.* when an agent may be thought of, who did the action suffered by the subject, as: das Kind iſt geholt worden, *the child has been fetched*; *somebody (the agent) has fetched the child.*

Examples of Compound Tenses of ſein and werden.

(Notice the English *to have* must here always be rendered by ſein, *to be*.)

1. *My father has been here.* [is here been].
2. *We had been in London.* [were . . . been].
3. *She had become very rich.* [was . . . become].
4. *This book has been bought.* [is bought become].
5. *The boy had been punished.* [was punished become].
6. *His son has become a father.* (Nominative).
7. *He is praised and not punished.* (Passive).
8. *It is sold; it is (being) sold (by somebody).*

1. Mein Vater iſt hier geweſen.
2. Wir waren in London geweſen.
3. Sie war ſehr reich geworden.
4. Dieſes Buch iſt gekauft worden.
5. Der Knabe war geſtraft worden.
6. Sein Sohn iſt ein Vater geworden.
7. Er wird gelobt und nicht geſtraft.
8. Es iſt verkauft, es wird verkauft.

The *Conditional Simple* of all German Verbs is formed by using the Imperfect Subjunctive of werden (see Lesson 9), and adding to it the Infinitive of the Verb. As in the *Future Simple*, this Infinitive must stand at the end of the sentence.

Examples.

ich würde es nicht kaufen, wenn. etc.   *I should not buy it, if, etc.*
Würden Sie den Mann loben, wenn. etc.   *Should you praise the man, if, etc.*

Exercise.

1. That teacher has been our teacher.
2. You had been very well-behaved.
3. The child had been (become) praised.
4. He has become my pupil.
5. Who bought the horse? It is sold (adj.).
6. The pencil has been used.
7. Do you use this book? or this pen?
8. They have not yet been discovered.
9. The king would have bought it, if, etc.
10. Would you hear the pupil, if, etc.

REFERENCE-PAGE G.

On the Adjective.

Adjectives after "to be" or "to become" never change **at** all (see **Rule** 10, Lesson 4), but **all adjectives, as well as** Present and Past Participles used adjectively, **have** changes when they **stand as** attributes before a noun, or are used **as nouns themselves.** These changes depend on **the article** or determinative word before the adjective. We have three forms:

FIRST FORM.

The adjective preceded by one of the "*Definite Article Group.*" (See Reference-Page C.)
der, dieser, jener, jeder, mancher, welcher?

Scheme for First Form.

	masc. Sing.	fem. Sing.	neut. Sing.	All Plurals.		m. s.	f. s.	n. s.	Plural.
Nom.	der gut·e	} die gut·e	das gut·e	die gut·en	N.	·e		·e	·en
Acc.	den gut·en				A.	·en	} ·e		·en
Gen.	des gut·en	der gut·en	des gut·en	der gut·en	G.	·en	·en	·en	·en
Dat.	dem gut·en	der gut·en	dem gut·en	den gut·en	D.	·en	·en	·en	·en

Notice.—Nom. **Sing. in ·e; all other forms in ·en, except fem. and neut.** sing. Accusative by 2, Lesson 1.

SECOND FORM.

The adjective preceded **by one of the "*Indefinite Article Group.*"** (See Reference-Page C.)
ein, kein, was für ein; mein, dein, sein, (ihr), unser, euer, ihr (Ihr):

Scheme for Second Form.

	masc. Sing.	fem. Sing.	neut. Sing.	All Plurals.		m. s.	f. s.	n. s.	Plural.
Nom.	dein gut·er	} deine gut·e	dein gut·es	keine gut·en	N.	·er		·es	·en
Acc.	deinen gut·en				A.	·en	} ·e		·en
Gen.	deines gut·en	deiner gut·en	deines gut·en	deiner gut·en	G.	·en	·en	·en	·en
Dat.	deinem gut·en	deiner gut·en	deinem gut·en	deinen gut·en	D.	·en	·en	·en	·en

Notice.—Nom. Sing. in ·er, ·e, ·es; all other forms in ·en, except fem. and neut. sing. **Acc.** by 2, Lesson 1.

THIRD FORM.

The adjective *not* preceded by any determinative of the Definite or Indefinite Article groups, or preceded by a definite or indefinite *numeral* [without one of the words of the "Definite" or "Indefinite" article groups before them], as: zehn, *ten*, etc.; einige, *several*; mehrere, *several*; viele, *many*; viel, *much*; wenige, *few*; wenig, *little*; etwas, *something*. This form is used also in the Vocative (= **Nominative**).

	masc. Sing.	fem. Sing.	neut. Sing.	All Plurals.
Nom.	gut·er	} gut·e	gut·es	gut·e
Acc.	gut·en			
Gen.	gut·en	gut·er	gut·en	gut·er
Dat.	gut·em	gut·er	gut·em	gut·en

Notice.—These terminations are those of the "*Definite Article group,*" see Reference-Page C., except in the Genitive Singular, masculine and neuter, where ·en displaces ·es for the sake of euphony.

Examples and Exercises on Reference-Page G.

N.B.—The declension of the adjective does not in any way influence that of the Determinative nor that of the Substantive.

First Form.—Decline alt, *old*, with der . . Vater; diese . . Frau; welches . . Buch?

Singular (masc.)
- N. der alte Vater, } *the old father*
- A. den alten Vater,
- G. des alten Vaters, *the old father's*
- D. dem alten Vater, *to the old father*

Singular (fem.)
- } diese alte Frau, *this old woman*
- dieser alten Frau, *of this old woman*
- dieser alten Frau, *to this old woman*

Singular (neuter.)
- } welches alte Buch? *which old book?*
- welches alten Buches? *of which old book?*
- welchem alten Buche? *to which old book?*

Plural.
- N. } die alten Väter, *the old fathers*
- A. }
- G. der alten Väter, **of the old fathers**
- D. den alten Vätern, *to the old **fathers***

Plural.
- } diese alten Frauen, *these old women*
- dieser alten Frauen, *of these old women*
- diesen alten Frauen, *to these old women*

Plural.
- } welche alten Bücher? *which old books?*
- welcher alten Bücher? *of which old books?*
- welchen alten Büchern? *to which old books?*

Exercise.—Decline glücklich, *happy*; with dieser . . Mann; jede . . Mutter (of course no plural), and jenes . . Land; also brav, *well-behaved*; with welcher . . Knabe?

Second Form.—Decline neu, *new*, with sein . . Hut; seine . . Feder; Was für ein . . Land?

Singular (masc.)
- N. sein neuer Hut, } *his new hat*
- A. seinen neuen Hut,
- G. seines neuen Hutes, *of his new hat*
- D. seinem neuen Hute, *to his new hat*

Singular (fem.)
- seine neue Feder, **no new pen**
- seiner neuen Feder, *of no new pen*
- seiner neuen Feder, *to no new pen*

Singular (neuter.)
- Was für ein neues Land? *What sort of new land?*
- Was für eines neuen Landes? *Of what sort of new land?*
- Was für einem neuen Lande? *To what sort of new land?*

Plural.
- N. } seine neuen Hüte, *his new hats*
- A. }
- G. seiner neuen Hüte, *of his new hats*
- D. seinen neuen Hüten, *to his new hats*

Plural.
- seine neuen Federn, *no new pens*
- seiner neuen Federn, *of no new pens*
- seinen neuen Federn, *to no new pens*

Plural.
- Was für **neue Länder**? *What sort of new lands?*
- [*Note.* Was für ein . . drops ein in the Plural, therefore the adjective changes according to the *Third Form* in Plural.]

Exercise.—Decline arm, *poor*, with Was für ein . . Graf?; meine . . Tochter; Ihr . . Kind: also groß, *tall*, with ein . . Hund. (No plural.)

Third Form.—Decline schlecht, with Wein, Schule, Brod.

Singular (masc.).
- N. schlechter Wein, } *bad wine*
- A. schlechten Wein,
- G. schlechten Weines, *of bad wine*
- D. schlechtem Weine, *to bad wine*

Singular (fem.).
- schlechte Schule, *bad school*
- schlechter Schule, *of (a) bad school*
- schlechter Schule, *to (a) bad school*

Singular (neuter).
- schlechtes Brod, **bad bread**
- schlechten Brodes, *of bad bread*
- schlechtem Brode, *to bad bread*

Plural.
- N. } **schlechte Weine, bad wines**
- A. }
- G. schlechter Weine, **of bad wines**
- D. schlechten Weinen, *to bad wines*

Plural.
- schlechte Schulen, *bad schools*
- schlechter Schulen, *of bad schools*
- schlechten Schulen, *to bad schools*

Plural.
- schlechte Brode, *bad loaves*
- schlechter Brode, *of bad loaves*
- schlechten Broden, *to bad loaves*

Exercise.—Decline schön, *beautiful*, with Brief (m.) *letter*; Milch (f.) *milk* **(no plural)**; Dorf (n.) *village*; also reich, *rich*, with König (m.), and with zehn . . Städte (no sing.).

SENTENCES AND EXERCISES ON THE USE OF THE ADJECTIVE AS AN ATTRIBUTIVE (Ref.-Page G.).

(Learn these Model Sentences carefully, and imitate them.)

FIRST FORM.

1. *The beautiful daughters of the dear mother.*
2. *Each good child loves its father.*
3. *Which beautiful letter will you fetch?*
4. *The rich count has many-a large village.*
5. *He has not heard this poor man.*

1. Die schönen Töchter der lieben Mutter.
2. Jedes gute Kind liebt seinen Vater.
3. Welchen schönen Brief werden Sie holen?
4. Der reiche Graf hat manches große Dorf.
5. Er hat diesen armen Mann nicht gehört.

Exercise on the First Form.

1. Which happy boys were there? These.
2. I have not fetched every large book.
3. Will you seek those beautiful letters.
4. Where were these rich counts? There.
5. Every poor man will be here.
6. Do you use this beautiful knife? No.
7. Who has heard that good young-man?
8. They bought these large pictures here.
9. Many-a happy child was there.
10. These well-behaved children are poor.

SECOND FORM.

1. *My old dog is sold.*
2. *Have you heard our good pupil?*
3. *We have not chosen your beautiful knife.*
4. *What a long letter you have!*
5. *Do not (thou) buy any large books!*

1. Mein alter Hund ist verkauft.
2. Haben Sie unseren guten Schüler gehört?
3. Wir haben Ihr schönes Messer nicht gewählt.
4. Was für einen langen Brief Sie haben!
5. Kaufe keine großen Bücher!

Exercise on the Second Form.

1. What a beautiful horse he has!
2. We have not heard your good brother.
3. Have you chosen our happy boy?
4. No, we have chosen his poor child.
5. Where is my poor, old dog? Not here.
6. What sort of an old knife have you?
7. Did you sell your large lands? No.
8. They love their good old house much.
9. He loved a poor but happy girl.
10. We have no rich boys here, not one.

THIRD FORM.

1. *Do you use much good money? Yes.*
2. *The men had little clear wine.*
3. *We fetched ten big, but poor men.*
4. *You have several good, old books.*
5. *My father said: Poor child, listen!*

1. Brauchen Sie viel gutes Geld? Ja.
2. Die Männer hatten wenig reinen Wein.
3. Wir holten zehn große, aber arme Männer.
4. Sie haben mehrere gute, alte Bücher.
5. Mein Vater sagte: Armes Kind, höre!

Exercise on the Third Form.

1. I say it to ten poor, old men.
2. Little good wine, but much bad.
3. Rich man, hear poor children!
4. They had something good there.
5. Well-behaved pupils have clean books.
6. Several old brothers of our boys are here.
7. Do you love good old wine?
8. Poor child, choose this large book!
9. Much old wine is not very good.
10. He deserves something beautiful.

Lesson 11.

33. Instead of the Conditional Simple, we often use in German the Imperfect Subjunctive, as in English. For example:

I would be rich, if, etc.   Ich würde reich sein, or, Ich wäre reich, wenn, etc.
He would have the book, if, etc.   Er würde das Buch haben, or, er hätte das Buch, wenn, etc.

34. The Present Participle of all German verbs is formed by adding -end to the root, as : hab-en, *to have ;* hab-end, *having ;* kaufen, *to buy ;* kauf-end, *buying.* It is, however, seldom used as a verb.

35. Both the Present Participle and the Past Participle may be used as adjectives; when thus standing before a noun, they conform to the rules given in Reference-Page G., as: das gekaufte Buch, *the bought book ;* ein liebender Freund, *a loving friend.*

36. The Perfect and Pluperfect Subjunctive are formed as in English, by using the Present and Imperfect Subjunctive of the auxiliary with the Past Participle of the Verb. Remember that this Past Participle must come last in the sentence [see 16]; and also be careful to remember that sein, *to be*, and werden, *to become*, as well as many other verbs, take sein, *to be*, for their auxiliary, though they may have in English the auxiliary *to have*.

Examples **on the Perfect and Pluperfect Subjunctive.**

1. Man sagte, ich hätte das schöne Pferd gekauft.	1. *They said, I had bought the beautiful horse.*
2. Sie hofften, du wärest reich geworden.	2. *They hoped, thou hadst become rich.*
3. Ich glaube, er sei ein reicher Graf gewesen.	3. *I believe, he has been a rich count.*
4. Glauben Sie, er wäre dort gewesen, wenn, etc.	4. *Do you think he would have been there, if,* etc.
5. Er sagt, er habe das geliebte Kind gesucht.	5. *He says, he has [23] sought the loved child.*
6. Wir hoffen, Sie werden dieses glauben.	6. *We hope, you will believe this.*
7. Sagt man, er sei arm geworden?	7. *Do they say, he has become poor?*
8. Man sagte, Sie wären dort gewesen.	8. *They said, you had been there.*
9. Hätten Sie das alte Pferd verkauft, wenn, etc.	9. *Would you have sold the old horse, if,* etc.
10. Wäre das große Buch geholt worden, wenn, etc.?	10. *Would the large book have been fetched, if,* etc.

Exercise.
Read up Rules 25, 31, 33.

1. They say, we have been (Subj.) there.	2. They said, we had become happy.
3. The old king hopes, he will become rich.	4. This well-behaved child has been (is . . . become) punished.
5. This loved man has been chosen.	6. Will you say, he has deserved it.
7. These rich men use their money here.	8. Do you hope they had praised the happy men.
9. My good father says, you have been there.	10. They say, the poor count would have been there.

Lesson 12.

37. The Second Future and Second Conditional are formed in German, as in English, by joining to the Past Participle of the Verb, the First Future and First Conditional of the auxiliary, as:

ich werde es gekauft haben } etc., Second Future, { *I shall have bought it.*
du wirst dort gewesen sein   { *Thou wilt have been there.*

ich würde das geglaubt haben } etc., Second Conditional, { *I should have believed that.*
du würdest reich geworden sein   { *Thou wouldst have become rich.*

38. The really conjugated Verb in these tenses is the auxiliary werden; this auxiliary therefore is the Assertion, and all rules as to the position of the Assertion apply to it, and not to the Infinitives sein or haben, nor to the Past Participle of the actual verb.

39. Instead of the Second Conditional, we may use the Pluperfect Subjunctive, as:
ich würde das geglaubt haben = ich hätte das geglaubt. *I should have believed that.*
du würdest reich geworden sein = du wärest reich geworden. *Thou wouldst have become rich.*

40. In every Primary or independent statement or question, containing a Past Participle and an Infinitive, the Infinitive must stand last of all in the sentence, and the Past Participle last but one.

Examples.

1. Man sagt, er werde ein Graf werden.
2. { Sie würden den Hund gekauft haben.
   { Sie hätten den Hund gekauft.
3. { Würde er arm geworden sein, wenn, etc.
   { Wäre er arm geworden, wenn, etc.
4. { Der Knabe würde gestraft worden sein.
   { Der Knabe wäre gestraft worden.
5. Du wirst das Geld gebraucht haben.
6. Wird der Mann nicht gewählt werden?
7. Die Frau wird ihr Kind gelobt haben.
8. Wir werden das nicht gesucht haben.
9. Er wird dem Brief nicht geglaubt haben.
10. Die Tochter wäre gelobt worden.

1. *They say, he will become a count.*
2. *They (or you) would have bought the dog.*
3. *Would he have become poor, if, etc.*
4. *The boy would have been (become) punished.*
5. *Thou wilt have used the money.*
6. *Will the man not be (become) chosen?*
7. *The woman will have praised her child.*
8. *We shall not have sought this.*
9. *He will not have believed the letter* (dat.).
10. *The daughter would have been praised.*

Exercise.

1. Will you not have sought your book?
3. This good boy will be praised.
5. Would he not have been chosen, if . . . ?
7. He fetched my old book, the good boy.
9. Where was our fine, happy child?

2. I would have sought it, if . . .
4. He would have been punished, if . . .
6. Yes, he would have been chosen, if .
8. He would not have fetched it, if . . .
10. It will not yet have been there.

Additional Exercises.

(To be written on repeating the work of the Second Term.)

On Lesson 7.

1. My boy, fetch that book there!
2. There is my horse; let us sell it.
3. Let the teacher (acc.) hear this child!
4. Do not use your pencil, child!
5. Seek my letter (acc.), do you hear?
6. What did you choose? Choose that.
7. Here is your father; he has the letter.
8. Let him be poor or rich, father!
9. Praise this pupil; he is well-behaved.
10. Let them hear their teacher!

On Lesson 8 and Ref.-Page D.

1. We say, these boys are not well-behaved.
2. They say, they have deserved rewards.
3. Those ladies hope, you are not poor.
4. I believe, he will fetch my horses.
5. We hope, you will buy those houses.
6. My books say, he was very poor.
7. The men believe, they will choose this.
8. Do the counts say, they are not rich?
9. These pupils say, they are very happy.
10. We believe, we have discovered the lands.

On Lesson 9 and Ref.-Page E.

1. I believe the boy (dat.); he said, it is there.
2. My father's dog is very large; they say so.
3. We hoped, you had your teacher's book.
4. I believed, this town was very old.
5. The child of this man said, it was happy.
6. Do they say, we were rich, or poor?
7. Did you hear, he sought my pictures?
8. No, but I heard, they bought those there.
9. The sons of those brothers were not rich.
10. We thought, the children were happy.

On Lesson 10 and Ref.-Page F.

1. Have you been there? Yes, we were there.
2. These wines have been bought here.
3. Would you, my child, have been happy?
4. No, I should not have been very happy.
5. Will you buy my father's horse?
6. Who will have become a count?
7. My child has become a man (nom.).
8. Would you have become my pupils, if ...
9. Which dog has been (become) bought?
10. Who will have used your money?

On Lesson 11 and Ref.-Page G.

1. Would this rich man have become poor, if ...
2. I believe he would have become a poor man.
3. Does he think, this good book is very old?
4. My poor son said, he was not happy.
5. These old horses have been bought here.
6. Would he seek my old hat? No.
7. Had you been there, my poor men?
8. Rich daughters of poor mothers.
9. Would you believe these rich counts?
10. We hope, they will sell their old houses.

On Lesson 12 and General.

1. I think, my good child will have a book.
2. The happy fathers would have been here.
3. Let these poor children choose books.
4. I should not have believed this.
5. Happy sons of happy, old fathers!
6. Much money, but few good dresses.
7. Should we not have been chosen.
8. I believe, you will be chosen there.
9. Would they have sold these old horses?
10. I sold it to those good, happy men.

REFERENCE-PAGE H.

The Regular Verb; root unchanged throughout.

1. Verbs with roots ending in ſ, ſch, z, insert a euphonic e before ſt, as: du tanzeſt.

2. Verbs with roots ending in d, t, chn, gn, thm, insert a euphonic e before the t of all terminations, as: er redeſt, he speaks; er redete, he spoke.

3. No ge is prefixed for the Past Participle if the verb begins with be-, ge-, emp-, ent-, er-, ver-, zer-, hinter-, miß-, voll-, wider-, (see Rule 19, lesson 6), nor is ge- prefixed to verbs ending in -iren, as: verdient, probirt.

4. In verbs conjugated with ſein, to be, simply substitute this auxiliary for haben, to have, (below) in all Compound Tenses, without any other change whatever.

Example of Regular Conjugation: ſag-en, *to say.*
(*N. B.*—es, *it,* shows the position of the Object or Predicate throughout.)

PRESENT INDICATIVE.	PRESENT SUBJUNCTIVE.	PERFECT INDICATIVE.	PERFECT SUBJUNCTIVE.
ich ſag-e es, *I say it*	ich ſag-e es, *I say it*	ich habe ⎫ *I have*	ich habe ⎫ *I have*
du ... -ſt es, *thou sayest it*	du ... -eſt es, *thou say it*	du haſt ⎬ *thou hast*	du habeſt ⎬ *thou have*
er ... -t es, *he says it*	er ... -e es, *he say it*	er hat ⎨ge-ſag-t *he has* ⎬ *said it*	er habe ⎨ge-ſag-t *he have* ⎬ *said it*
wir ... -en es, *we say it*	wir ... -en es, *we say it*	wir haben ⎬ *we have*	wir haben ⎬ *we have*
ihr ... -t es, *ye say it*	ihr ... -et es, *ye say it*	ihr habet ⎬ *ye have*	ihr habet ⎬ *ye have*
ſie ... -en es, *they say it*	ſie ... -en es, *they say it*	ſie haben ⎭ *they have*	ſie haben ⎭ *they have*

IMPERFECT INDICATIVE.	IMPERFECT SUBJUNCTIVE.	PLUPERFECT INDICATIVE.	PLUPERFECT SUBJUNCTIVE.
ich ſag-te es, *I said it*	ich ſag-te es, *I said it*	ich hatte ⎫ *I had*	ich hätte ⎫ *I had (or would have)*
du ... -teſt es, *thou saidst it*	du ... -teſt es, *thou saidst it*	du hatteſt ⎬ *thou hadst*	du hätteſt ⎬ *thou hadst*
er ... -te es, *he said it*	er ... -te es, *he said it*	er hatte ⎨ge-ſag-t *he had* ⎬ *said it*	er hätte ⎨ge-ſag-t *he had* ⎬ *said it*
wir ... -ten es, *we said it*	wir ... -ten es, *we said it*	wir hatten ⎬ *we had*	wir hätten ⎬ *we had*
ihr ... -tet es, *ye said it*	ihr ... -tet es, *ye said it*	ihr hattet ⎬ *ye had*	ihr hättet ⎬ *ye had*
ſie ... -ten es, *they said it*	ſie ... -ten es, *they said it*	ſie hatten ⎭ *they had*	ſie hätten ⎭ *they had*

FIRST FUTURE INDICATIVE.	FIRST FUTURE SUBJUNCTIVE.	SECOND FUTURE INDICATIVE.	SECOND FUTURE SUBJUNCT.
ich werde ⎫ *I shall*	ich werde ⎫ *I shall*	ich werde ⎫ *I shall*	ich werde ⎫ *I shall*
du wirſt ⎬ *thou wilt*	du werdeſt ⎬ *thou wilt*	du wirſt ⎬ *thou wilt*	du werdeſt ⎬ *thou wilt*
er wird ⎨es ſag-en *he will* ⎬ *say it*	er werde ⎨es ſag-en *he will* ⎬ *say it*	er wird ⎨ge-ſag-t haben *he will* ⎬ *have said it*	er werde ⎨ge-ſag-t haben *he will* ⎬ *have said it*
wir werden ⎬ *we shall*	wir werden ⎬ *we shall*	wir werden ⎬ *we shall*	wir werden ⎬ *we shall*
ihr werdet ⎬ *ye will*	ihr werdet ⎬ *ye will*	ihr werdet ⎬ *ye will*	ihr werdet ⎬ *ye will*
ſie werden ⎭ *they will*	ſie werden ⎭ *they will*	ſie werden ⎭ *they will*	ſie werden ⎭ *they will*

IMPERATIVE.	FIRST CONDITIONAL.	SECOND CONDITIONAL.	INFINITIVE.
(no First Person Singular.)	ich würde ⎫ *I should*	ich würde ⎫ *I should*	es ſag-en, *to say it*
ſag-e es! *say (thou) it!*	du würdeſt ⎬ *thou wouldst*	du würdeſt ⎬ *thou wouldst*	es ge-ſag-t haben, *to have said it*
laßt es ihn ſagen! *Let him say it!*	er würde ⎨es ſag-en *he would* ⎬ *say it*	er würde ⎨ge-ſag-t haben *he would* ⎬ *have said it*	
ſagen wir es! *Let us say it!*	wir würden ⎬ *we should*	wir würden ⎬ *we should*	PRESENT PARTICIPLE.
ſag-t es! ⎫ *Say (you) it*	ihr würdet ⎬ *ye would*	ihr würdet ⎬ *ye would*	es ſag-end, *saying it*
ſagen Sie es! ⎭			
laßt es ſie ſagen! *Let them say it!*	ſie würden ⎭ *they would*	ſie würden ⎭ *they would*	PAST PARTICIPLE.
			ge-ſag-t, *said*

REFERENCE-PAGE I.

haben, *to have*. PRESENT PARTICIPLE : hab-end, *having*. PAST PARTICIPLE : ge-hab-t, *had* (regular).
Conjugated exactly like the Regular Verbs, root : hab-; except in the—

PRESENT INDICATIVE.	IMPERFECT INDICATIVE.	IMPERF. SUBJUNCTIVE.	Thus Regular are :
ich hab-e es, *I have it*	ich hatte es, *I had it*	ich hätte es, {*I had it* / *shd.* **have it**}	FUTURE SIMPLE.
du hast es, *thou hast it*	du hattest es, *thou hadst it*	du hättest es, *thou hadst it*	ich werde es haben, *I shall have it*
er hat es, *he has it*	er hatte es, *he had it*	er hätte es, *he had it*	FIRST CONDITIONAL.
wir hab-en es, *we have it*	wir hatten es, *we had it*	wir hätten es, *we had it*	ich würde es haben, *I should have it*
ihr hab-t es, *ye have it*	ihr hattet es, *ye had it*	ihr hättet es, *ye had it*	IMPERATIVE.
sie hab-en es, *they have it*	sie hatten es, *they had it*	sie hätten es, *they had it*	habe! *have (thou)*!

In the COMPOUND TENSES **haben** is its own auxiliary, as : ich habe es gehabt, *I have had it* (etc.).

sein, *to be*. PRESENT PARTICIPLE : sei-end, *being* (rarely used). PAST PARTICIPLE : gewesen, *been*.

PRESENT INDICATIVE.	PRES. SUBJ.	IMPERF. INDIC.	IMPERF. SUBJUN.	IMPERATIVE.
ich bin es, *I am it (it is I)*	ich sei es,	ich war es,	ich wäre es,	sei es, *be (thou) it*
du bist es, *thou art it*	du seiest es,	du warst es,	du wärest es,	(regular)
er ist es, *he is it*	er sei es, *(I am) be it, etc.*	er war es, *I was it (it was I), etc.*	er wäre es, *I were it, etc.*	—
wir sind es, *we are it*	wir seien es,	wir waren es,	wir wären es,	seien wir es, *let us be it*
ihr seid es, *ye are it*	ihr seiet es,	ihr waret es,	ihr wäret es,	seid es, {*be (you) it*}
sie sind es, *they are it*	sie seien es,	sie waren es,	sie wären es,	seien sie es, (regular)

In the Future Simple and First Conditional, **sein** is regular ; in the COMPOUND TENSES it is its own auxiliary.

PERFECT INDICATIVE.	PERFECT SUBJUNCTIVE.	SECOND FUTURE INDICATIVE.
ich bin es gewesen, *I have been it*	ich sei es gewesen, *I have been it*	ich werde es gewesen sein, *I shall have been it*
PLUPERFECT INDICATIVE.	PLUPERFECT SUBJUNCTIVE.	SECOND CONDITIONAL.
ich war es gewesen, *I had been it*	ich wäre es gewesen, *I had been it*	ich würde es gewesen sein, *I should have been it*

werden, *to become*. PRES. PARTIC. : werd-end, *becoming*. PAST PART. : (ge)worden (see Rule 31), *become*.
Conjugated exactly like the Regular Verbs, root : werd-; except in the—

PRESENT INDICATIVE.	IMPERF. INDIC.	IMPERF. SUBJUN.	Thus Regular are :
ich werde es, *I become it*	ich wurde es,	ich würde es,	PRESENT SUBJUNCTIVE.
du wirst es, *thou becomest it*	du wurdest es, *I became it, etc.*	du würdest es, *I became it, should, etc.*	ich werde es, *I become it*
er wird es, *he becomes it*	er wurde es,	er würde es,	du werdest es, *thou becomest it*
wir werden es, *we become it*	wir wurden es,	wir würden es,	FUTURE SIMPLE INDICATIVE.
ihr werdet es, *ye become it*	ihr wurdet es,	ihr würdet es,	ich werde es werden, *I shall become it*
sie werden es, *they become it*	sie wurden es,	sie würden es,	du wirst es werden, *thou wilt become it*

In the COMPOUND TENSES, **werden** is conjugated with **sein**, *to be*.

PERFECT INDICATIVE.	PERFECT SUBJUNCTIVE.	SECOND FUTURE CONDITIONAL.
ich bin es geworden, *I have become it*	ich sei es geworden, *I have become it*	ich werde es geworden sein, *I shall have become it*
PLUPERFECT INDICATIVE.	PLUPERFECT SUBJUNCTIVE.	SECOND CONDITIONAL.
ich war es geworden, *I had become it*	ich wäre es geworden, *I had become it*	ich würde es geworden sein, *I should have become it*

Conversational Sentences.

(To be learnt in small portions again and again during the Term.)

1.	Wie weit ist es von hier nach Berlin?	*How far is it from here to Berlin?*
2.	**Es ist noch mehr als zwanzig Meilen.**	*It is still more than twenty miles.*
3.	Ich bin müde; das Reisen ermüdet sehr.	*I am tired; travelling tires one very much.*
4.	Sind Sie hungrig? Nein, aber ich bin durstig.	*Are you hungry? No, but I am thirsty.*
5.	Es regnete stark, es hat gestern geschneit.	*It rained heavily, it snowed yesterday.*
6.	Heute ist es aber recht schönes Wetter.	*To-day, however, it is very beautiful weather.*
7.	Sie kommen mit uns; nicht wahr?	*You are coming with us, are you not?*
8.	Ja, ich werde mit Vergnügen kommen.	*Yes, I shall come with pleasure.*
9.	**Gehen Sie heute Abend in's Conzert?**	*Will you go to the concert this evening?*
10.	Nein, wir werden in's **Theater** gehen.	*No, we are going to the theatre.*
11.	Sehen Sie das schöne Dorf dort unten?	*Do you see the beautiful village down there?*
12.	Hier auf dem Berge **ist es** sehr schön.	*Here on the mountain it is very nice.*
13.	Setzen Sie **sich da auf diese Bank.**	*Sit down here on this bench.*
14.	Danke, mein Herr, setzen Sie sich auch.	**Thank you, Sir, sit down also.**
15.	Wie hat es Ihnen in Wien gefallen?	**How did you like Vienna?**
16.	Es gefiel mir außerordentlich gut.	*I liked it very much indeed.*
17.	**Wie lange blieben Sie in der Stadt?**	*How long did you remain in the town?*
18.	Ich blieb einen **ganzen Monat** dort.	*I remained a whole month there.*
19.	Sind Sie schon in der Schweiz gewesen?	**Have you already been in Switzerland?**
20.	Nein, aber wir gehen nächstes Jahr hin.	**No, but we go there next year.**
21.	Wir werden im Juli abreisen.	**We shall set out in July.**
22.	Mein Freund ist nach Amerika gegangen.	**My friend is gone to America.**
23.	Er wird wahrscheinlich fünf Jahre fort sein.	**He will probably be away five years.**
24.	**Es tut mir leid, aber ich kann nicht bleiben.**	**I am sorry, but I cannot remain.**
25.	Ich fürchte, Sie sind nicht ganz wohl.	*I fear you are not quite well.*
26.	Nein, ich habe starkes Kopfweh.	*No, I have a violent headache.*
27.	Mein Kopf tut mir sehr weh.	*My head pains me very much.*
28.	Ich bitte, geben Sie mir etwas Wasser.	*I beg you to give me some water.*
29.	Hier ist ganz kaltes, frisches Wasser.	*Here is some quite cold, fresh water.*
30.	Ach, das ist gut, ich danke Ihnen bestens.	*Oh, that is good, I thank you sincerely.*
31.	Fühlen Sie sich wieder etwas besser?	*Do you feel a little better again?*
32.	Oh ja, aber ich will nach Hause gehen.	**O yes, but I will go home.**
33.	Ich glaube, man wird jetzt fortgehen.	*I believe, people are going away now.*
34.	**Adieu, mein lieber Freund, auf Wiedersehen.**	*Good-bye, my friend, au revoir.*
35.	**Auf baldiges Wiedersehen, lieber Heinrich.**	*I hope to see you again soon, dear Henry.*
36.	Ich hoffe, dich recht bald wiederzusehen.	*I hope to see you again very soon.*

POEMS.

(To be learnt in small portions until thoroughly known.)

Schäfer's Sonntagslied. (Uhland.)

Das ist der Tag des Herrn!
Ich bin allein auf weiter Flur;
Noch eine Morgenglocke nur
Nun Stille nah' und fern.

Anbetend knie' ich hier.
O süßes Grau'n! Geheimes Weh'n!
Als knieten Viele ungeseh'n,
Und beteten mit mir.

Der Himmel, nah' und fern,
Er ist so klar und feierlich;
So ganz, als wollt' er öffnen sich.
Das ist der Tag des Herrn.

The Shepherd's Sunday Song.
(Literal Translation.)

This is the day of the Lord!
I am alone on the wide plain;
Yet one morning-bell only,
Now silence near and far.

Worshipping **I kneel here.**
O sweet awe! **Mysterious breathings!**
As if many knelt unseen,
And were praying along with me.

Heaven, near and far away,
Is so clear and solemn-looking;
So altogether, as if it were going to open.
That is the Lord's **day.**

Der Gute Kamerad. (Uhland.)

Ich hatt' einen Kameraden,
Einen bessern find'st du nit. (or nicht)
Die Trommel schlug zum Streite,
Er gieng an meiner Seite
In gleichem Schritt und Tritt.

Eine Kugel kam geflogen,
Gilt's mir oder gilt es dir?
Ihn hat sie weggerissen,
Er liegt mir vor den Füßen,
Als wär's ein Stück von mir.

Will mir die Hand noch reichen,
Derweil ich eben lad'!
Kann dir die Hand nicht geben,
Bleib' du im ew'gen Leben,
Mein guter Kamerad!

The Good Comrade.
(Literal Translation.)

I had a comrade,
***A** better one you could not find.*
The drum beat for the battle,
***He** marched at my side*
With equal step (and tread).

***A** (cannon) ball came flying (towards us),*
*Is it my turn or is **it yours?***
Him it has torn away,
He lies in front of my feet,
Just as if it were a piece of myself.

He wants to give me his hand once more,
Just whilst I am loading (my gun);
I cannot give you my hand.
Remain in eternal life (hereafter),
My good comrade.

Reference-Page J.

SEQUENCE OF WORDS in the PRIMARY or PRINCIPAL Sentence.

(Recapitulation of Syntax Rules given hitherto.)

The student must, of course, be able without hesitation to recognise a **member** of a sentence as the **Subject**, or the **Object**, or the **Predicate**, etc. He must also carefully remember that the **Assertion** is **never** an Infinitive or Past Participle, but always a verb or auxiliary conjugated, *i.e.* expressing Person, Number, and Tense.

A. Natural order in Statements. (Learn this order by heart.)

1	2	3	4	5	6	7
Subject, with all its enlargements.	*Assertion* i.e. Conjugated Verb or Auxiliary.	*Objects* with their enlargements. (Noun with preposition) Noun in oblique Case. See *Notice* (a) below.	*Adverbs* or *Adverbials*. See *Notice* (b) below.	*Predicate* with its enlargements. [Separable prefix] Nom. of nouns. Adj. invariable.	*Past Partic.* If more than one, put that of the Auxiliary last.	*Infinitive.* If more than one, put that of the Auxiliary last.
Der gute Knabe	kauft	seine Bücher	heute.	none	none	none
Mein alter Vater	hat	dem Knaben	nicht	none	geglaubt	none
Die Kinder	sind	von dem Lehrer	gestern	none	gelobt worden.	none
Er	war	none	schon	ein alter Mann.	none	none
Diese Männer	würden	none	dort	nicht reich	geworden	sein.
Die Sonne	gieng	none	none	heute spät auf.	none	none

B. Inverted order, *i.e.* Assertion before Subject, without any other change. This takes place (a) in Questions; (b) when any other **member of the sentence, except the Subject**, stands **at the beginning of the** sentence for **emphasis.**

3, 4, 5, 6, or 7	2	1	3	4	5	6	7
	INVERSION.						
	Assertion	*Subject.*	*Objects.*	*Adverbs.*	*Predicate.*	*Past Partic.*	*Infinitive.*
Geglaubt	kauft	der gute Knabe	seine Bücher	heute?	none	none	none
Von dem Lehrer	hat	mein alter Vater	dem Knaben	nicht.	none	(at beginning)	none
Ein alter Mann	sind	die Kinder	(at beginning)	gestern	none	gelobt worden.	none
Dort	war	er	none	schon.	(at beginning)	none	none
Heute	würden	diese Männer	none	(at beginning)	nicht reich	geworden	sein.
	gieng	die Sonne	none	none	spät auf.	none	none

Notice.—(a) If there are more than one *Object*, Person precedes Thing, Pronoun precedes Noun, Dative precedes Accusative. (b) As to *Adverbials*, adverbs of time precede all **others, and even** stand often before the Objects; the adverb **nicht** generally precedes other adverbs, **or** it may stand before the word it negatives; [noch nicht, *not yet*, is rarely separated]. (c) Principal sentences joined by—**und,** *and*; **oder,** *or*; **denn,** *for, because*; **aber, allein,** *but*; and **sondern,** *but* (after a negative, and *not* introducing a complete sentence), preserve the same sequence of words in each sentence as given above.

N.B.—The above Sequence of words is sometimes slightly interfered with by a desire to make any word specially emphatic by placing it where it ought not to stand according to Rule.

THIRD TERM

THE pupil ought now to begin with translating very easy pieces of German, using a Dictionary. Every word ought, with the assistance of the teacher (especially in the Irregular Verbs) to be parsed *viva voce*. The Reference-Pages ought to be constantly referred to in this parsing. A few words should be parsed *in writing* for each translation lesson, and a "Vocabulary" should be begun by the pupil, into which he should write down the English of every *new* word he meets with in each lesson set in translation.

A few sentences from page 61, and a few words of the Dictionary on pages 58, 59, should still form an integral part of every Grammar lesson set, also the Poem on page 62.

N.B.—Reference-Page **J**, page 38, ought now to be constantly referred to in doing the Exercises in this Term, the words for which will be found in the Dictionary on pp. 58, 59.

Example of Parsing.

Translate:—Du haſt zwei Ohren und nur einen Mund; Vieles ſollſt du hören, und wenig darauf ſagen. Du haſt zwei Augen und nur einen Mund: denn Manches ſollſt du ſehen und dabei ſchweigen. Zwei Hände haſt du, und einen Mund: Zur Arbeit ſind zwei da, zum Eſſen nur Einer.

PARSING.

Of *Nouns* give number and case in **the text**; and **Nominative** Singular with definite **article** and English; also Genitive Singular and **Nominative** Plural.—Of *Verbs* give Person, number, tense, and mood in the text, and **Infinitive with the** English, 3d Person Singular Present Indicative; Imperfect Indicative; and Perfect Indicative.

N.B.—For some time the Infinitive of Irregular Verbs met with in Translation must be given by the teacher to the pupil, who will then be able to parse the verb by looking them out on Reference-Page **N**.

[The letters in () refer to the Reference-Pages, which must be consulted in the Parsing.]

du (Q.), Personal Pronoun, Nom. Sing. 2d person, *thou (you)*.
haſt (I.), Auxiliary, 2d pers. Sing., Pres. Indic. of haben, *to have*.
   er hat, er hatte, er hat gehabt, *hast*.
zwei (R.), Numeral adjective, *two*.
Ohren (D. a.), Noun, accusative Plural of:
   das Ohr, des —es, die —en, *ears*.
und, co-ordinate Conjunction, *and*.
nur, adverb of limitation, *only*.
einen (C. b.), Indef. Article, masc. Sing. acc., *a, one*.
Mund (D. a.), Noun, accusative Singular of:
   der Mund, des —es, die —e, *mouth*.
Vieles, Indef. adjective, neut. acc. Sing., *much*.
ſollſt (K.), Auxiliary, 2d pers. Sing. Pres. Ind., of:
   ſollen, er ſoll, er ſollte, er hat geſollt, *shalt*.
hören (H.), Infinitive **regular** Verb:
   er hört, hörte, hat gehört, *(to) hear*.
wenig, Indefinite Pronoun, *little*.
darauf (Q. 5.), **contraction for auf es**, Preposition with acc. neut. Pers. Pron., *about it*.
ſagen (H.), Infinitive, regular Verb.
   er ſagt, ſagte, hat geſagt, *(to) say*.
Augen (D. b.), Noun, accusative Plural **of**:
   das Auge, des —s, die —n, *eyes*.

denn, co-ordinate Conjunction, *for* (because).
Manches (C. a.), Indef. adj. neut. Acc. Sing., *many a (thing)*.
ſehen (N.), Infinitive irregular Verb.
   er ſieht, ſah, hat geſehen, *(to) see*.
dabei (Q. 5.), contraction for bei dem, Preposition with dat. Sing. of relative, "*by it,*" *withal*.
ſchweigen (N.), Infinitive irregular Verb, *be silent*.
   er ſchweigt, ſchwieg, hat geſchwiegen.
Hände (D. b.), Noun, accusative Plural of:
   die Hand, der —, die'—e, *hands*.
zur (O. N.B.—2.), **contraction** of zu der, Preposition with dative singular feminine article, *for* (*the*).
Arbeit (D. b.), Noun, dative singular of
   die Arbeit, der —, die —en, *work*.
ſind (I.), Auxiliary, 3d plural Present Indicative of:
   ſein, er iſt, war, iſt geweſen, *are*.
da, Adverb of place, *there, here*.
zum (O. N.B.—2.), contraction of zu dem, Preposition with dative singular masculine Article, *for* (*the*).
Eſſen, Infinitive used as a noun, dative singular of:
   das Eſſen, des —s, [die —], *eating*.
Einer (C. b. 2.), Indefinite article used as a noun masculine Singular Nominative *one*.

Literal Translation.

You have two ears, and only one mouth; much you should hear, and say little about it. You have two eyes, and only one mouth; for many a thing you should see and be silent withal. Two hands you have, and one mouth; for work there are two, for eating only one.

REFERENCE-PAGE K.

The Auxiliaries of Mood.

Besides haben, *to have*, sein, *to be*, and werden, *to become*, the German language has, like the English, *auxiliary verbs*, to express the **mode** of an action. Unlike the English auxiliaries of mood, the German auxiliaries have a complete conjugation, and require the actual verb in the *Infinitive without* zu (*to*...). There are seven such auxiliaries: **dürfen**, *to be allowed ;* **können**, *to be able ;* **mögen**, *to like ;* **müssen**, *to be obliged ;* **sollen**, *(to) ought ;* **wollen**, *to be willing ;* and **lassen**, *to let*.

Of these lassen is altogether irregular, and will be given among the irregular verbs ; the other six are **regular** verbs throughout, except in the *Singular Present Indicative ;* the first four however drop the modification of their root vowel for the Imperfect Indicative, but resume it for the Imperfect Subjunctive ; sollen and wollen cannot modify at all ; **mögen** changes g into ch in the Imperfects and Past Participle.

In all other respects they are conjugated like sagen. (See Reference-Page H.)

dürfen, *to be allowed, may*
PRESENT INDICATIVE.
ich darf, — *I am allowed to*
du darfst, — *thou mayest*
er darf, — *he may*
wir dürfen, — *we are allowed to*
ihr dürft, — *ye may*
sie dürfen, — *they are allowed to*
(es laufen — *buy it*)
IMP. IND. ich durfte, *I was allowed*
IMP. SUB. ich dürfte, *I { might / should } be allowed*
PAST PARTIC. gedurft, *allowed*

können, *to be able, can*
PRESENT INDICATIVE.
ich kann, — *I am able to*
du kannst, — *thou canst*
er kann, — *he is able to*
wir können, — *we can*
ihr könnt, — *ye are able to*
sie können, — *they can*
(es hören — *hear it*)
IMP. IND. ich konnte, *I could*
IMP. SUB. ich könnte, *I would be able to*
PAST PARTIC. gekonnt, *been able*

mögen, *to like, may*
PRESENT INDICATIVE.
ich mag, — *I like to*
du magst, — *thou mayest*
er mag, — *he may*
wir mögen, — *we like to*
ihr mögt, — *ye like to*
sie mögen, — *they may*
(es glauben — *believe it*)
IMP. IND. ich mochte, *I liked to*
IMP. SUB. ich möchte, *I should like to*
PAST PARTIC. gemocht, *liked*

müssen, *to be obliged, must*
PRESENT INDICATIVE.
ich muß, — *I am obliged to*
du mußt, — *thou must*
er muß, — *he is obliged to*
wir müssen, — *we must*
ihr müßt, — *ye must*
sie müssen, — *they are obliged to*
(es nicht sagen — *not say it*)
IMP. IND. ich mußte, *I was obliged to*
IMP. SUB. ich müßte, *I should be obliged to*
PAST PARTIC. gemußt, *obliged*

sollen, *ought, should*
PRESENT INDICATIVE.
ich soll, — *I should*
du sollst, — *thou shouldst*
er soll, — *he is to*
wir sollen, — *we are to*
ihr sollt, — *ye should*
sie sollen, — *they are to*
(es holen — *fetch it*)
IMP. IND. ich sollte, *I ought to*
IMP. SUB. ich sollte, *I ought to*
PAST PARTIC. gesollt, *ought*

wollen, *to wish, be willing*
PRESENT INDICATIVE.
ich will, — *I wish to*
du willst, — *thou wilt*
er will, — *he wishes to*
wir wollen, — *we will*
ihr wollt, — *ye will*
sie wollen, — *they wish to*
(es verlaufen — *sell it*)
IMP. IND. ich wollte, *I wished to*
IMP. SUB. ich wollte, *I wanted to*
PAST PARTIC. gewollt, *wished*

Though easy of conjugation, these auxiliaries present great difficulties as to their employment.

EXAMPLES AND EXERCISES ON REFERENCE-PAGE K.

Example.—Write out in full—(1) the Present Subjunctive, (2) the Imperfect Subjunctive, (3) the Future Simple Indicative, (4) the Conditional Simple, of **dürfen**; also (5) the Compound Future Indicative, (6) the Perfect Subjunctive, (7) the Compound Conditional, of **können**.

(1) PRESENT SUBJUNCTIVE.
ich dürfe, *I am (be) allowed*
du ...est, *thou mayest*
er ...e, *he may*
wir ...en, *we are allowed*
ihr ...et, *ye may*
sie ...en, *they may*

(2) IMPERFECT SUBJUNCTIVE.
ich dürfte, *I might, would*
du ...est, *thou wouldst*
er ...e, *he would*
wir ...en, *we should*
ihr ...et, *ye might*
sie ...en, *they might*
} *be allowed*

(3) FUT. SIMPLE INDICAT.
ich werde ⎫ *I shall*
du wirst ⎪ *thou wilt*
er wird ⎬ *he will* } *dürfen* } *be allowed*
wir werden ⎪ *we shall*
ihr werdet ⎪ *ye will*
sie werden ⎭ *they will*

(4) CONDITIONAL SIMPLE.
ich würde ⎫ *I should*
du ...est ⎪ *thou wouldst*
er ...e ⎬ *he would* } *dürfen* } *be allowed*
wir ...en ⎪ *we should*
ihr ...et ⎪ *ye would*
sie ...en ⎭ *they would*

(5) COMPOUND FUTURE INDICAT.
ich werde ⎫ *I shall*
du wirst ⎪ *thou wilt*
er wird ⎬ *he will* } *gekonnt* } *have been able*
wir werden ⎪ *we shall*
ihr werdet ⎪ *ye will*
sie werden ⎭ *they will*

(6) PERFECT SUBJUNCTIVE.
ich habe ⎫ *I have*
du habest ⎪ *thou have*
er habe ⎬ *he have* } (lesen) können, gekonnt } *been able (to read), been able*
wir haben ⎪ *we have*
ihr habet ⎪ *ye have*
sie haben ⎭ *they have*

(7) COMPOUND CONDITIONAL.
ich würde ⎫ *I should*
du würdest ⎪ *thou wouldst*
er würde ⎬ *he would* } haben (lesen) können, gekonnt } *have been able (to read), have been able*
wir würden ⎪ *we should*
ihr würdet ⎪ *ye would*
sie würden ⎭ *they would*

Exercise.—Write out in full—(1) Future Simple Indicative, (2) Future Simple Subjunctive, (3) Present Subjunctive, of **mögen**; also (4) Imperfect Subjunctive, (5) Pluperfect Indicative, (6) Perfect Indicative, of **müssen**.

Examples.

1. Darf der Knabe diese Bücher kaufen?
2. Er hat sie kaufen dürfen * (nor geburft).
3. Wir mögen diese Bilder nicht sehen.
4. Er sollte morgen nach London gehen.
5. Sie haben es so gewollt, mein Herr.
6. Möchten Sie nach Paris reisen?

1. *Is the boy allowed to buy these books?*
2. *He has been allowed to buy them.*
3. *We do not like to see these pictures.*
4. *He ought to go to London to-morrow.*
5. *You have wished it thus, Sir.*
6. *Should you like to travel to Paris?*

* *Notice carefully:* When these auxiliaries are used in the Compound Tenses, along with the Infinitive of a Verb, the Past Participle of the auxiliary is replaced by its Infinitive.

Exercise.

(See Rules on Reference-Page K; also above.)

1. Was the man allowed to see those dogs?
2. Yes, he has been allowed to see them.
3. We wished to sell our old horse.
4. They have not wished to go to London.
5. My father does not like his new wine.
6. You ought not to be idle, my boys.
7. They say you are obliged to do this.
8. Your daughter did not like to sing.
9. Were they allowed to choose their books?
10. Yes, they have been allowed to choose.

Additional Notes on Reference-Page K.

Differences in the idiomatic use of the auxiliaries in English and German.

(Learn and digest these sample sentences carefully.)

1. Sie haben Recht, mein Herr; ich hatte Unrecht.
2. Es ist dunkel geworden, und es wird kalt.
3. Darf ich es sagen? Du darfst es nicht sagen.
4. Ich hätte mein Pferd verkaufen können.
5. Können Sie Deutsch? Ich kann es noch nicht.
6. Sie mag reich sein. Möchte sie glücklich sein!
7. Ich hätte den Knaben gern sehen mögen.
8. Wir haben das Haus verkaufen müssen.
9. Mein Sohn soll jetzt Französisch anfangen.
10. Du sollst deinen Nächsten lieben!
11. Er soll ausgewandert sein.
12. Er will nach Australien gehen.
13. Wir werden es morgen kaufen.

1. *You are right, Sir ; I was wrong.*
2. *It has got dark, and it is getting cold.*
3. *May I say it? You must not say it.*
4. *I could have sold my horse.*
5. *Do you know German? I do not know it yet.*
6. *She may be rich. O that she were happy!*
7. *I should have liked to see the boy.*
8. *We were obliged to sell the house.*
9. *My son is now to begin French.*
10. *Thou shalt love thy neighbour!*
11. *He is said to have emigrated.*
12. *He intends to go to Australia.*
13. *We shall buy it to-morrow.*

Conjugate like **dürfen**:
bedürfen, *to need*; er bedarf,
er bedurfte, er hat bedurft,
followed by a noun in the Genitive, as:
ich bedarf des Buches, *I need the book.*

Conjugate like **mögen**:
vermögen *to be able*; er vermag,
er vermochte, er hat vermocht,
followed by an Infinitive with zu, as:
ich vermag es zu thun, *I am able to do it.*
(This verb admits of zu before the Infinitive.)

Exercise on the above.

1. My father will be right, I shall obey.
2. Are you not wrong, my dear friend?
3. It is getting late; it has got night.
4. You may say it to your kind teacher.
5. We needed a friend, and you are one.
6. O that these children were diligent!
7. My little son knows a little German.
8. Does he also know French? No, not yet.
9. He is to learn French soon.
10. The men could have chosen their friends.
11. We were obliged to go to Paris.
12. Were they not also obliged to go?
13. Was she able to do this work?
14. No, she has not been able to do it (*fem.*).
15. Have you needed your money, Sir?
16. Did you wish to buy my horse?
17. I have not wished to buy it.
18. It may be cheap, but I need no horse.
19. He is said to be in Berlin.
20. Why was he not allowed to go?

Notice.—The words for the Exercises in this term will be found in the Dictionary on pages 58, 59; or in that on page 12.

REFERENCE-PAGE L.

Hints for recognising **as** regular or irregular any verb [not an **auxiliary** or one of the **half-regular** Verbs (Ref.-Page **M**, *N.B. b* and *c*)] met with in Translation.

Auxiliaries, **and the** nine half-regular verbs [see Ref.-Page **M**, *N.B. b* and *c*] are not comprised in the following hints, which ought to be very carefully learnt, as they are very useful.

Any verb **is** regular—

I. If the 1st or 3d person Singular IMPERFECT ends in *ste*. (No exceptions.)
With the exception of tun, *to do*, and the Verbs (about 20 altogether) which **have** a root ending in d or t; the terminations -test, -ten, -tet of the Imperfect also betray a regular verb.

II. If the PAST PARTICIPLE ends in -t. (No exceptions, as all irreg. Past Part. end in -n.)

III. If the INFINITIVE has: (Learn the exceptions by heart.)

   (a) *Root-Vowel*: o; except only kommen, *to come*; stoßen, *o push*.
               u; except only rufen, *to call*; tun, *to do*.
               eu, äu; without any exceptions.
               ä; except only gähren, *to ferment*; gebären, *to bring forth*.
               ö; except only erlöschen, *to become extinguished*; schwören, *to swear*.
               ü; except only betrügen, *to cheat*; lügen, *to lie, tell a lie*.
               au; except only hauen, *to hit*; laufen, *to run*; schnauben, *to snort*; saufen, *to drink (of animals)*; and saugen, *to suck*.

   (b) *Termination*: ...den; except only backen, *to bake*; erschrecken, *to be frightened*.
               ...chten; except only fechten, *to fight*; flechten, *to weave*.
               ...zen; except only sitzen, *to sit, be seated*.
               ...gnen; ...eln; ...ern; ...igen; ...iren; these without exceptions.

Notes on the *auxiliary* to be used in the *Compound Tenses*:

The English often differs from the German in the use of *to have* or *to be*, as we have seen already, **thus:** *I have been* = ich bin gewesen (*I am been*).

Neuter verbs of motion or of condition mostly take sein in the compound tenses.

   (a) *Of motion*: [Root verbs only are given here; the derivatives also take sein.]

begegnen (reg.), *to meet*	fliehen, *to shun, flee*	reisen (reg.), *to travel*	stürzen (reg.), *to fall headlong*
fahren, *to take a drive*	gehen, *to go*	reiten, *to take a ride*	wandern (reg.), *to wander*
fallen, *to fall*	kommen, *to come*	schwimmen, *to swim*	and a few more.
fliegen, *to fly* (with wings)	laufen, *to run*	steigen, *to mount*	

   (b) *Of condition or state*:

aufwachen (reg.), *to wake up*	einschlafen, *to fall asleep*	genesen, *to recover*	stehen, *to stand*
bleiben, *to remain*	erschrecken, *to be frightened*	sein, *to be*	werden, *to become*

N.B.—**Many of** these may, with a slight change, be turned into transitive verbs, when they take haben as their auxiliary, as: einschläfern, *to send to sleep*, etc.

Examples and Exercises on Reference-Page L.

Example:—Are the following regular or irregular verbs, and why?

ich glaubte, *I believed,*	regular,	∵	1st pers. Singular Imperfect ending in ‑te.
er erschuf, *he created,*	irregular,	∵	3d pers. Sing. Imperfect *not* ending in ‑te.
Sie riefen, *you called,*	irregular,	∵	Plural Imperfect *not* ending in ‑ten or ‑tet.
gelebt, *lived,*	regular,	∵	Past Participle ending in ‑t.
er bat, *he begged,*	irregular,	∵	3d pers. Sing. Imperfect *not* ending in ‑te.
gegangen, *gone,*	irregular,	∵	Past Participle *not* ending in ‑t.
er betete, *he prayed,*	regular,	∵	3d pers. Sing. Imperfect ending in ‑te.
kommen, *to come,*	irregular,	∵	Exception to root vowel o being regular.
toben, *to rage,*	regular,	∵	Root vowel of Infinitive o.
erlauben, *to permit,*	regular,	∵	Root vowel of Infinitive ‑au (not an exception).
versuchen, *to attempt,*	regular,	∵	Root vowel of Infinitive u.
tanzen, *to dance,*	regular,	∵	Termination of Infinitive ‑zen.
begegnen, *to meet,*	regular,	∵	Termination of Infinitive ‑gnen.
fügen, *to join,*	regular,	∵	Root vowel of Infinitive ü.
studiren, *to study,*	regular,	∵	Termination of Infinitive ‑iren.
schwören, *to swear,*	irregular,	∵	Exception to root vowel ö being regular.

Exercise.—Are the following regular or irregular verbs, and why?

gewähren, *to grant*	beugen, *to bend*	geraubt, *robbed*	laufen, *to run*
sitzen, *to sit*	ich kam, *I came*	rufen, *to call*	dichten, *to compose*
er hob, *he lifted*	er fragte, *he asked*	fechten, *to fight*	verlassen, *forsaken*
er dankte *he thanked*	betrügen, *to cheat*	er schrieb, *he wrote*	rauschen, *to rustle*
glücken, *to succeed*	tun, *to do*	führen, *to lead*	ich gieng, *I went.*

to have in English, in the **Compound** Tenses, **sein** in German.

I have met my friend, **he has come.**	Ich bin meinem Freund begegnet; er ist gekommen.
He had fallen, *he was frightened.*	Er war gefallen, er war erschrocken.
The child has gone *to sleep, **it has been tired.***	Das Kind ist eingeschlafen, es ist müde gewesen.
We have wandered through the whole of Europe.	Wir sind durch ganz Europa gewandert.
The enemies have fled; *we have remained.*	Die Feinde sind geflohen; wir sind geblieben.

Given: fliehen, *to flee;* floh, ist geflohen. bleiben, *to remain;* blieb, ist geblieben.

Exercise.

1. **Have** you remained there? No, Sir.
2. Where **have** you been, my little friend?
3. Who **has** fled? The enemy **has** fled.
4. **Have** you met your brother? (Dative.)
5. No, **I have** not yet met my brother. (Dat.)
6. I should have remained if . . .
7. We **have** gone to England. (Page 22, foot.)
8. Will you believe, we **have** (subj.) remained?
9. **Have** they travelled far, your friends?
10. **He has** fallen [headlong] into the river.
    (in with *acc.*)

Reference-Page M.
The Irregular Verb.

The Irregular **Verbs** are irregular only in the Imperfect Indicative, the Imperfect Subjunctive, and the Past **Participle**. But most of those, which have a, au, o or e, for their root vowel modify a into ä, au into äu, o into ö, and e into i or ie, for the 2d and 3d [*never* the 1st] persons Singular of the *Present Indicative*; and the 2d person Singular *Imperative*, if contracted.

*Examples of the **Irregularities** of Irregular Verbs.*

sehen, *to see.*

PRESENT INDICATIVE.	IMPERFECT INDICATIVE.	IMPERFECT SUBJUNCTIVE.	IMPERATIVE.
ich seh-e es, *I see it*	ich sah es, *I saw it*	ich säh-e es, *I saw it*	sieh! *see* (thou)!
du sieh-st es, *thou seest it*	du sah-st es, *thou sawest it*	du säh-est es, *thou sawest it*	(rest regular)
er sieh-t es, *he sees it*	er sah es, *he saw it*	er säh-e es, *he saw it*	
wir seh-en es, *we see it*	wir sah-en es, *we saw it*	wir säh-en es, *we saw it*	PAST PARTICIPLE.
ihr seh-t es, *ye see it*	ihr sah-t es, *ye saw it*	ihr säh-et es, *ye saw it*	gesehen, *seen*
sie seh-en es, *they see it*	sie sah-en es, *they saw it*	sie säh-en es, *they saw it*	

All other tenses are always regular, *i.e.* as given on Reference-Page **H**.

It will therefore be sufficient to give of irregular verbs only the

INFINITIVE PRESENT.	3d SING. PRES. INDIC.	3d SING. IMPF. INDIC.	3d SING. PERF. INDIC.	to show what auxiliary to use.
sehen, *to see*	er sieht	er sah	er hat gesehen	

Remembering carefully the following Rules.

1. Where the 3d person Singular of Present Indicative shows a modification of root vowel, the same modification occurs in the 2d person Singular of the same tense, and the 2d person Singular Imperative **if contracted**.

2. The Imperfect Subjunctive is throughout formed from the Imperfect Indicative in the same way as shown above, modifying a into ä, o into ö, and u into ü.

3. All other tenses are regular, as shown in Reference-Page **H**.

N.B.—(a) The following verbs do not modify the root vowel in 2d and 3d person Singular *Present Indicative* (**of** course verbs with i, ie, ei, eu cannot do **so**). *Regular Verbs* never do so, nor do the half-regular Verbs **below, nor** verbs with u for root vowel, of which two **only** are irregular:

bewegen, *to move;* genesen, *to recover;* heben, *to lift;* schaffen, *to create;* stehen, *to stand;* gehen, *to go;* hauen, *to hit;* pflegen, *to nurse;* stecken, *to stick;* weben, *to weave.*

(b) The following Verbs have a *root-vowel* change, but are otherwise *quite* **regular**:

brennen, *to burn;* brannte, gebrannt
kennen, *to know;* kannte, gekannt
nennen, *to call;* nannte, genannt

rennen, *to run;* rannte, gerannt
senden, *to send;* sandte, gesandt
wenden, *to turn;* wandte, gewandt

(c) To these may be added the following:

denken, *to think;* dachte, gedacht
bringen, *to bring;* brachte, gebracht

wissen, *to know;* wußte, gewußt, with irreg. *Pres. Ind.*, Sing. only, ich weiß, du weißt, er weiß

NOTES TO REFERENCE-PAGE M.

The Irregular Verb.

The learner will find that the best way **to acquire a knowledge** of the irregular verbs **is to constantly** repeat the "Headline" **of** each, and **enlist the ear in the** service of memory. The **alphabetical** list should be gone over again and again in small portions.

We may distinguish **four** conjugations, **according to the root vowel in the Imperfect Indicative.**

1st Conjugation: Imperfect: **a** (about 60 verbs, *i.e.* root-verbs):

    (a) e(i)   a   e   as: lesen, *to read*; las, gelesen   (about 15 verbs)
    (b) e(i)   a   o   as: helfen, *to help*; half, geholfen   (about 28 verbs)
    (c) i   a   u   as: finden, *to find*; fand, gefunden   (about 16 verbs)

2d Conjugation: Imperfect: ie or i (about 50 verbs):

    (a) ei   i   i   as: leiden, *to suffer*; litt, gelitten   (about 20 verbs)
    (b) ei   ie   ie   as: schreiben, *to write*; schrieb, geschrieben   (about 15 verbs)
    (c) (a)   ie   a   as: schlafen, *to sleep*; schlief, geschlafen   **(about 15 verbs)**

3d Conjugation: **Imperfect:** o (about 40 verbs):

    (a) ie   o   o   as: verlieren, *to lose*; verlor, **verloren**   (about 20 verbs)
    (b) (e)   o   o   as: heben, *to lift*; hob, gehoben   (about 20 verbs)

4th Conjugation: **Imperfect:** u (9 verbs)

    all: a   u   a   as: fahren, *to drive*; fuhr, gefahren

The following have irregularities in addition **to root-vowel changes:**

(a) Lengthening of vowel and consequently omission of double consonant:

    bitten, *to beg*; bat, gebeten   schaffen, *to work*; schuf, (geschaffen)
    kommen, *to come*; kam, (gekommen)   treffen, *to hit, meet*; traf, (getroffen)
                   sitzen, *to sit*; saß, (gesessen)

(b) **The** change ei into i is generally accompanied by a doubling of the consonant:

    greifen, *to grasp*; griff, gegriffen   gleiten, *to glide*; glitt, geglitten
    kneifen, *to pinch*; kniff, gekniffen   pfeifen, *to whistle*; pfiff, gepfiffen
    reiten, *to ride*; **ritt**, geritten   schleifen, *to grind*; schliff, geschliffen
    schreiten, *to stride*; schritt, geschritten   streiten, *to quarrel*; stritt, gestritten
    Thus also d into tt: leiden, *to suffer*; litt, gelitten
    schneiden, *to cut*; schnitt, geschnitten   sieden, *to **boil***; sott, gesotten

(c) Still further irregularities have—

INFINITIVE.	ENGLISH.	PRESENT INDICATIVE SINGULAR.	3D SINGULAR IMPERFECT INDICATIVE.	3D SINGULAR PERFECT INDICATIVE.
gehen	*to go*	(reg.) er geht	er gieng	er ist gegangen
hauen	*to strike*	(reg.) er haut	er hieb	er hat gehauen
nehmen	*to take*	ich nehme, du nimmst, **er nimmt**	er nahm	er hat genommen
stehen	*to stand*	(reg.) er steht	er stand	er ist gestanden
tun	*to do, make*	ich tue, du tust, er tut	er tat	er hat getan
ziehen	*to pull*	(reg.) er zieht	er zog	er hat gezogen

Examples and Exercises on Reference-Page M.

Example.—*Given:* lesen, *to read;* er liest, las, hat gelesen
and: gehen, *to go;* er geht, gieng, ist gegangen
write out in full—(1) **Present** Indicative; (2) **Imperfect** Subjunctive; (3) **Imperative**; (4) **Perfect Indicative**;
(5) **Perfect Subjunctive**; (6) **Compound Future Indicative**; (7) **Future Simple Subjunctive** of each.

(1) Pres. Indicative.	(2) Impf. Subjunctive.	(3) Imperative.	(7) Future Simple Subj.
ich lese, *I read*	ich läse, *I* {might / should} *read*	none	ich werd-e *I shall read*
du liesest, *thou readest*	du ...est, *thou wouldst* ...	lies (or lese), *read (thou)*	du ... est *thou wilt* ...
er liest, *he reads*	er ...e, *he would* ...	lasst ihn / er soll } lesen, *let him read*	er ... e *he will* ...
wir lesen, *we read*	wir ...en, *we should* ...	lesen wir, *let us read*	wir ... en *we shall* ...
ihr leset, *ye read*	ihr ...et, *ye would* ...	leset (lesen Sie) *read (you)*	ihr ... et *ye will* ...
sie lesen, *they read*	sie ...en, *they would* ...	lasst sie / sie sollen } lesen, *let them read*	sie ... en *they will* ...

Same of : gehen, *to go*.

(1) Pres. Indicative.	(2) Impf. Subjunctive.	(3) Imperative.	(7) Future Simple Subj.
ich geh-e, *I go*	ich gieng-e, *I* {might / should} *go*	none	ich werd-e *I shall go*
du ... st, *thou goest*	du ... est, *thou wouldst* ...	geh' (or gehe) *go (thou)*	du ... est *thou wilt go*
er ... t, *he goes*	er ... e, *he would* ...	lasst ihn / er soll } gehen, *let him go*	er ... e *he will go*
wir ... en, *we go*	wir ... en, *we should go*	gehen wir, *let us go*	wir ... en *we shall go*
ihr ... t, *ye go*	ihr ... et, *ye would go*	gehet (gehen Sie), *go (you)*	ihr ... et *ye will go*
sie ... en, *they go*	sie ... en, *they would go*	lasst sie / sie sollen } gehen, *let them go*	sie ... en *they will go*

(4) Perfect Indicative.	(5) Perfect Subjunctive.	(6) Compd. Future Indicative.
ich habe *I have read*	ich habe *I have read*	ich werde *I shall*
du hast *thou hast read*	du ... est *thou have* ...	du wirst *thou wilt*
er hat *he has read*	er ... e *he have* ...	er wird *he will*
wir haben } gelesen *we have read*	wir ... en } gelesen *we have* ...	wir werden } gelesen haben *we shall have read*
ihr habt *ye have read*	ihr ... et *ye have* ...	ihr werdet *ye will*
sie haben *they have read*	sie ... en *they have* ...	sie werden *they will*

Same of : gehen, *to go*.

(4) Perfect Indicative.	(5) Perfect Subjunctive.	(6) Compd. Future Indicative.
ich bin *I have gone*	ich sei *I have gone*	ich werde *I shall*
du bist *thou hast* ...	du seiest *thou have* ...	du wirst *thou wilt*
er ist *he has* ...	er sei *he have* ...	er wird *he will*
wir sind } gegangen *we have* ...	wir seien } gegangen *we have* ...	wir werden } gegangen sein *we shall have gone*
ihr seid *ye have* ...	ihr seiet *ye have* ...	ihr werdet *ye will*
sie sind *they have* ...	sie seien *they have* ...	sie werden *they will*

Exercise.—*Given:* stehen, *to stand;* er steht, stand, ist gestanden
and : verlieren, *to lose;* er verliert, verlor, hat verloren
write out in full—(1) **Present Indicative**; (2) **Perfect Subjunctive**; (3) **Conditional Compound**; (4) **Imperfect Subjunctive** of each.

REFERENCE-PAGE **N**.

Alphabetical List of the Irregular Verbs.

Notes. 1. Root-verbs only are given here, not their derivatives; thus the pupil will find : finden, *to find;* but not emp=finden, *to feel.*

2. Auxiliaries are not given (except laffen, *to let*), nor are the half-regular verbs, as fennen, *to know*, etc. [These nine will be found on Ref.-Page **M**. *N.B. b.c.*]

3. Of each verb the Infinitive, and the 3d pers. Sing. of—Pres. Indic.; Imperfect Indic.; and Perfect Indic.; are given: these parts suffice to conjugate the verb fully, if we remember the following Rules, which have been already given or hinted at:—

(*a.*) *The* **Present Indicative**: 1st pers. Sing. adds =e to the *root of the Infinitive*; 2d pers. Sing. substitutes =ft for the =t of the given 3d person; *Plurals* add =en, =(e)t, =en to *Infinitive Root.*

(*b.*) *The* **Imperfect Indicative**: 1st pers. Sing. always like the given 3d person; 2d pers. Sing. adds =ft to the given 3d person; *Plurals* add =en, =et, =en to the given 3d person.

(*c.*) *The* **Imperfect Subjunctive**: adds (without any exception) =e, =eft, =e; =en, =et, =en, to the given 3d person of the Imperfect Indicative, *modifying* a, o, u *into* ä, ö, ü.

(*d.*) *The* **Imperative** is generally regular, as : gebe, *give thou.* But sometimes a contracted form is used for the 2d pers. Singular only, as : *gieb, *give thou;* whenever this is the case, the vowel is modified as in the given 3d pers. Sing. of the Present Indicative; in fact it is then the 3d pers. Sing. of the Pres. Indic. with the =t cut off. **see * in the List.**

[All the other tenses are formed *regularly*, as given in Reference-Page **H**.]

The **Perfect Indicative** shows both the *Past Participle* and the **auxiliary** used for all the Compound tenses—(as *adjectives*, the Past Participles are used always with **fein,** *to be*)—and in the *passive voice* with **werden,** *to become.*

This List ought to be learnt over and over again in small portions.

Infinitive.	3d pers. Sing. Pres. Indic.	3d pers. Sing. Impf. Ind.	3d person Sing. Perfect Indicative.	Infinitive.	3d pers. Sing. Pres. Indic.	3d pers. Sing. Impf. Ind.	3d person Sing. Perfect Indicative.
baden, *to bake*	er bädt	bud	hat gebaden	binden, *to bind*	er bindet	band	hat gebunden
befehlen, *to command*	*er befiehlt	befahl	hat befohlen	bitten, *to beg*	er bittet	bat	hat gebeten
befleißen (fich) *to apply (oneself)*	er befleißt (fich)	befliß (fich)	hat (fich) befliffen	blafen, *to blow*	er bläft	blies	hat geblafen
				bleiben, *to remain*	er bleibt	blieb	ift geblieben
beginnen, *to begin*	er beginnt	begann	hat begonnen	braten, *to roast*	er brät	briet	hat gebraten
beißen, *to bite*	er beißt	biß	hat gebiffen	brechen, *to break*	*er bricht	brach	hat gebrochen
bergen, *to hide*	*er birgt	barg	hat geborgen	dingen, *to hire*	er dingt	(dingte)	hat gedungen
berften, *to burst*	es birft	barft	ift geborften	drefchen, *to thrash*	*er drifcht	drafch	hat gedrofchen
bewegen, *to induce*	er bewegt	bewog	hat bewogen	dringen, *to urge*	er dringt	drang	ift gedrungen
biegen, *to bend*	er biegt	bog	hat gebogen	empfehlen, *to recommend*	*er empfiehlt	empfahl	hat empfohlen
bieten, *to offer*	er bietet	bot	hat geboten				

Reference-Page N.—List of Irregular Verbs—*Continued.*

Infinitive	3d pers. Sing. Pres. Indic.	3d pers. Sing. Impf. Ind.	3d person Sing. Perfect Indicative.	Infinitive	3d pers. Sing. Pres. Indic.	3d pers. Sing. Impf. Ind.	3d person Sing. Perfect Indicative.
erbleichen, to **turn pale**	er erbleicht	erblich	ist erblichen	hauen, to hit, hew	er haut	hieb	hat gehauen
				heben, to lift	er hebt	hob	hat gehoben
erlöschen, **to become extinguished**	es erlöscht	erlosch	ist erloschen	heißen, to be called	er heißt	hieß	hat geheißen
				helfen, to help	*er hilft	half	hat geholfen
erschallen, to resound	es erschallt	erscholl	ist erschollen	klemmen, to pinch	er klemmt	(klomm)	(hat geklemmt)
erschrecken, to become frightened	*er erschrickt	erschrak	ist erschrocken	klimmen, to climb	er klimmt	klomm	ist geklommen
				klingen, to sound	es klingt	klang	hat geklungen
essen, to eat	*er ißt	aß	hat gegessen	kneifen, to pinch	er kneift	kniff	hat gekniffen
fahren, to take a drive	er fährt	fuhr	ist gefahren	kreischen, to scream	er kreischt	(krisch)	hat gekrischen
fallen, to fall	er fällt	fiel	ist gefallen				(also regular)
fangen, to catch	er fängt	fieng	hat gefangen	kommen, to come	er kommt	kam	ist gekommen
fechten, to fight	er ficht	focht	hat gefochten	kriechen, to creep	er kriecht	kroch	ist gekrochen
finden, to find	er findet	fand	hat gefunden	küren, to elect	er kürt	kor	hat gekoren
flechten, to weave, plait	er flicht	flocht	hat geflochten	laden, to load	er ladet	lud	hat geladen
				lassen, to let, allow	er läßt	ließ	hat (ge)lassen
fliegen, to fly (wings)	er fliegt	flog	ist geflogen	laufen, to run	er läuft	lief	ist gelaufen
fliehen, to shun, flee	er flieht	floh	ist geflohen	leiden, to suffer	er leidet	litt	hat gelitten
fließen, to flow	(er) fließt	floß	ist geflossen	leihen, to lend	er leiht	lieh	hat geliehen
fressen, to eat (of animals)	*(er) frißt	fraß	hat gefressen	lesen, to read	*er liest	las	hat gelesen
				liegen, to lie, be laid	er liegt	lag	ist gelegen
frieren, to freeze	es friert	fror	hat gefroren	lügen, to tell a lie	er lügt	log	hat gelogen
gähren, to ferment	es gährt	gohr	hat gegohren	meiden, to shun	er meidet	mied	hat gemieden
gebären, to bring forth	sie gebiert	gebar	hat geboren	melken, to milk	er milkt	molk	hat gemolken
				messen, to measure	*er mißt	maß	hat gemessen
geben, to give	*er giebt	gab	hat gegeben	nehmen, to take	*er nimmt	nahm	hat genommen
gebieten, to command	er gebietet	gebot	hat geboten	pfeifen, to whistle	er pfeift	pfiff	hat gepfiffen
gedeihen, to thrive	er gedeiht	gedieh	ist gediehen	pflegen, to nurse	er pflegt	pflog	hat gepflogen
gefallen, to please	er gefällt	gefiel	hat gefallen	preisen, to praise	er preist	pries	hat gepriesen
gehen, to go	er geht	gieng	ist gegangen	quellen, to gush forth	es quillt	quoll	ist gequollen
gelingen, to succeed	es gelingt	gelang	ist gelungen	raten, to advise	er rät	riet	hat geraten
gelten, to be worth	es gilt	galt	hat gegolten	reiben, to rub	er reibt	rieb	hat gerieben
genesen, to recover (health)	er geneft	genas	ist genesen	reißen, to tear	er reißt	riß	hat gerissen
				reiten, to take a ride	er reitet	ritt	ist geritten
genießen, to enjoy	er genießt	genoß	hat genossen	riechen, to smell	es riecht	roch	hat gerochen
geschehen, to happen	es geschieht	geschah	ist geschehen	ringen, to struggle (wring)	er ringt	rang	hat gerungen
gewinnen, to gain, win	er gewinnt	gewann	hat gewonnen				
				rinnen, to run	es rinnt	rann	ist geronnen
gießen, to pour	er gießt	goß	hat gegossen	rufen, to call	er ruft	rief	hat gerufen
gleichen, to resemble	er gleicht	glich	hat geglichen	saufen, to drink (of animals)	er säuft	(soff)	hat gesoffen
gleiten, to glide	er gleitet	glitt	ist geglitten				
glimmen, to glow	es glimmt	glomm	hat geglommen	saugen, to **suck**	er saugt	sog	hat gesogen
graben, **to** dig	er gräbt	grub	hat gegraben	schaffen, **to work (create)**	er schafft	schuf	hat geschaffen
greifen, to seize	er greift	griff	hat gegriffen				
halten, to hold	er hält	hielt	hat gehalten	scheiden, **to separate (depart)**	er scheidet	schied	(ist) geschieden
hangen, to be hanging	er hängt	hieng	ist gehangen				

Reference-Page N.—List of Irregular Verbs—*Concluded*.

Infinitive.	3d pers. Sing. Pres. Indic.	2d pers. Sing. Impf. Indic.	3d person Sing. Perfect Indicative.	Infinitive.	3d pers. Sing. Pres. Indic.	2d pers. Sing. Impf. Ind.	3d person Sing. Perfect Indicative.
scheinen, *to seem*	er scheint	schien	hat geschienen	springen, *to spring*	er springt	sprang	ist gesprungen
schelten, *to scold*	*er schilt	schalt	hat gescholten	stechen, *to sting, prick*	*er sticht	stach	hat gestochen
scheeren, *to shear* (concern)	er scheert	schor	hat geschoren	stecken, *to stick*	er steckt	stad	(hat gesteckt)
				stehen, ***to stand***	er steht	stand	ist gestanden
schieben, *to push*	er schiebt	schob	hat geschoben	stehlen, ***to steal***	*er stiehlt	stahl	hat gestohlen
schießen, *to shoot*	er schießt	schoß	hat geschossen	steigen, *to mount*	er steigt	stieg	ist gestiegen
schlafen, *to sleep*	er schläft	schlief	hat geschlafen	sterben, *to die*	*er stirbt	starb	ist gestorben
schlagen, *to hit*	er schlägt	schlug	hat geschlagen	stieben, *to fly off*	er stiebt	stob	(hat) gestoben
schleichen, *to sneak*	er schleicht	schlich	ist geschlichen	stinken, *to stink*	es stinkt	stank	hat gestunken
schleifen, *to grind* (knives)	er schleift	schliff	hat geschliffen	stoßen, *to push*	er stößt	stieß	hat gestoßen
				streichen, *to stroke*	er streicht	strich	hat gestrichen
schließen, *to conclude, shut*	er schließt	schloß	hat geschlossen	streiten, *to quarrel*	er streitet	stritt	hat gestritten
				tun, *to do, make*	er tut	tat	hat getan
schlingen, *to surround*	er schlingt	schlang	hat geschlungen	tragen, *to carry*	er trägt	trug	hat getragen
schmeißen, *to throw*	er schmeißt	schmiß	hat geschmissen	treffen, *to hit*	*er trifft	traf	hat getroffen
schmelzen, *to melt*	*er schmilzt	schmolz	hat geschmolzen	treiben, *to drive*	er treibt	trieb	hat getrieben
schnauben, *to snort*	er schnaubt	schnob	hat geschnoben	treten, *to step*	*er tritt	trat	ist getreten
schneiden, *to cut*	er schneidet	schnitt	hat geschnitten	triefen, *to drip*	er trieft	troff	hat getroffen
schreiben, *to write*	er schreibt	schrieb	hat geschrieben				(also regular)
schreien, *to cry, shout*	er schreit	schrie	hat geschrieen	trinken, *to drink*	er trinkt	trank	hat getrunken
schreiten, *to stride, proceed*	er schreitet	schritt	ist geschritten	trügen, *to cheat*	er trügt	trog	hat getrogen
				verderben, *to spoil*	*er verdirbt	verdarb	hat verdorben
schweigen, *to be silent*	er schweigt	schwieg	hat geschwiegen	verdrießen, *to **annoy***	es verdrießt	verdroß	hat verdrossen
schwellen, *to swell*	es schwillt	schwoll	ist geschwollen	vergessen, *to forget*	*er vergißt	vergaß	hat vergessen
schwimmen, *to swim*	er schwimmt	schwamm	ist geschwommen	verlieren, *to loose*	er verliert	verlor	hat verloren
schwinden, *to vanish*	er schwindet	schwand	ist geschwunden	wachsen, *to grow*	er wächst	wuchs	ist gewachsen
schwingen, *brandish, swing*	er schwingt	schwang	hat geschwungen	wägen, *to weigh*	er wägt	wog	hat gewogen
				waschen, *to wash*	er wäscht	wusch	hat gewaschen
schwören, *to swear*	er schwört	schwor	hat geschworen	weben, *to weave*	er webt	wob	hat gewoben
sehen, *to see*	*er sieht	sah	hat gesehen	weichen, *to yield*	er weicht	wich	ist gewichen
sieden, *to boil*	er siedet	sott	hat gesotten	weisen, ***to** show, point out*	er weist	wies	hat gewiesen
singen, *to sing*	er singt	sang	hat gesungen				
sinken, *to sink*	er sinkt	sank	ist gesunken	werben, *to **recruit***	*er wirbt	warb	hat geworben
sinnen, *to meditate*	er sinnt	sann	hat gesonnen	werfen, *to throw*	*er wirft	warf	hat geworfen
sitzen, *to sit*	er sitzt	saß	ist gesessen	wiegen, *to weigh*	er wiegt	wog	hat gewogen
speien, *to spit*	er speit	spie	hat gespieen	winden, *to wind*	er windet	wand	hat gewunden
spinnen, ***to spin***	er spinnt	spann	hat gesponnen	zeihen, *to accuse*	er zeiht	zieh	hat geziehen
sprechen, ***to speak***	*er spricht	sprach	hat **gesprochen**	ziehen, *to pull*	er zieht	zog	hat gezogen
sprießen, ***to shoot up***	er sprießt	sproß	ist gesprossen	zwingen, *to **force***	er zwingt	zwang	hat gezwungen

REFERENCE-PAGE O.

On the Prepositions.

All prepositions govern either Accusative, **or** Genitive, **or** Dative in the nouns with which **they are connected.** [The most commonly used are here given first in each list.]

I. Prepositions requiring their noun (with its enlargements) in the **Accusative Case:**

durch..., *through*...
für..., *for*...
gegen..., *against...towards*
ohne..., *without*...
um..., *about,* **around**...
wider..., *against*

Notice: The following, **used** with Verbs of motion only, stand *after* their noun, which must be in the *accusative:*
...hinauf, herauf, *up*... ; hinunter, herunter, *down*
...hinab, herab, *down*... ; hindurch, *through* (rare)
...entlang, *alongside,* along...

N.B. hin... means *away from,* her...means *towards,* the speaker.

II. Prepositions requiring their noun (with its enlargements) in the **Genitive Case:**

anstatt (or statt)..., *instead of*...	diesseits..., *this side of*...	vermittelst..., *by means of*...	zufolge..., *in consequence of*...
längs..., *alongside of*...	jenseits, *that side of*...	außerhalb..., *outside of*...	unweit..., *not far from*...
trotz..., *in spite of*...	um...willen, *for the sake of*...	innerhalb..., *inside of*...	unfern..., *not far from*...
während..., *during*	ungeachtet..., *notwithstanding*...	oberhalb..., *above*...	inmitten..., *in the middle of*...
wegen..., *on account of*...	vermöge, *by the power of*...	unterhalb..., *below*...	hinsichtlich..., *with regard to*...

III. Prepositions requiring their noun (with its enlargements) in the **Dative Case:**

aus..., *out of, from*...	zu..., *to, at*	The following stand after their noun, which must be in the *Dative:*
bei..., *at, near*...	außer..., *beside, except*	...gegenüber, *opposite to*...
mit..., *with*...	nebst..., *beside*	or gegenüber..., *vis-à-vis*
nach..., *after, to*...	sammt..., *together with*	...entgegen, *against*...
seit..., *since* (of time)	nächst..., *nearest to, next*	...gemäß, *in accordance with*...
von..., *of, from, by*...	binnen..., *within* (of time)	...zufolge, *in consequence of*...	...zuwider, *against*...

IV. The following *nine* prepositions of locality or **position** require their noun, etc., in **the Accusative, if the** verb in the sentence implies **a** change or motion with regard to the substantive (or pronoun) which stands after the preposition; but they require it in the **Dative,** if the verb in the sentence does not imply such change or motion. [Remember the change or motion must be in regard to the noun after the preposition.]

an..., *towards, to; at*
auf..., *upon, on to; on*
in..., *into; in*

neben..., *to the side of; by, near*
über..., *over, across..; over, above*
unter..., *below, beneath*

hinter..., *behind; after*
vor..., *to the front of; in front of, before*
zwischen..., *between*

N.B. (1.) In speaking of *Time,* vor (*ago, before*), and in (*in*), always take dative, as: vor zehn Tagen (dative Plural), *ten days ago;* in einer Minute, *in a minute.*

(2.) Preposition and Definite Article are often contracted, as: am = an dem; an's = an das; auf's = auf das; beim = bei dem; durch's = durch das; im = in dem; in's = in das; vom = von dem; zum = zu dem; zur = zu der. (Other contractions are very rare indeed.)

Examples and Exercises on Reference-Page O.

I. 1. Er führte den alten Mann durch den Wald.
    2. Sie gieng den Berg hinauf, den Bach entlang.
    3. Es geht gegen meinen Willen.

    1. He led the old man through the forest.
    2. She went up the mountain, along the brook.
    3. It goes against my will.

Exercise on the Accusative.

1. This is for your good, kind teacher.
2. Go through the town towards the church.
3. He bought this without my permission.
4. He has (is) gone along this rapid river.
5. The child fell down the hill yesterday.
6. We shall travel round the world.

II. 1. Sie sind trotz des Verbotes gegangen.
    2. Tue es, um deines Vaters willen.
    3. Er kam während meiner Stunde.

    1. You have gone in spite of the prohibition.
    2. Do it, for your father's sake.
    3. He came during my lesson.

Exercise on the Genitive.

1. He lives this side of the mountain.
2. We went, in consequence of the command.
3. The boy came on account of his brother.
4. The house lies above the village.
5. He died in the midst of the enemies.
6. We were walking alongside of the river.

III. 1. Er gieng aus dem Hause zu dem Mann.
     2. Wir werden nach einer Stunde kommen.
     3. Sie wohnen Ihrem Hause gegenüber.

     1. He went out of the house to the man.
     2. We shall come after an hour.
     3. They live opposite your house.

Exercise on the Dative.

1. Come out of the room after the lesson.
2. Will you go with your father?
3. We shall do it within three days.
4. The soldiers went against the enemy.
5. Charles was (became) loved by his teacher.
6. I spoke to those idle boys yesterday.

IV. 1. Der Vogel fliegt über das Dach dort.
    2. Stehen Sie nicht an dem Fenster.
    3. Kommen Sie an das Fenster, Karl.

    1. The bird flies over the roof there.
    2. Do not stand at the window.
    3. Come to the window, Charles.

Exercise.

1. Those books lie on the chair in my room.
2. Bring them into this room, my good boy.
3. We go to (into the) school; they are in (the) church.
4. We were between two fires.
5. They went (have...gone) across the sea, a week ago.
6. I shall come to London in a few days.

General Exercise on the Prepositions.

1. Were these boys in the room with the man?
2. Yes, but they went soon out of the house.
3. Where do you live? Opposite that church.
4. Why did you not go to London?
5. We remained here against our will.
6. Let us go along this beautiful brook!
7. You have not been in (the) town. Why not?
8. It was on account of our poor friend.
9. He has been on the mountain.
10. Are you also going on the mountain?

REFERENCE-PAGE **P.**

On Inseparable and Separable Verbs.

I. Inseparable Verbs.

(a.) We have already seen that verbs beginning with the *unaccented* prefixes : be .., ge .., emp .., ent .., er .., ver .., zer .., hinter .., miß .., voll .., wider, (Ref.-Page **H.**) are inseparable, *i.e.* these prefixes never leave the root-verb throughout the conjugation, nor is ge .. prefixed for the Past Participle, as :

(zu) verlieren (irreg.) *to loose;* er verliert, verlor, hat verloren.
(zu) zerstören (reg.) *to destroy;* er zerstört, zerstörte, hat zerstört.

(b.) There are, besides, some ten inseparable verbs with *accented* prefixes, as : ant'worten, *to answer*. These are *all regular* verbs and admit of ge .. for the Past Participle :

(zu) antworten, *to answer;* er antwortet, antwortete, hat geantwortet.
(zu) frühstücken, *to breakfast;* er frühstückt, frühstückte, hat gefrühstückt.
(zu) handhaben, *to handle;* er handhabt, handhabte, hat gehandhabt.

N.B.—wider .., against, is *always* inseparable; wieder .., again, is *always* separable, except only in wiederholen, *to repeat*.

II. Separable Verbs.

Many root-verbs combine with prepositions or adverbs, the latter generally retaining their meaning and being accented, as : auf=stehen, *to stand up, rise*. Such verbs are **separable**, *i.e.*

(1.) In *Primary sentences*, if the tense have **no** auxiliary in it, they throw their prefix off, and it stands where a Predicate would stand (see Rules 10 and 11, on page 38); as : er steht heute nicht auf, *he does not get up to-day*.

(2.) In the *Past Participle* they take .. ge .. between the prefix and the root; as : er ist aufgestanden, *he has got up*.

(3.) In the Infinitive, if zu (*to, in order to*) be used, zu is placed between the prefix and the root; as : ich hoffe morgen aufzustehen, *I hope to get up to-morrow*.

N.B.—This insertion of ge .. or zu is not called separation.

Separation never *takes place* in Past Participle *and in* Infinitive.

Note—There are *four* prefixes which, in some verbs, are separable and in others inseparable, they are : durch, über, um, and unter.

(a.) They are inseparable **when belonging to** *active* or *transitive* verbs conjugated in the Compound tenses with haben, as :
ich habe die Schweiz durchreist, *I have travelled through (all over) Switzerland*.
er übergieng den Fehler, *he overlooked the mistake (missed it)*.

(b.) They are **separable when belonging to neuter or intransitive verbs**, conjugated in the Compound tenses with sein, as :
ich bin durch die Schweiz gereist, *I have travelled through Switzerland*.
er gieng zum Feind über, *he went over to the enemy*.

Examples and Exercises on Reference-Page P.

I. *Inseparable Verbs.* (For Irregular Verbs, see Alphabetical List, Reference-Page N.)

erhalten (see halten), to receive
empfinden (see finden), to feel
belohnen (reg.), to reward
entgehen (see gehen), to escape

gelingen (irreg.), to succeed
verdienen (reg.), to deserve
mißbrauchen (reg.), to misuse
vollbringen (see p. 46), to accomplish

hinterlassen (see lassen), to bequeath
zerstören (reg.), to destroy
widerstehen (see stehen), to withstand
widersprechen (see sprechen), to contradict

zerreißen (see reißen), to tear
empfangen (see fangen), to receive
entführen (reg.), to carry off
geloben (reg.), to promise

Examples.

1. Erhält der Knabe eine Strafe? Sie ist verdient.
2. Wann frühstückten Sie? Er hat noch nicht gefrühstückt.
3. Was hat er geantwortet? Er antwortete Nichts.
4. Sie haben das Geld empfangen und mißbraucht.

1. Does the boy get (a) punishment; it is deserved.
2. When did you breakfast? He has not yet breakfasted.
3. What has he answered? He answered nothing.
4. You have received and misused the money.

Exercise.

1. Will the boy be (become) rewarded?
2. No, I believe he has deserved punishment.
3. Do not withstand (to) your faithful friend (Dat.).
4. He has contradicted his brother (Dative).
5. That town has been (become) destroyed.
6. We have accomplished the deed.
7. What has be bequeathed to his daughter (Dative)?
8. He bequeathed her (ihr) a large fortune.
9. Did she receive her fortune?
10. Yes, and she misused it.

II. *Separable Verbs.* (Conjugated like their root verbs, which look out on Reference-Page **N**, if irregular.)

ab'schlagen, to refuse
an'kleiden (reg.), to dress
auf'stehen, to rise, get up
auf'geben, to rise (of stars)
aus'geben, to spend (money)

bei'tragen, to contribute
ein'nehmen, to take in, earn
fort'setzen (reg.), to continue
her'bringen, to bring hither
hin'legen (reg.), to lay there

los'lassen, to let free, go
mit'gehen, to go with (one)
nach'sehen, to look after
nieder'lassen (sich), to settle
vorstellen (reg.), to introduce

weg'tragen, to carry away
weg'bleiben, to remain away
wieder'kommen, to come again
zu'bringen, to spend (time)
zu'machen (reg.), to close

Examples.

1. Kleiden Sie das Kind an! Es ist angekleidet.
2. Wann stehen Sie auf? Er wird mitgehen.
3. Geben Sie viel Geld aus? Ich habe kein Geld.
4. Wo bringen Sie Ihre Zeit zu? Im Hause.

1. Dress the child! It is dressed.
2. When do you get up? He will go with (us).
3. Do you spend much money? I have no money.
4. Where do you spend your time? In the house.

Exercise.

1. Do not refuse his request! Let the bird loose (go).
2. Bring my book into my room hither (hierher).
3. I have introduced him (ihn) to the count (Dative).
4. Get up; the sun has (is) risen.
5. We have spent this money.
6. I contributed to the work (zu with Dative).
7. They have come again. (Use sein.)
8. Will you introduce the man to the king?
9. I have already introduced him (ihn).
10. We do not earn much money?

Exercise on durch..., über..., um..., unter...

1. We have translated (übersetzen, insep.) the exercise.
2. They have crossed (über'setzen sep.) (over) the river.
3. The milk has run over (über'laufen, sep.).
4. I returned (um'kehren, sep.) and went away.
5. The man was (became) run over (überfahren, insep.).
6. Those ships have sunk (unter'gehen, sep.).

REFERENCE-PAGE Q.

Personal Pronouns.

FIRST PERSON.

	SINGULAR.	PLURAL.
Nom.	ich, *I*	wir, *we*
Acc.	mich, *me, myself*	uns, *us, ourselves*
Gen.	meiner, *of me*	unser(er), *of us*
Dat.	mir, *to me*	uns, *to us, ourselves*

SECOND PERSON.

	SINGULAR.	PLURAL.
Nom.	du, *thou*	ihr, *ye*
Acc.	dich, *thee, thyself*	euch, *ye*
Gen.	deiner, *of thee*	euer(er), *of ye (you)*
Dat.	dir, *to thee*	euch, *to ye (you)*

THIRD PERSON.

	SINGULAR MASCULINE.	SINGULAR FEMININE.	SINGULAR NEUTER.	PLURAL M. F. and N.
Nom.	er, *he*	sie, *she (Acc. her)*	es, *it*	sie (*they*); Sie, *you*
Acc.	ihn, *him*			
Gen.	seiner, *of him*	ihrer, *of her*	[seiner, *of it*]	ihrer, *of them*; Ihrer, *of you*
Dat.	ihm, *to him*	ihr, *to her*	[ihm, *to it*]	ihnen, *to them*; Ihnen, *to you*

Notes on the Personal Pronouns.

(1) Remember that **the 3d person** Plural is used in addressing a stranger politely, as:
   Werden Sie gehen? *Will you go?* **Ich bringe Ihnen das Buch,** *I bring (to) you the book.*

(2) **Be careful to make the** possessive adjective agree with the Personal pronoun in person, as:
   Du hast deinen Rock, *thou hast thy coat.* **Sie sehen Ihre Söhne,** *you see your sons.*
   [Of course this rule only applies to a case where the same person (or persons) is referred to.]

(3) Personal pronouns must strictly agree in *Gender* with the nouns they refer to; thus the English *it* may be er, or sie, or es, according as it refers to a masculine, feminine, or neuter Noun, as:
   Wo ist der Hut? *Where is the hat?* **Er ist hier,** *It is here* (etc.)

(4) The oblique cases (Accusative, Genitive, Dative) **may be governed** by prepositions, as: von ihm, *from him.*
   Notice *however,* **that when** the Personal Pronoun refers to a *thing*, it is preferable to use Genitive and Dative of derselbe, or dieselbe, or dasselbe, in which the definite article is declined, **and** selbe is merely **an adjective** in the First form (see Ref.-Page G), as:
   Where is my stick? *I am in need of it.* **Wo ist mein Stock?** **Ich bedarf desselben.**

(5) Moreover, if the thing referred to be an abstract, or of the *neuter gender*, the Dative and Accusative pronouns are replaced by da... (dar... before a vowel) or hier... as prefixes to the preposition, as:
   Haben Sie davon gehört? *Have you heard of it (there-of).*

Reflexive Pronouns.

myself, thyself, ourselves, and *yourselves* are borrowed from the Personal Pronouns above; BUT *himself, herself, itself, themselves,* have only one *invariable* form: sich (Dative and Accusative) **ich freue mich,** *I rejoice (myself)*, but: er freut sich (*not* ihn); Sie freuen sich.

N.B.—(a) All *reflexive verbs* take **"haben"** in their Compound tenses, and **all**, except ten, govern the Accusative of the reflexive pronoun.

   (b) **selbst is often** added to strengthen the reflexive pronoun, as: **er liebt sich selbst.**

   (c) **If *myself*,** etc., are *not* reflective, they are rendered by selbst without any pronoun, as:
   The king himself, der König selbst; *I shall go myself,* ich werde selbst gehen.

Examples and Exercises on Reference-Page Q.

I. *On the Personal Pronouns.*

Some verbs govern the *Genitive* in German, which do not in English, as: bedürfen, *to want;* gedenken, *to remember;* spotten, *to make fun of,* *laugh at.*

1. Wir haben seiner und Ihrer bedurft.
2. Werden Sie seiner spotten? Nein, ich bedarf seiner.
3. Die Frau hat unserer gedacht (or an uns .).
4. Geben Sie mir das Buch und nicht ihm.
5. Sahen Sie ihn? Nein, aber ich habe Sie gesehen.

We have wanted him and you.
Will you laugh at him? No, I need him.
The woman has remembered (thought of) us.
Give the book to me and not to him.
Did you see him? No, but I saw you.

Exercise.

1. I beg you, give me (Dat.) your pen. Here it is.
2. Where did you hear him? In the town.
3. He will bring you (Dat.) our exercises.
4. Do not laugh at him (Gen.); he is very ill.
5. I hope, you will believe us (Dat.) and not him (Dat.).
6. Are you going to (zu) him? No, to her.
7. Here is your ring. Take it (masc.).
8. Here is her book. Do you need it?
9. I have not heard of it (there-of = davon).
10. Are you satisfied with it? (there-with.)

II. *On the Reflexive Verbs.*

Some reflexive verbs govern a genitive (besides the **Acc. of** the reflexive Pronoun), as: sich erinnern, *to remember;* sich erbarmen, *to pity;* sich erfreuen, *to enjoy,* etc.

1. Wir erinnerten uns seiner und ihrer.
2. Bitte, erbarmen Sie sich unser(er).
3. Kleide dich an! Ich habe mich angekleidet.
4. Haben Sie sich schon gewaschen? Ja mein Herr.
5. Wir erfreuen uns sehr guter Gesundheit.

We remembered him and her.
Pray, take pity on us (pity us).
Dress yourself! I have dressed myself.
Have you already washed yourself? Yes, Sir.
We enjoy very good health.

Exercise.

1. Do you remember me, my dear friend?
2. O yes! I remember you very well (gut).
3. Does he enjoy good health?
4. No, he has caught cold (sich erkälten).
5. We have refused to (zu) go there (dahin).
6. We have resolved not to go there.
7. You must not praise yourself.
8. Take pity on (Pity) her, Sir.
9. Have they resolved, to **do this**? (Inf. last.)
10. No, they refuse to do that (that to do).

Difference between *myself, thyself,* etc., as *reflexive* and **as** *not-reflexive* Pronouns. Sie selbst haben mich gerufen (not reflexive), *You yourself have called me.*

Exercise. *See* Q. (*N.B. b and c*).

1. We saw you ourselves (not reflexive).
2. We dressed ourselves (reflexive).
3. You yourself came to (zu) us.
4. I have washed myself, myself (emphatic).
5. Thou hast seen it thyself.
6. She remembered you and him.
7. The men sold the horses themselves.
8. They cheated themselves (emphatic).

Dictionary of Words (not on page 12) for the Exercises.

(To be learnt in small portions, set for each lesson, through the Term.)

to be able, können (K.), vermögen (K.)
above, über (Dat. and Acc.) (O.)
to accomplish, vollbringen (sep.)
on account of, wegen (Gen.) (O.)
after, nach (Dat.) (O.)
again, wieder
against, wider... (insep.) (P.)
—— gegen (Acc.) (O.)
ago, seit... (Dat.) (O.)
to allow, erlauben (reg.)
to be allowed, dürfen (K.)
along(side of), längs (O.), entlang
also, auch (conjunction)
bad, schlecht (adj. and adverb)
to beg, bitten (irreg.) (N.)
to bequeath, hinterlassen (insep.)
Berlin, Berlin
between, zwischen (O.) (Dat and Acc.)
the Bible, die Bibel, —, —n
the bird, der Vogel, —s, =
the boy, der Knabe, —n, —n
brightly, hell (adj. and adverb)
to bring, bringen (p. 46)
the brook, der Bach, —es, =e
the brother, der Bruder, —s, =
to burn, brennen (p. 46)
by (agent), von (O.) (Dat.)
to call, rufen (irreg.) (N.)
can, können (K.)
to catch cold, sich erkälten (Q.) (reg.)
the chair, der Stuhl, —s, =e
Charles, Karl
cheap, billig (adj. and adverb)
to cheat, betrügen (irreg.) (N.)
the church, die Kirche, —, —n
to come, kommen (irreg.) (N.)

to command, befehlen (irreg.) (N.)
in consequence of, zufolge (O.)
to contradict, widersprechen (Dat.)
to contribute, bei'tragen (sep.)
to copy, ab'schreiben (sep. irreg.)
to create, erschaffen (irreg.)
the day, der Tag, —es, —e
dear, lieb (adj.)
the deed, die Tat, —, —en
to destroy, zerstören (reg.)
to die, sterben (irreg.) (auxil.: sein)
diligent, fleißig
to do, make, tun (irreg.)
to dress, ankleiden (reg.)
—— sich ankleiden (refl.)
to drink, trinken (irreg.)
to earn, verdienen (reg.)
the earth, die Erde, —, —n
to eat, essen (irreg.)
the enemy, der Feind, —es, —e
England, England
to enjoy, sich (Gen.) erfreuen
the exercise, die Aufgabe, —, —en
faithful, treu (adj.)
to fall, fallen (irreg.)
to fall-headlong, stürzen (reg.)
far, weit, fern (adv.)
a few, einige, wenige
the fire, das Feuer, —s, —
to flee, fliehen (irreg.)
to fly (with wings), fliegen (irreg.)
for, für (preposition) (O.)
for, denn (conjunction)
to forsake, verlassen (irreg.)
the fortune (luck), das Glück, —es
(property, money), das Vermögen
French, französisch (adj.)

the friend, der Freund, —es, —e
the garden, der Garten, —s, =
the gentleman, der Herr, —n, —en
German, Deutsche (adj.)
to get (= become), werden
—— (= receive), erhalten (irreg.)
to get up, auf'stehen (irreg.)
to give, geben (irreg.)
to go, gehen (irreg. with sein)
to go to sleep, ein'schlafen (irreg.)
God, Gott [der—, des—es, die=er]
health, die Gesundheit, —, —en
heaven, der Himmel, —s, —
heavy (of rain), stark (adj.)
here (= hither), hierher (motion)
the hill, der Hügel, —s, —
to hope, hoffen (reg.)
the house, das Haus, —es, =er
idle (lazy), träge (adj.)
ill, krank (adj.)
into (in), in (with acc.) (O.)
to introduce, vor'stellen (sep. reg.)
kind, gut, gütig (adj.)
to know, kennen (p. 46)
—— wissen (p. 46)
large, groß (adj.)
late, spät (adv. or adj.)
to laugh (at), lachen (reg.) (über)
lazy, träge (adj.)
to learn, lernen (reg.)
the lesson, die Aufgabe, —, —n
to let, lassen (irreg.) (auxiliary)
to lie (tell a lie), lügen (irreg.)
—— (be situated), liegen (irreg.)
the light, das Licht, —es, —er
to like, lieben, gern haben
little (adj.) klein (adv. = wenig)

Dictionary—continued.

a little, ein wenig (adverb)
to live, leben, wohnen (reg.)
London, London
loose, frei (frei'lassen)
may, können, dürfen (K.)
meet, begegnen (reg. with Dat.)
  in the midst of, inmitten (Gen.) (O.)
Miss, (mein) Fräulein
the mountain, der Berg, —es, —e
to need, brauchen (with acc.) (reg.)
—— bedürfen (with gen.) (p. 43)
new, neu (adj.)
the night, die Nacht, —, ⸚e
now, jetzt, nun
to be obliged, müssen (K.)
on, auf (Dat. and Acc.) (O.)
opposite, gegenüber (Dat.) (O.)
ought, sollen (K.)
out (of), aus (Dat.) (O.)
over (across), über (Dat. Acc.) (O.)
Paris, Paris
the permission, die Erlaubniß
to pity, sich erbarmen (Gen.)
the pond, der Teich, —es, —e
the prohibition, das Verbot, —es
the rain, der Regen, —s
rapid, schnell, reißend
to receive, erhalten (irreg.)
to recommend, empfehlen (irreg.)
to refuse, verweigern (reg.)
to remain, bleiben (irreg.)
to remember, sich erinnern (reg.)
to request, bitten (irreg.)
to resolve, sich entschließen (irreg.)
to return, zurück'kehren (reg.)
to be right, Recht haben
to rise (of men), auf'stehen (sep.) (of stars, sun), auf'gehen (sep.)

the river, der Fluß, —sses, ⸚sse
round, rund (adj.)
turn-round, um'kehren (reg.)
satisfied, zufrieden (adj.)
the school, die Schule, —, —n
the sea, das Meer, —es, —e
to see, sehen (irreg.)
self (selves), selbst
to send, schicken (reg.) senden (46)
several, mehrere (adj.)
this side of, diesseits (Gen.) (O.)
that side of, jenseits (Gen.) (O.)
to sing, singen (irreg.)
Sir! mein Herr!
to sit, sitzen (irreg.)
to go to sleep, einschlafen (irreg.)
the soldier, der Soldat, —en, —en
soon, bald (adv.)
to speak, sprechen (irreg.)
to spend (time), zu'bringen
to spend (money), aus'geben
in spite of, trotz (Gen.) (O.)
to steal, stehlen (irreg.)
still, noch (adv.)
the sun, die Sonne, —, —n
to take, nehmen (very irreg.)
to thank, danken (Dat.) (reg.)
there = (thither), dorthin
three = drei
through, durch (Acc.) (O.)
to, zu; nach; in (into)
too, zu (emphatic)
towards, nach, gegen (O.)
to translate, übersetzen (insep.)
to travel, reisen (reg.)
the village, das Dorf, —es, ⸚er
to walk, gehen (irreg.)
to want, brauchen (Acc.) (reg.)

to want, bedürfen (Gen.) K. (43)
to wash, waschen (irreg.)
the week, die Woche, —, —n
well, wohl, gut (adverbs)
why? warum?
the will, der Willen, —s, —
to wish, wünschen (with zu)
—— wollen (without zu)
with, mit (Dat.) (O.)
within (of time), binnen (Dat.)
—— (*of place*), in (O) [hinein]
without, ohne (O.) (Acc.)
to withstand, widerstehen (insep.)
the work, die Arbeit, —, —en
to work, arbeiten (reg.)
the world, die Welt, —, —en
wrong, unrecht
I am wrong, ich habe Unrecht
yesterday, gestern

NOTICE.

In using the Dictionary, refer to the Reference-Pages indicated; in the Irregular Verbs the alphabetical list (N) will give all that is necessary. As to separable or inseparable Verbs, refer to Reference-Page P and study it again.

Of the Nouns, the Nominative Singular is given, and the Genitive Singular and Nominative Plural are indicated.

As to changes of Adjectives refer to Reference-Page G, pp. 28 and 29.

Additional Exercises.

(To be written, on reviewing the Reference-Pages **K** *to* **Q** *[see page 38 in all for the sequence of words].)*

To Reference-Page K (and page 43).

1. Was your father wrong? No, he was right.
2. Did you need (bedürfen, Gen.) my knife?
3. The Bible says, Thou shalt not steal.
4. They are said (sollen) to have lived very long.
5. Were you obliged to punish the boys?
6. You must (dürfen) not go without us.
7. Was he able (vermögen) to (zu) go there?
8. He could not go; he was poor.

To Reference-Page L.

1. They met their friends (Dat.) in Paris.
2. Have the enemies fled? No, we fled.
3. He has forsaken his father and his mother.
4. When did the child go-to-sleep? (Use Perfect.)
5. Where did you remain, (my) Miss?
6. We remained several days in Paris.
7. Did the little girl fall into the river?
8. No, she (it) fell into the pond.

To Reference-Page M.

1. Did the light burn brightly?
2. It has not burnt very well, Sir.
3. Did you know (wissen) this, dear friend?
4. No, but I know (wissen) it now.
5. He knows (wissen) too much.
6. I did not know (kennen) this gentleman.
7. But he has known (kennen) you long.
8. Who has sent me this beautiful ring?

To Reference-Page N.

1. Who recommended you to this man?
2. He, my friend, has recommended me.
3. What have you eaten this (Acc.) day?
4. Do not give this to your son.
5. Who has called? I did not call.
6. God created heaven and earth.
7. Let us drink to (auf, Acc.) his health!
8. Have (Are) you sat on that chair?

To Reference-Page O.

1. Will you go with your friend, Charles?
2. No, I shall go without my friend.
3. See the birds fly over that house.
4. The knife was lying (lay) on this table.
5. They did this in spite of the prohibition.
6. Go into the house; I remain in the garden.
7. Why did you not come to (zu) me?
8. It was on account of the heavy rain.

To Reference-Page P.

1. Had the enemy destroyed that town?
2. See, the sun rises over (Dat.) the hills.
3. Come, rise, ye lazy boys! (2d pers. Pl.).
4. Have you come again?
5. I have returned to you (zu, Dat.).
6. How have you spent your time?
7. I have copied this letter here.
8. I have also translated this exercise.

To Reference-Page Q.

1. Do you want (bedürfen) my friend or me?
2. I thank you (Dat.); I want your friend.
3. Will he come with me or with you?
4. He has resolved to go with them.
5. Did you remember (Reflexive) me? (Gen.).
6. No, I have not remembered you.
7. Has he enjoyed (Reflexive) good health? (Gen.).
8. No, he is still in very bad health. (Dat.)

CONVERSATIONAL SENTENCES.

(To be learnt in small portions, set for every Lesson, through the Term.)

1. Es klopft. Jemand klopft an die Türe. — There is a knock. Some one is knocking at the door.
2. Herein! Kommen Sie herein. — Come in! Come in! (Enter!)
3. Wer ist da? Ich bin es, mein Lieber. — Who is there? It is I, my dear.
4. Ah! Mein lieber Karl. Komm' herein. — Ah! My dear Charles, come in.
5. Es freut mich, dich wieder einmal zu sehen. — I am pleased to see you once again.
6. Wo bist du denn gewesen, seit ich dich sah? — Where have you been since I saw you?
7. Ich bin viel heruntgereist seit Weihnachten. — I have travelled about much since Christmas.
8. Ich war auch einige Tage in München. — I was also a few days in Munich.
9. Und wie hat es dir dort gefallen, Karl? — And how did you like it, Charles?
10. Oh! Sehr gut, danke; ich traf viele Freunde. — Oh! very well, thanks; I met many friends.
11. Sahst du auch unseren alten Müller? — Did you see our old Müller also?
12. Ja, und er läßt dich freundlichst grüßen. — Yes, and he sends his kindest regards.
13. Wie geht es ihm in seiner neuen Heimath? — How is he getting on in his new home?
14. Ziemlich gut, er hat ein gutes Geschäft. — Tolerably well; he has a good business.
15. Hast du den Sohn des reichen B. getroffen? — Did you meet the son of the rich B.?
16. Nein, er hatte die Universität verlassen. — No, he had left the University.
17. Er war auf Reisen, in Italien, glaub' ich. — He was travelling, in Italy, I believe.
18. Man sagt, es gehe ihm wieder etwas besser. — They say, he is a little better again.
19. Was hatte er denn? War er krank? — What was the matter? Was he ill?
20. Er litt an täglichem Kopfweh. — He suffered from daily headaches.
21. Er soll zu viel studirt haben, sagt man. — He is said to have studied too much.
22. Nun, das war nie der Fall mit uns. — Well, that was never the case with us.
23. Drum haben wir auch nicht so viel Kopfweh. — That is why we have not so much headache.
24. Und wird der junge B. lange fortbleiben? — And will young B. remain away long?
25. Nein, ich glaube, er wird bald zurückkehren. — No, I believe he will return soon.
26. Dann wird er in's Geschäft eintreten. — Then he will enter the business.
27. So hat er seine Studien ganz aufgegeben? — So he has given up his studies entirely?
28. Ja, er soll Geschäftsmann werden. — Yes, he is to become a business man.
29. Darf ich dir eine Cigarre anbieten? — May I offer you a cigar?
30. Nein, ich habe mir das Rauchen abgewöhnt. — No, I have given up smoking.
31. Wirst du heute Abend in's Casino kommen? — Will you come to the casino (club) this evening?
32. Ja, mit Vergnügen. Adieu einstweilen. — Yes, with pleasure. Good-bye meanwhile.
33. Auf Wiedersehen diesen Abend um sieben. — To the pleasure of seeing you this evening at seven.
34. Empfiehl' mich deiner Fräulein Schwester. — Give my kind regards to your sister.
35. Ja gerne, und du mich deiner Frau Mutter. — Yes, willingly, and you mine to your mother.
36. Danke. Adieu. Also auf diesen Abend. — Thanks. Good-bye. Then this evening.

POEM.

(To be learnt by heart during this Term.)

Das Gewitter. Von Gustav Schwab.

1. Urahne, Großmutter, Mutter und Kind
   In dumpfer Stube beisammen sind;
   Es spielet das Kind; die Mutter sich schmückt;
   Großmutter spinnet; Urahne, gebückt,
   Sitzt hinter dem Ofen im Pfühl:
   Wie weben die Lüfte so schwül!

2. Das Kind spricht: „Morgen ist Feiertag!
   „Wie will ich spielen im grünen Hag!
   „Wie will ich springen durch Thal und Höh'n!
   „Wie will ich pflücken viel Blumen schön!
   „Dem Anger, dem bin ich hold!"
   Hört ihr's, wie der Donner grollt?!

3. Die Mutter spricht: „Morgen ist Feiertag!
   „Da halten wir Alle fröhlich' Gelag;
   „Ich selber, ich rüste mein Feierkleid;
   „Das Leben, es hat auch Lust nach Leid,
   „Dann scheint die Sonne wie Gold!"
   Hört ihr's, wie der Donner grollt?!

4. Großmutter spricht: „Morgen ist Feiertag!
   „Großmutter hat keinen Feiertag!
   „Sie kochet das Mahl; sie spinnet das Kleid;
   „Das Leben ist Sorg' und viel Arbeit;
   „Wohl dem, der tat, was er sollt'!"
   Hört ihr's, wie der Donner grollt?!

5. Urahne spricht: „Morgen ist Feiertag!
   „Am liebsten morgen ich sterben mag;
   „Ich kann nicht singen und scherzen mehr;
   „Ich kann nicht sorgen und schaffen schwer;
   „Was tu' ich noch auf der Welt?!"
   Seht ihr, wie der Blitz dort fällt?!

6. Sie hören's nicht, sie sehen's nicht;
   Es flammet die Stube wie lauter Licht.
   Urahne, Großmutter, Mutter und Kind
   Vom Strahl mit einander getroffen sind.
   Vier Leben endet ein Schlag:—
   Und Morgen ist's Feiertag!

The Thunderstorm. *(Literal translation.)*

1. *Great-grandmother, grandmother, mother and child*
   Are together in the close **room** *;*
   The child is playing; the mother is decking herself out;
   Grandmother is spinning; great-grandmother, bent,
   Is sitting behind the oven in the cushions:
   How oppressive the air (is blowing) feels!

2. *The child says: "To-morrow is (a) holiday!*
   " How I will play in the green meadow!
   " How I will skip through vale and hill!
   " How I will gather many beautiful flowers!
   " The green fields, of them I am fond!"
   Do you hear, how the thunder growls (angrily)?!

3. *The mother says: "* **To-morrow is** *holiday!*
   " Then we all will keep up the merry feast;
   " I myself, I am preparing my holiday-dress;
   " Life, it has still joy after sorrow,
   " Then the sun shines, even as gold!"
   Do you hear, how the thunder roars!?

4. *Grandmother says: " To-morrow is holiday!*
   " Grandmother has no holiday!
   " She must cook the dinner, and spin (for) the dress;
   " Life is (but) cares and much work!
   " Happy is he, who did what he ought to have done"!
   Do you hear, how the thunder roars!?

5. *Great-grandmother says: " To-morrow* **is** *holiday!*
   " Most of all I should like to die to-morrow;
   " I can no longer sing nor joke;
   " I cannot be busy nor work hard;
   " What good am I any longer in **the world** *?!"*
   Do **you** *see, how the lightning* **strikes** *there?!*

6. *They hear it not, they see it not;*
   The room is aflame, is nothing but light.
   Great-grandmother, grandmother, mother **and child**
   All together are struck by the flash of lighting.
   One stroke terminates four lives:—
   And to-morrow is holiday!

FOURTH TERM

The student should test his knowledge of Grammar continually in the Translation lesson by parsing and analysing.

Some few words from pages 86 and 87, a few sentences from page 88, and a few lines of the poems on pages 89 and 90, should still form an integral part of every lesson in Grammar.

The Dictionaries, Sentences, and Poems given in Terms 1, 2, and 3 might also with advantage be repeated.

REFERENCE-PAGE R.

The Numerals.

A. All Numerals are based upon the *Cardinal Numbers*, used for counting:

1 = einſ	6 = fechſ	11 = elf (or eilf)	21 = ein und zwanzig	100 = ein hundert
2 = zwei	7 = sieben	12 = zwölf	22 = zwei und zwanzig	200 = zwei hundert
3 = drei	8 = acht	13 = dreizehn	30 = dreißig	1000 = ein tausend
4 = vier	9 = neun	14 = vierzehn, etc.	40 = vierzig	2000 = zwei tausend
5 = fünf	10 = zehn	20 = zwanzig	50 = fünfzig, etc.	1,000,000 = eine Million

The above will enable the intelligent pupil to form all numbers up to a million.

All cardinal numbers are invariable, but **zwei** and **drei**, if used without any determinative before a noun (expressed or understood) become: *Genitive* —er, *Dative* —en. **One** in counting dates, etc., is **einſ**; if used before a noun, it is **ein, eine, ein**; if used without a noun, it is **einer, eine, eines**; *one after an adjective is **never** translated*.

B. From the above Cardinal Numbers are formed:

1. The **Ordinal Numbers**; add **—te** up to nineteen, and **—fte** from twenty upwards, as: der (die, das), zweite, *the second;* der ein und zwanzigste, *the twenty-first*, except only der erste, *the first*, and der dritte, *the third*.

   Notice.—All these are adjectives, and may be declined as such [see 3 forms, Ref.-Page G].

2. The **Multiplicatives**: (These may be used as adjectives, —mal then becomes —malig.)
   (a) add **—mal** without exception [einſ drops =ſ, *first*] as: zehnmal, *ten times*.
   (b) add **—fach** or **fältig** [einſ drops =ſ, *first*] as: einfach, *one-fold*, simple; sechsfach, *six-fold*; vierfältig, *four-fold* [=fach and =fältig are synonymous].

3. The **Variatives**: (always invariable) add: **—erlei** [einſ drops =ſ, *first*] otherwise no exceptions: einerlei, *one kind (all the same)*; zwölferlei, *twelve kinds*.

4. The **Distinctives**: (always invariable) add: **—tens** to the Cardinals up to nineteen, and **—stens** from twenty upwards (seldom used), as: zweitens, *secondly;* zwanzig, **—stens**, *twentiethly*. Only exceptions: erstens, *firstly;* and drittens, *thirdly*.

5. The **Fractionals**: (always invariable) (really compounds of der Teil, *the part*, abbreviated into **—tel**); add **—tel** to the Cardinals up to nineteen, and **—stel** from twenty upwards, as: ein sechstel, *a sixth;* ein dreißigstel, *one-thirtieth*. Only exception, ein drittel, *a third*.

Note.—*half* as an adjective is **halb**; as: das halbe, *the half*; ein halbes, *a half*. Notice: *half a...*, *half the...*, must be translated *a half...*, *the half....* The *half* (a noun) is die Hälfte.
  1½ is either ein und ein halb [with halb declined] or anderthalb, [invariable] (*half of the second*).
  2½ is either zwei und ein halb or dritthalb (*half of the third*).
  3½ is either drei und ein halb or vierthalb (*half of the fourth*).
      (These are **the only peculiarities of this kind**.)

EXAMPLES AND EXERCISES ON REFERENCE-PAGE R.

A. *Examples:*
1. *Write out German for:* **56, 27.** Sechs und fünfzig. Sieben und zwanzig.
2. *In the year 1886.* Im Jahre achtzehnhundert sechs und achtzig.
3. *At what o'clock did he go? At 9 o'clock.* Um wie viel Uhr gieng er? Um neun Uhr.
4. *How old was the boy? Which one? This one.* Wie alt war der Knabe? Welcher? Dieser.
5. *We have one good knife and one bad one.* Wir haben ein gutes Messer und ein schlechtes.
6. *32 and 76 are 108.* Zwei und dreißig und sechs und siebenzig sind ein hundert und acht.
7. *The books of two or three boys.* Die Bücher zweier oder dreier Knaben.
8. *The books of these* **two boys and this one.** Die Bücher dieser zwei Knaben und dieses.
9. *At 9.15 or 9.30.* **Um ein Viertel nach neun** Uhr, oder um halb zehn Uhr.
10. *No, at a quarter to ten.* **Nein, um ein Viertel vor** (or bis) zehn Uhr.

Exercise.

1. 36 and 142 are 178.
2. How old are you? I am 16 years old.
3. At what o'clock will they come?
4. I believe they will come at 5.15 or 5.30.
5. You have **two** diligent boys and an idle [one].
6. Yes, and you have only two idle [ones].
7. We went there at a quarter to seven.
8. You were late, you should have come at 6.30.
9. When did he die? In the year 1715.
10. Three boys' caps are here. (The caps of 3 boys.)
11. Do you see **the dog of** these two children?
12. Give me a new pen, and not an old [one].

B. *Examples:*
1. *Henry III. or IV.* Heinrich der Dritte oder der Vierte.
2. *What day of the month is to-day?* Der wievielte des Monats ist heute?
3. *What day of the month had we yesterday?* Den wievielten des Monats hatten wir gestern?
4. *It is the 23d of March to-day.* Es ist der drei und zwanzigste März heute.
5. *7 times 5 is 35.* Siebenmal fünf sind fünf und dreißig.
6. *Will you have two or three kinds of paper?* Wollen Sie zweierlei oder dreierlei Papier?
7. *I paid this threefold or fourfold.* Ich habe dies dreifach oder vierfach bezahlt.
8. *Fourthly: he is a fool.* Viertens: er ist ein Narr.
9. *On the 16th of July he* **died.** Am sechzehnten Juli starb er (Inversion, see p. 38).
10. *We waited half an hour* **or more.** Wir warteten eine halbe Stunde oder mehr.
11. *This is only the half of your book.* Dieses (O. a. 2) ist nur die Hälfte Ihres Buches.
12. ⅔ *and* 3/10 *are* 39/30. Zwei drittel und drei Zehntel sind neun und zwanzig dreißigstel.

Exercise.

1. Henry the Eighth of (von) England.
2. What day of the month have we **to-day**?
3. We have the 31st [of] March.
4. What are (Was sind) 9 times 12? 108.
5. You have six kinds [of] knives there.
6. He is firstly poor and secondly ill.
7. They (are) died on the 27th of July.
8. Give me one-half (subst.) of your apple.
9. He gave me half an (a half) apple.
10. It is 5 minutes past (after) seven o'clock.
11. What are ½ and ⅔? ¾.
12. I will not pay him ten times [over].

N.B.—**Omit** the words in [brackets], and write the numbers, etc., fully **out in words.**

REFERENCE-PAGE S.

I. Possessive Pronouns.

Distinguish *Adjectives* (before a noun) from *Pronouns* (not before a noun). The Possessive Adjectives, mein, bein, *my*, *thy*, etc., are given and declined in Reference-Page O. *b*. The Possessive Pronouns are, if preceded by definite article, formed by adding ‑ige to the adjectives, as: der meinige, der deinige, *mine*, *thine*, etc. These are declined like adjectives in the 1st Form (see Reference-Page G). They are often abbreviated into der meine, der deine, etc.; or if *not* preceded by the definite article, into meiner, meine, meines, etc., declined like dieser. Thus we have: *mine* = der (die, das) meinige, *or*: der (die, das) meine, *or*: meiner ‑e ‑es; *thine* = der (die, das) deinige, *or*: der (die, das) deine, *or*: deiner (deine, deines), etc.

Remember: The Possessive Pronoun must agree in *gender*, as well as in *number*, with the thing possessed, but its *case* depends on its own verb, as:

dies ist mein Hund; hier ist der seinige; haben Sie den Ihrigen verloren?

Note.—The English Possessive is sometimes rendered by the definite article, with the verb reflexive, as: wir haben uns die Hände gewaschen, *We have (to ourselves) washed our (the) hands.*

II. Demonstrative Pronouns.

dieser and jener may be used as adjectives, *i.e.* before nouns, and also as Pronouns, *i.e.* not before a noun. The Declension is the same, given in Reference-Page O. *a*. [Remember to use it neuter singular invariable when separated by sein from its noun.] To the above two we may add the following, used either as adjectives or pronouns, but always agreeing with their noun in *gender* and *number*, and with their verb in *case*: derjenige, diejenige, dasjenige, diejenigen, *this*, *these*, *those*; and varied in the same way: derselbe, *the same*; der nämliche, *the same*. In these decline the definite article der, die, das as if it stood alone, and decline: jenige, selbe, nämliche, as adjectives in the 1st Form (see Reference-Page G.).

N.B. derjenige has an abbreviated form: der, die, das; die; declined thus:

	M. S.	F. S.	N. S.	PLURAL	M. S.	F. S.	N. S.	PLURAL
Nom.	der	die	das	die	derjenige	diejenige	dasjenige	diejenigen
Acc.	den	die	das	die	denjenigen	diejenige	dasjenige	diejenigen
Gen.	dessen	deren	dessen	derer	desjenigen	derjenigen	desjenigen	derjenigen
Dat.	dem	der	dem	denen	demjenigen	derjenigen	demjenigen	denjenigen

Where not differing in form from the definite article, the pronoun der, etc., is pronounced emphatically.

III. Interrogative Pronouns.

The adjectives, welcher? *which*, etc., can also be used without nouns after them [see O. *a. b.*], but: Was für ein...? *what sort of*...? becomes: Was für einer? eine? eines? as pronoun.

There is besides these only one real Interrogative Pronoun, wer? *who*? was? *what*? of which the Genitive only, wessen? *whose*? can be used before a substantive.

Declension of Wer? *who*?

Nom.	Wer? *who*?	Was? *what*?
Acc.	Wen? *whom*?	Was? *what*?
Gen.	Wessen? *whose*?	Wessen? *of what*?
Dat.	Wem? *to whom*?	[Was? *to what*?]

Examples and Exercises on Reference-Page S.

I.

1. *This is my ring,* where is hers?
2. *He was not in your* house, but in mine.
3. *Your houses and theirs are old.*
4. *She* has wounded her hand.
5. *Have you lost your pencil or mine?*

1. Dieſes iſt mein Ring. Wo iſt der ihrige.
2. Er war nicht in Ihrem Hauſe, ſondern in dem meinigen.
3. Ihre Häuſer und die ihrigen ſind alt.
4. Sie hat ſich die Hand verwundet.
5. Haben Sie Ihren Bleiſtift verloren oder den meinigen.

Exercise.

1. Is this (C. a. 2) your dog **or his**?
2. It is his. I have lost mine.
3. He will bring his brother, and I mine.
4. Was he in my house? No, in (the) his.
5. Have you your books? Yes, we **have ours**.
6. I have brought my boots and **yours**.
7. They have washed their hands **(see 4 above)**.
8. Why do you ask my brother **and not his**?
9. Who has a friend? **I have lost mine.**
10. Ours died a year **ago (vor with dat.).**
11. These (dieſ) are your **pens, not ours.**
12. This is my pencil; **where is yours?**

II.

1. *These are our friends, not Charles'* (those of Charles).
2. *The man, whom we remember* (with gen.).
3. *Was it this boy, or (that of) that gentleman's?*
4. *Have you my letter or (that of) my brother's?*
5. *I have (that of) your brother's.*

1. Dieſes* ſind unſere Freunde, nicht diejenigen von Karl.
2. Der Mann, deſſen wir uns erinnern.
3. War es dieſer Knabe oder derjenige jenes Herrn?
4. Haben Sie meinen Brief oder den meines Bruders?
5. Ich habe denjenigen Ihres Bruders.

** or Dies, or Das.

Exercise.

1. This **is my book, not (that of) Charles'**.
2. Give me (dat.) your knife and (that of) Henry's.
3. We saw your son and (that of) this gentleman's.
4. This house is not (that of) my brother's.
5. These are your pictures or (those of) your friend's.
6. Where is that boy, whom (gen.) you remembered?
7. Have you your own gloves?
8. Yes, but she has (those of) (von) Mary's.
9. Is this the same town? Yes, it is the same.
10. Will they have the same punishment?
11. Why have you not brought your dog?
12. I have brought (that of) my neighbour's.

III.

1. *What sort of pencil have you?*
2. *She has a dress. What sort (of dress)?*
3. *To whom has he given the apple?*
4. *Whose books are these?* Mine.
5. *He lost his friend.* Which?

1. Was für einen Bleiſtift haben Sie?
2. Sie hat ein Kleid; was für eines?
3. Wem hat er den Apfel gegeben?
4. Weſſen Bücher ſind das? Meine?
5. Er verlor ſeinen Freund. Welchen?

Exercise.

1. She had a new dress. What sort (of dress)?
2. Whose exercises are these? They are his.
3. Whom do you call? My friend (acc.).
4. What are you doing? Nothing.
5. To whom does he give these gloves?
6. What sort of dog have you **lost**?
7. (Of) whom do you remember (yourself)?
8. Who is there? Whose house is this?

General Exercise.

1. Whose dog have you there? (da)
2. I have my dog, not my son's (that of my son).
3. It is not my garden, it is his.
4. Have you my roses or yours?
5. I have mine, yours are in your room.
6. Why do you lose my knife and not yours?

REFERENCE-PAGE T.

The Comparison of Adjectives.

As in English, Adjectives may be in the Positive, Comparative, or Superlative.

A. The Adjective used as a PREDICATE, *i.e.* invariable (after "to be," or "to become").

1. POSITIVE.	2. COMPARATIVE.			3. SUPERLATIVE.	
	(a) *of Superiority.*	(b) *of Equality.*	(c) *of Inferiority.*	(a) *of Superiority.*	(b) *of Inferiority.*
as: { lang / long	(⸚er) er als / länger als / longer than	ebenſo (—) als / ebenſo lang als / as long as	weniger (—)als / weniger lang als / less long than	am (⸚)ſten / am längſten / the longest	am wenigſten (—) / am wenigſten lang / the least long

Of these only 2 (*a*) and 3 (*a*) **offer any** peculiarities, as follows:—

(i) Adjectives of more than one syllable, and those ending in au can never modify.

(ii) Most adjectives of **one syllable**, having a, o, u as vowel, modify these vowels; *except*:

blaß, *pale*	froh, *merry*	lahm, *lame*	roh, *raw, coarse*	ſchlank, *slim*	voll, *full*
bunt, *variegated*	hold, *loveable*, **kind**	matt, *languid*	rund, *round*	ſtolz, *proud*	zahm, *tame*
falſch, *false*	klar, *clear*	plump, *plump*	ſanft, *soft*	toll, *mad*	and a few rarely used ones besides

(iii) For the sake of euphony, adjectives ending in ‑el in the Positive, drop e before adding ‑er to the l for the Comparative 2, (*a*), as: eitel, *vain*: eitler, *vainer*; also adjectives ending in d, ß, z, or in more than two consonants, insert ‑e before adding ‑ſten for the Superlative, 3 (*a*); as: ſüß, *sweet*, am ſüßeſten, *the sweetest*.

(iv) The following eight adjectives have further irregularities:—

1.	2 a.		3 a.	1.	2 a.		3 a.	
bald, *soon*	{ eher, früher, } *sooner*		am eheſten, *the soonest*	hoch, *high*	höher, *higher*		am höchſten, *the highest*	
gern, *willingly*	lieber, *rather*		am liebſten, (*best*)	nahe, *near*	näher, *nearer*		am nächſten, *the nearest*	
groß, *great*	größer, *greater*		am größten, *the greatest*	viel, *much*	mehr, *more*		am meiſten, *the most*	
gut, *good*	beſſer, *better*		am beſten, *the best*	wenig, *little*	{ weniger, minder, } *less*		am wenigſten, am mindeſten, } { *the least*	

N.B.—If two qualities are compared, 2 *a* is formed with mehr ... als invariably.

B. The Adjective used as ATTRIBUTE, *i.e.* before a noun, must, after its Comparative or Superlative is formed according to the above rules, strictly change **for** gender, case, and number, as the Positive does, in the three forms (see Reference-Page **G.**); thus—

Form (i): der größere Mann, *the greater man*; ich habe den ſchöneren Hund, *I have the more beautiful dog*.

Form (ii): ein älteres Schloß, *an older castle*; er iſt mein liebſter Bruder, *he is my dearest brother*.

Form (iii): beſſerer Wein, *better wine*; wir haben längere Aufgaben, *we have longer exercises*.

N.B.—If used *attributively*, the "**am**" in the Superlative is **dropped**.

C. The Adjective used as an ADVERB has the same comparison exactly as when a Predicate (see **A.** above); as: er ſchrieb am längſten, *he wrote the longest*. There are, moreover, two adverbial forms of *some* adjectives in the Superlative:

(i) auf's beſte,   auf's höchſte, etc.   And (ii) beſtens,   höchſtens.
    (*in the best way*).   (*in the highest degree*).   (*in the best manner*).   (*at the most*).

Examples and Exercises on Reference-Page T.

A. *Example:*

(i) Compare fully: ſchön, *beautiful;* ſchlecht, *bad;* gut, *good;* edel, *noble.*

Positive.	Comparative			Superlative	
	of Superiority.	*of Equality.*	*of Inferiority.*	*of Superiority.*	*of Inferiority.*
ſchön	ſchöner als	ebenſo ſchön als	weniger ſchön als	am ſchönſten	am wenigſten ſchön
ſchlecht	ſchlechter als	ebenſo ſchlecht als	weniger ſchlecht als	am ſchlechteſten	am wenigſten ſchlecht
gut	beſſer als	ebenſo gut als	weniger gut als	am beſten	am wenigſten gut
edel	edler als	ebenſo edel als	weniger edel als	am edelſten	am wenigſten edel

(ii) Compare shortly: ſtolz, *proud;* alt, *old;* hoch, *high;* finſter, *dark.*

Positive.	Comparative.	Superlative.	Positive.	Comparative.	Superlative.
ſtolz	ſtolzer	am ſtolzeſten	hoch	höher	am höchſten
alt	älter	am älteſten	finſter	finſterer	am finſterſten

Exercise.

Compare fully: falſch, *false;* groß, *great;* kurz, *short;* bald, *soon.*
Compare shortly: wenig, *little;* blaß, *pale;* jung, *young;* viel, *much.*

B. *Example:*

Decline, *Singular* and *Plural:* der edlere Graf, *the nobler count;* ein jüngeres Mädchen, *a younger girl;* mein ſchönſtes Meſſer, *my most beautiful knife;* and beſſerer Wein, *better wine.*

	Singular (adj. 1st Form).	*Singular* (2d Form).	*Singular* (2d Form).	*Singular* (3d Form).
Nom.	der edlere Graf	ein jüngeres Mädchen	mein ſchönſtes Meſſer	beſſerer Wein
Acc.	den edleren Grafen			beſſeren Wein
Gen.	des edleren Grafen	eines jüngeren Mädchens	meines ſchönſten Meſſers	beſſeren Weines
Dat.	dem edleren Grafen	einem jüngeren Mädchen	meinem ſchönſten Meſſer	beſſerem Weine
	Plural (1st Form).	*Plural* (3d Form).	*Plural* (2d Form).	*Plural* (3d Form).
Nom. Acc.	die edleren Grafen	jüngere Mädchen	meine ſchönſten Meſſer	beſſere Weine
Gen.	der edleren Grafen	jüngerer Mädchen	meiner ſchönſten Meſſer	beſſerer Weine
Dat.	den edleren Grafen	jüngeren Mädchen	meinen ſchönſten Meſſern	beſſeren Weinen

Notice: Decline article and noun according to their own rules; and the adjective according to Reference Page G.

Exercise.

Decline, *Singular* and *Plural:* ſein größter Freund, *his greatest friend;* dieſe ſanftere Frau, *this more gentle woman;* ſtrengſtes Verbot, *most severe prohibition.*

General Exercise.

1. Have you seen my most beautiful dog?
2. I have never seen a more beautiful dog.
3. I have lost my dearest brother.
4. Have you ever (je) heard a falser word?
5. No, he is the falsest man in the town.
6. Has he given (to) you [any] freſher water?
7. You ought (ſollten) to sell the younger horse.
8. He is (the) most proud; she is (the) most gentle.
9. We are at the most (see T., C.) twenty men.
10. I am astonished in the highest degree.

REFERENCE-PAGE U.

Indefinite Pronouns and Adjectives.

I. Used with or without a noun after them; in the latter case often with a Capital initial.

Those marked with an asterisk (*) are indeclinable.

Declined like Adjectives:
der eine, *the one*
der andere, *the other (one)*
der nämliche, *the same (one)*
die meisten, *most (men)*

alles, *everything*
alle, *all (people)*
beide, *both*
einige, *several*
*etwas, *something*

jeder (-e, -es), *each (one)*
kein (-er, -e, -es), *no (one)*
mancher, *many a (one)*
*mehr, *more*
mehrere, *several*

*nichts, *nothing*
viel, *much (singular)*
viele, *many (men)*
wenig, *little (singular)*
wenige, *few (men)*

Thus: Hier sind beide Knaben; ich habe beide gesehen. *Here are both [the] boys; I have seen both.*

N.B.—gar before nichts or wenig makes them emphatic, as: gar Nichts, *nothing at all.* irgend increases the indefinite, uncertain meaning of etwas; also of Einer and Jemand. Er hat irgend Etwas gekauft, *he has bought some thing or other.*

II. Used as nouns, and *never* followed by a noun:

Jedermann, *every one;* Jemand, *some one;* man, *some one;* Niemand, *no one.*

N.B.—man is the French on; it stands for the English *we, they, somebody;* or the Passive, and must have its verb in 3d pers. Singular, as: man sagt = *they say, one says, it is said, people are saying,* etc. *one's,* before a noun, is sein = *his. One loses one's money.* Man verliert sein Geld.

Notice: (i) Jedermann, Jemand and Niemand take -es for Genitive, and do not change for the other cases; as: Er ist Jedermanns Freund, *he is everybody's friend.*

(ii) *not anything cannot be* rendered by nicht etwas, *nor not anybody by* nicht Jemand; they must be rendered by *nothing* = nichts, and *nobody* = Niemand.

Adverbs.

Most English adverbs have exact equivalents in German, which the Dictionary will readily furnish. Here are mentioned a few only of each class:

A. Pure Adverbs.

PLACE.	TIME.	AFFIRMATION.	NEGATION.	DOUBT.	QUANTITY.	INTERROGATION.
rechts, *to the right*	sonst, *formerly*	ja, *yes*	nein, *no*	vielleicht, *perhaps*	wenig, *little*	wo? *where*
links, *to the left*	jetzt, *now*	gewiß, *certainly*	keineswegs, *by no means*	schwerlich, *hardly*	ganz, *wholly*	wie viel? *how much*
da, *here*	einst, *once*	freilich, *of course*	nicht, *not*	wahrscheinlich, *probably*	genug, *enough*	wohin? *whither*
vorn, *in front*	seitdem, *since*	wahrlich, *indeed*	durchaus nicht, *by no means*	zweifelhaft, *doubtful*	kaum, *scarcely*	woher? *whence*
außen, *outside*	noch, *still, yet*	jedenfalls, *certainly*			ungefähr, *about*	[see p. 78.]

B. Adverbial Expressions.

In these German is very rich; a few only are given here:

PLACE: zu Hause, *at home;* nach Hause, *home.*
TIME: eines Tages, *one day;* von Zeit zu Zeit, *from time to time;* heut zu Tage, *now-a-days.*
AFFIRMATION: auf jeden Fall, *in every case;* ohne Zweifel, *without doubt.*
NEGATION: auf keinen Fall, *in no case.*

Notice: Most adjectives may be used as Adverbs of manner,—they are then invariable.

N.B.—With verbs of motion, *where?* is wohin? (*whither*); *there* is dahin or dorthin; *here* is hierher or daher [*where is* we. only with verbs of rest]. See also Ref.-Page O. *Where is he?* Wo ist er? but *Where is he going?* Wohin geht er?

EXAMPLES AND EXERCISES ON REFERENCE-PAGE U.

On I. *Examples:*

1. *Most men love themselves.* Die meisten Menschen lieben sich selbst.
2. *Give him some thing or other, pray.* Geben Sie ihm irgend Etwas, bitte.
3. *Few are satisfied with little.* Wenige sind mit Wenig (or Wenigem) zufrieden.
4. *Many a one wished something impossible.* Mancher wünschte etwas Unmögliches.
5. *He has little, I have nothing at all.* Er hat wenig; ich habe gar Nichts.

Exercise.

1. Several boys brought me (Dat.) beautiful presents.
2. The one or the other has done this.
3. Something is better than nothing at all.
4. I have seen the same man several *times* (mal).
5. No one likes this idle boy here.
6. We punished both boys too (zu) little.
7. All blamed that vain man.
8. Many-a-one fears his own shadow.
9. The one and the other have seen him.
10. Much wishes often [for] more.

On II. *Examples:*

1. *He has not found anything there.* Er hat dort Nichts gefunden.
2. *It is every one's duty to do his best.* Es ist Jedermanns Pflicht sein Bestes zu thun.
3. *People say he has died in Africa.* Man sagt, er sei in Afrika gestorben.
4. *I cannot give you anything.* Ich kann Ihnen Nichts geben.
5. *Some one has stolen my little dog.* Jemand hat meinen kleinen Hund gestohlen.

Exercise.

1. I cannot give him anything to-day.
2. Have you found anybody in the house?
3. No, I have not found anybody there.
4. Everybody's friend is nobody's friend.
5. They say he has killed somebody.
6. People said, everybody loved that boy.
7. Nobody has lost money in this affair.
8. I blame nobody.
9. Do not blame anybody.
10. Will people say, he was a good man?

On Adverbs. *Examples:*

1. *To the right lies the church.* Rechts liegt die Kirche.
2. *He will probably be in school.* Er wird wahrscheinlich in der Schule sein.
3. *Where are you going? Where do you come from?* Wohin gehen Sie? Woher kommen Sie?
4. *We shall visit that town perhaps.* Wir werden jene Stadt vielleicht besuchen.
5. *I do not by any means know it.* Ich weiß (kenne) es keineswegs.

Exercise.

1. It lies in front, before the table.
2. He certainly will not do it.
3. Formerly he was (was he) a very good man.
4. The boys have wholly *forgotten* it.
5. How much has he bought at (auf, Dat.) the market?
6. He has not by any means bought much (see 5 immediately above, in *Examples*).
7. Now he is (is he) very happy and contented.
8. Indeed; I do not know it.
9. He has never played since.
10. We shall certainly go about twenty miles to-day.

Reference-Page V.
Relative Pronouns.

As in English so in German, Nouns or Pronouns are often accompanied by relative clauses, introduced by *who* or *which*, welcher, etc., der, etc.

These relative pronouns welcher, der must agree with **their noun or** pronoun (*i.e.* their *antecedent*) in *gender* and *number*; but in *case* (unless followed **by** a noun themselves) they are **governed by** the verb in their own clause, or its preposition.

	MASC. SINGULAR.	FEM. SINGULAR.	NEUTER SINGULAR.	PLURAL M. F. N.	ENGLISH.
Nom.	welcher or der	welche or die	welches or das	welche or die	who, which
Acc.	welchen or den	welche or die	welches or das	welche or die	whom, which
Gen.	dessen	deren	dessen	deren	of whom, of which
Dat.	welchem or dem	welcher or der	welchem or dem	welchen or denen	to whom, to which

Remember these three rules most carefully:

(i) Relative clauses do not in any way alter the order of words in the Principal Sentence, as:

$$\overset{1}{\text{Der Mann,}} \quad \text{welcher (or der) hier wohnt,} \quad \overset{2}{\text{gab dem Kind}} \overset{3}{\text{einen Apfel.}}$$

The man, who lodges here, gave the child an apple.

(ii) The relative **clause** itself must *begin* **with the relative pronoun** (or its preposition, if there be one) and must END with its ASSERTION (*not* the Infinitive or Past Participle), as:

Die Stadt, von der ich spreche, liegt in Böhmen.
The town, of which I speak, lies in Bohemia.

Der Fluß, dessen Ufer Sie so schön gefunden haben, ist der Rhein.
*The river, **the** banks of which you have found so beautiful, is the Rhine.*

(iii) Separable verbs NEVER separate in Relative clauses, as:

Der Knabe, der zu spät aufstand, ist bestraft worden.
The boy, who got up too late, has been (become) punished.

Notice: Except the sentence be very short, place the relative clause always immediately after its antecedent, as:

Ich habe den Mann, welcher meinen Hund stahl, gestern in der Stadt gesehen.
I saw the man, who stole my dog, yesterday in the town.

But we might say, finishing the *short* principal sentence first:

Ich habe den Mann gesehen, welcher den Hund stahl.

[*N.B.*—Among the oblique cases of *which* must be included some of the *interrogatives* on **page 78 when** used as *relatives*.]

Correlative Pronouns.

The antecedents of Relative Pronouns are sometimes Demonstrative Pronouns, as: derjenige, etc., derselbe, etc., der nämliche, etc. **These two kinds** of pronouns, as: derjenige, welcher..., are sometimes styled Correlative; **each of them is** declined according to its own rules (see above, **and Reference-Page 8.), and dependent on its own verb, as:**

Ich liebe denjenigen, der mein Freund ist. *I love that one (him) who is my friend.*

N.B.—derjenige, welcher is often contracted (only Nominative) into wer, as: derjenige, welcher zufrieden **ist, ist glücklich,** *He who is* content, *is happy;* better: **Wer** zufrieden ist, ist glücklich. Thus also "**was**" for **dasjenige, welches.**

Examples and Exercises on Reference-Page V.

Remember to look to page 38 or 83 for the Order of Words, both in the Principal and the Relative Sentence; in the latter the *Assertion* stands last of all in its own clause. The order in the Principal Sentence is *not* in any way altered by the insertion of a Relative Clause. (*N.B.* The relative pronoun *must never* be omitted.)

I. Relatives. *Examples:*

1. Wir haben den Knaben nicht gesehen, welcher den **Preis erhalten hat**.
   We have not seen the boy, who received the prize.
2. Haben Sie die Zeitung, welche ich Ihnen schickte, noch nicht gelesen?
   Have you not yet **read the newspaper,** [*which*] *I sent you.*
3. Das Land, dessen Schönheiten Sie bewunderten, ist mein Vaterland.
   The country, the beauties of which you admired, is my country.
4. Der Mann in London, dessen Sie sich erinnern, ist letzte Woche gestorben.
   The gentleman in London, whom you remember, died last week.

Exercise.

1. We bought the picture, which (of which) you remembered; it is not dear.
2. Here is the dog, of which (von, Dat.) you speak; it (he) is very ugly.
3. Have you seen the man, whose house we bought yesterday?
4. The present, we have received **to-day,** is very beautiful.
5. Will you visit the land, the beauties of which every one praises?
6. That oak, the leaves of which are so green, is in our garden.
7. The town (which) we admired most, is Florence in Italy. (Florenz, Italien.)
8. Will they accept the rings which we brought them (Dat.)?

II. Correlatives. *Examples:*

1. Es ist das nämliche, welches ich so bewunderte. *It is the same which I admired so.*
2. Wir tadeln diejenigen, welche träge sind. *We blame those who are idle.*
3. Der Lehrer straft **den,** der dies gethan hat. *The teacher punishes him who did this.*
4. Er lobt denjenigen heute, den er gestern tadelte. *He praises him to-day whom he blamed yesterday.*

Exercise.

1. Will you see these books, or the one (that) which I have here?
2. Let us love what is beautiful and good [that which = was].
3. That one ought (sollte) to be happy, who is in good health.
4. I shall give this to the one, who is most diligent (am fleißigsten).
5. He who (wer) answers best, will receive the prize.
6. They remember (remember themselves of **that which) what you have written.**
7. The boys bought what was most costly.
8. Do not speak of what (that which) you **ought to forget.**

K

Reference-Page W.

Conjunctions.

Besides pure conjunctions, as *and*, und, etc., many adverbs and some prepositions may be used as **conjunctions**. All these are here **enumerated**.

Conjunctions may affect the position of the Assertion in the sentence which they begin, *but do not interfere with any other parts*. We must distinguish three **classes**:

1. Conjunctions which **do not alter the** order of words at all, and allow of the separation of separable verbs in the Simple **tenses**. These are marked (1) in the alphabetical list below. *Example:*

$\overset{1}{\text{Der Vater}} \overset{2}{\text{liest,}} \mid \text{und} \overset{1}{\text{die Mutter}} \overset{2}{\text{geht}} \overset{5}{\text{aus.}}$ *The father reads, and the mother is going out.*

2. Conjunctions which [like all **adverbs or other parts of the** sentence (except the Subject), when first in the sentence, see **Reference-Page J.**, page 38] require the *Inversion*, i.e. Assertion before Subject in the **clause they begin**; these allow of the separation of separable verbs in the Simple Tenses. They are marked **(2)** in the alphabetical list. *Example:*

$\overset{1}{\text{Der Vater}} \overset{2}{\text{liest,}} \mid \text{unterdessen} \overset{2}{\text{geht}} \overset{1}{\text{die Mutter}} \overset{5}{\text{aus.}}$ *The father reads, meanwhile the mother goes out.*

3. Conjunctions which **throw the Assertion** in the clause they begin to the very end of it; these do **not** allow **of separation of separable verbs in any case.** They are marked (3) in the alphabetical list. *Example:*

$\overset{1}{\text{Der Vater}} \overset{2}{\text{liest,}} \mid \text{wenn} \overset{1}{\text{die Mutter}} \text{am} \overset{4}{\text{Abend}} \text{in die} \overset{4}{\text{Stadt}} \overset{2}{\text{ausgeht.}}$
The father reads, when the mother in the evening goes out into the town.

Notice.—When the clause beginning with one of these (3) Conjunctions precedes the other, i.e. the Principal **sentence**, then in *this latter*, i.e. in the Principal *sentence*, **the** *Inversion takes place* [just as if it began **with an adverb** or other part of the sentence (except the Subject), see Reference-Page J., page 38]. *Example:*

$\overset{1}{\text{Wenn}} \text{die Mutter} \overset{2}{\text{ausgeht,}} \mid \text{(so)} \overset{2}{\text{liest}} \overset{1}{\text{der Vater.}}$ *If (when) the mother goes out, the father reads.*

Alphabetical List of Conjunctions and Words used as Conjunctions.

Notice.—Those **marked (1) do not alter the order**; those marked **(2) require simple** Inversion of Assertion and Subject; those marked **(3) throw the Assertion to the end of their** clause. [See 1, 2, 3, above.]

(*N.B.*—Subj. means Subject.)

according as (3), **je nachdem** (Subj.) ...... (Assertion).
after (3), nachdem (Subj.) ...... (Assertion).
also, too (2), auch (Assertion) (Subj.) ......
although **(3),** { obgleich, obwohl, wenn (Subj.) auch, obschon, wiewohl, wenn (Subj.) schon, wenn (Subj.) gleich.

and (1), und (Subj.) (Assertion, etc.).
as if (3), als ob,* als wenn,* wie wenn.*
[* These three require Imperfect Subjunctive.]
as long as... (3), so lange (als) (Subj.)...
as often as... (3), so oft (als) (Subj.)...
as soon as... (3), so bald (als) (Subj.)...

REFERENCE-PAGE W.—*continued.*

Alphabetical List of Conjunctions.—*continued.*

because, for (1), denn (Subj.) (Assertion).
because, as, since (cause) (3), weil, da...
before (3), bevor, ehe...
besides, moreover (2), außerdem, überdieß.
both... and... (1), sowohl (1st subj.) als auch.
but (1), aber, allein [jedoch, 1 or 2].
but (after negative) (1), sondern (with incomplete clause).
but that (3), (after negative or zu and adj.), als daß...
either (2), entweder... [or = oder (1)].
even if (3), selbst wenn...
furthermore (2), ferner...
how... (3), wie.
however (= as to the rest) (2), übrigens...
however (with adj.) (3) wie (adj.) auch...
however much (3) { so sehr (Subj.) auch...
{ wenn (Subj.) auch noch so..
if (3), wenn* { requires its verb, if in a past tense, to be in the *Imperfect Subjunctive.*
in case (that) (3), falls, wofern...
indeed ('t is true) (2), zwar... [aber (1)].
in order to (Infin.) (3), um (Obj.), zu (Infin.).
instead of (...ing) (3), anstatt daß (Subj.).
just as (Subj.) (3), sowie, gleichwie...
lest (= so that not) (3), damit (Subj.) nicht...
likewise (2), desgleichen (Assert.) (Subj.).
meanwhile (2), unterdessen...
{ *notwithstanding* (2), dessenungeachtet...
{ *nevertheless* (2), nichtsdestoweniger...
nor (2), noch, auch (Assert.) (Subj.) nicht...
not only... (2) { nicht nur..., nicht bloß...
{ nicht allein...
(but also (1)], {sondern (Subj.) (Assert.) auch.

notwithstanding (3), ungeachtet daß...
on the other hand (2), dagegen, hingegen...
or (1), oder.
otherwise (else) (2), sonst...
partly... (2), theils...
provided that (3), vorausgesetzt, daß...
rather (2), vielmehr...
scarcely (2), kaum...
since (time) (3), seit or seitdem...
so (= then) (2), so...
sometimes... sometimes (2), bald.. bald...
so that (3), so daß, damit* (with Subjunctive).
still (yet) (2), doch..., dennoch..., gleichwohl.
that (= so that) (3), daß.
the (comparative), *the* (comparative), Notice carefully:
(3) je (comparative)..., desto (2) (comparative)...
then... (2) dann..., da.
therefore (2) { also, daher, darum
thus { deßhalb, demnach
{ folglich, mithin
{ deßwegen [all (2)].
unless (3) { wofern (Subj.) nicht...
{ ohne daß..., wenn (Subj.) nicht.
unless (1), außer* (Subj.) (Assertion in Subjunctive).
until (3) { bis, bis daß...
{ (after negative), als bis...
when (with Imperfect Tense) (3), als...
when (with Pres. or Future) (3), wenn, wann.
whether (3), ob (with Subjunctive).
while (3), während, indem.
whilst (3), während.

[*N.B.*—To the above must be added in class (3) all the indirect interrogatives; see Reference-Page **X**.]

The Student will notice that many of the above are Adverbs, and some Prepositions, but all used as Conjunctions.

Most common Conjunctions.

1st Class: und, aber, oder, denn, [jedoch], sondern (after negative).
2d Class: zwar, sonst, also, darum, folglich, deßhalb, unterdessen.
3d Class: als, bis, damit, seit, ob, wenn, daß, weil, während.

EXAMPLES AND EXERCISES ON REFERENCE-PAGE **W**.

[*For General Sequence of Words in* **all** *sentences see page* 38 *or* 83.]

1. *Conjunctions marked* (1) : **No alteration** in sequence of words.   *Examples :*

    1. *My father is rich, but my uncle is a very poor man.*
    1. $\overset{1}{\text{Mein}}$ $\overset{2}{\text{Vater}}$ $\overset{5}{\text{ist reich,}}$ | aber (allein, jedoch) $\overset{1}{\text{mein}}$ $\overset{2}{\text{Oheim}}$ $\overset{5}{\text{ist ein sehr armer Mann.}}$

    2. *He cannot come now, for he has lost all his money.*
    2. $\overset{1}{\text{Er}}$ $\overset{2}{\text{kann}}$ $\overset{4}{\text{jetzt nicht}}$ $\overset{7}{\text{kommen,}}$ | denn $\overset{1}{\text{er}}$ $\overset{2}{\text{hat}}$ $\overset{3}{\text{all sein Geld}}$ $\overset{6}{\text{verloren.}}$

    3. *My friend has sent me these letters, and I am very thankful to him.*
    3. $\overset{1}{\text{Mein Freund}}$ $\overset{2}{\text{hat}}$ $\overset{3}{\text{mir diese Briefe}}$ $\overset{6}{\text{geschickt,}}$ | und $\overset{1}{\text{ich}}$ $\overset{2}{\text{bin}}$ $\overset{3}{\text{ihm sehr}}$ $\overset{5}{\text{dankbar.}}$

Exercise on (1).

1. Will you go with your brother, or will you remain at home (zu Hause)?
2. He is not going to Africa, but his brother will go there next year (nächstes Jahr).
3. This little boy has not brought his books, but those of his friend.
4. You cannot go with me, my child, for I must go alone (allein).
5. Will the enemies destroy **both** the town **and also** the villages?
6. My friends, we must obey (Dat.) the king **or** the emperor (Dat.).

2. *Conjunctions marked* (2) : **Assertion before Subject** in the clause they introduce.
Examples :

    1. *He has no friends ; besides, he is not a rich man.*
    1. $\overset{1}{\text{Er}}$ $\overset{2}{\text{hat}}$ $\overset{3}{\text{keine Freunde;}}$ | überdies $\overset{2}{\text{ist}}$ $\overset{1}{\text{er}}$ $\overset{3}{\text{nicht}}$ $\overset{5}{\text{ein reicher Mann.}}$

    2. *He told them to go ; nevertheless they remained in the house.*
    2. $\overset{1}{\text{Er}}$ $\overset{2}{\text{befahl}}$ $\overset{3}{\text{ihnen}}$ $\overset{7}{\text{zu gehen,}}$ | dennoch (nichtsdestoweniger) $\overset{2}{\text{blieben}}$ $\overset{1}{\text{sie}}$ $\overset{4}{\text{im Hause.}}$

    3. *The enemy defeated us last year, on the other hand we gained a victory now.*
    3. $\overset{1}{\text{Der Feind}}$ $\overset{2}{\text{besiegte}}$ $\overset{3}{\text{uns}}$ $\overset{4}{\text{letztes Jahr,}}$ | dagegen $\overset{2}{\text{gewannen}}$ $\overset{1}{\text{wir}}$ $\overset{4^*}{\text{jetzt}}$ $\overset{3}{\text{einen Sieg.}}$

    * *N.B.*—Adverbs of time sometimes precede the object.

Exercise on (2).

1. He died soon, **otherwise** he would now **be a rich man**.
2. They are not our friends, **still** they are just towards (gegen, Acc.) **us**.
3. That little boy brought us the newspaper, **then** (dann) he went away (fort).
4. 'Tis true, he is not a clever boy, **yet** (dennoch) he writes his exercises well (**gut**).
5. Not only was the English general brave, but (1) he was also cautious.
6. We wrote to him last (letzte) week, **therefore** he went to **Liverpool**.

3. *Conjunctions marked* (3) : **Assertion at the very end** of their clause.   *Examples :*

    1. *We shall not praise him, as long as he is such a lazy boy.*
    1. $\overset{1}{\text{Wir}}$ $\overset{2}{\text{werden}}$ $\overset{3}{\text{ihn nicht}}$ $\overset{4}{\text{loben,}}$ $\overset{7}{}$ | so lange (als) $\overset{1}{\text{er}}$ $\overset{5}{\text{ein so träger Knabe}}$ $\overset{2}{\text{ist.}}$

    2. *You have believed this although your friend has told you the contrary.*
    2. $\overset{1}{\text{Sie}}$ $\overset{2}{\text{haben}}$ $\overset{3}{\text{dieses}}$ $\overset{6}{\text{geglaubt,}}$ | obgleich $\overset{1}{\text{Ihr Freund}}$ $\overset{3}{\text{Ihnen}}$ $\overset{3}{\text{das Gegenteil}}$ $\overset{6}{\text{gesagt}}$ $\overset{2}{\text{hat.}}$

EXAMPLES AND EXERCISES ON REFERENCE-PAGE **W**.—*continued.*

Exercise on (3).

1. Will you go on (auf, Acc.) the ice, notwithstanding that your **friend has warned you**?
2. We are doing this, in order to try his courage.
3. Write to (an, Acc.) him, so that he may know (wiſſen) the whole affair.
4. You do not know (wiſſen) how much we have loved that unfortunate man.
5. These boys played (were playing), whilst those ladies wrote their letters.
6. Will you wait, **until** the whole **town** knows (of) this affair (Acc.)?
7. I would not **have believed it, if he had not shown** me the letter.
8. These men **would not have (been) gone, unless we had forced them.**
9. He will do it, provided that you pay **him well.**
10. They have **been ill since I** saw them last (zuletzt).

General Sentences on the Conjunctions and Relatives.

Examples: [See Notice on page 74, attached to No. 3.]

1. $\overset{1}{\text{Wenn}}\ \overset{}{\text{der Schnee}}\ \overset{2}{\text{ſchmilzt}},\ |\ \overset{2}{\text{ſo}}\ \overset{}{\text{wird}}\ \overset{1}{\text{der Frühling}},\ |\ \overset{1}{\text{auf den}}\ \overset{2}{\text{wir}}\ \overset{4}{\text{hoffen}},\ |\ \overset{7}{\text{bald kommen}}.$
 *When the snow melts, the spring, for which we hope, **will come soon.***
2. $\overset{2}{\text{Entweder}}\ \overset{}{\text{wird}}\ \overset{1}{\text{der Mann}}\ \overset{7}{\text{kommen}},\ |\ \overset{1}{\text{oder ich}}\ \overset{2}{\text{werde}}\ \overset{3}{\text{ihn}}\ \overset{7}{\text{ſtrafen}}.$
 Either the man will come, or I shall punish him.
3. $\overset{1}{\text{Wer}}\ \overset{2}{\text{kann}}\ \overset{7}{\text{wiſſen}},\ |\ \overset{1}{\text{ob der Angeklagte}},\ |\ \overset{4}{\text{der}}\ \overset{2}{\text{hier}}\ \overset{}{\text{ſteht}},\ |\ \overset{5}{\text{ſchuldig}}\ \overset{2}{\text{iſt}}\ \text{oder nicht?}$
 Who can know (it), whether the accused, who is standing here, is guilty or not?
4. $\overset{1}{\text{Während}}\ \overset{}{\text{der Feind}}\ \overset{3}{\text{die Stadt}},\ |\ \overset{1}{\text{die}}\ \overset{2}{\text{wir}}\ \overset{2}{\text{lieben}},\ |\ \overset{2}{\text{zerſtörte}},\ |\ \overset{}{\text{gewannen wir einen Sieg}}.$
 *Whilst the enemy **was** destroying the town, which we love, we gained a victory.*
5. $\overset{1}{\text{Als die Nachricht}}\ \overset{4}{\text{hier}}\ \overset{2}{\text{ankam}},\ |\ \overset{2}{\text{war}}\ \overset{1}{\text{der Soldat}}\ \overset{4}{\text{ſchon}}\ \overset{6}{\text{verurtheilt}}.$
 *When the news **arrived here,** the soldier was already condemned.*

Exercise.

Be careful to examine which is the "*Principal Sentence*;" it never begins **with a conjunction; except ſo** (**not** translated in English). It is printed in italics here:—

1. *The enemy,* who gained this victory, *would have fled,* if we had been more cautious.
2. *Whilst you* (were writing) wrote this letter, *he was reading the newspaper.*
3. *I shall wait,* until the boy, whom I sent to (auf, Acc.) the post, comes back.
4. *Have you seen the letter,* which my son wrote, or *have you not seen it* (ihn) *yet?*
5. When the news, **which** we expected, arrived, *we were no longer* (nicht mehr) *there.*
6. *We sent you a letter,* so that you might (ſollten) not expect us.
7. Scarcely was the door opened, *when* (ſo) *the* **boys** *rushed in* (hinein'ſtürzen).
8. *We hoped,* you would do this, because you have been our friend hitherto (bisher).

REFERENCE-PAGE X.

Indirect Speech (*Oratio Obliqua*).

A statement, request, or command, and a question may be mentioned, as it was uttered, i.e. direct (*Oratio Recta*), as:

Statement: ich sagte dir: „ Er hat es gethan." *I told you:* "*He has done it.*"
Request: er bat ihn: „ Gieb mir ein Buch!" *He asked him:* "*Give me a book!*"
Command: der Vater befahl: „ Geht in's Haus!" *The father commanded:* "*Go into the house.*"
Question: Sie fragten mich: „ Hast du das Geld?" *You asked me:* "*Have you the money?*"

If the direct words are not used, all these become *Indirect Speech*.

The following Rules hold good in all Indirect Speech.

1. The order in the Indirect Speech clause is unchanged, if it is *not* introduced **by any conjunction**, *but* **if a conjunction begins the** clause, the assertion, i.e. the *conjugated verb or auxiliary, is thrown to the very end of it.*

2. The *Subjunctive* is used in the dependent clause, particularly if it is *not* introduced by a conjunction [unless the **quotation is mentioned as an emphatic fact**; then the Indicative may be used in some cases].

3. The *Present Subjunctive* is preferred to the *Imperfect*, particularly in the third person Singular [unless the action referred to is emphasised as being a past action; then the Perfect is used].

4. Always **complete** the Principal Sentence entirely, before beginning the clause containing the Indirect Speech.

Statements: either not introduced by a conjunction, or introduced by **daß**, *that*, as:
ich sagte dir, er habe es gethan; or:..., daß er es gethan habe (or hat).

Requests or Commands: either not introduced by **a conjunction, or** introduced by **daß,** *that*. The dependent clause generally contains **sollen,** *ought*, as:
er bat ihn, daß er ihm ein Buch **gebe; or:** ..., er **solle ihm** ein Buch geben.
der Vater befahl, daß sie in's Haus gehen sollten; or: ..., sie sollten in's Haus gehen.

Questions: always introduced by **ob,** *whether, if;* or by one of the *interrogative conjunctions* below; all these throw the assertion to the end of their clause, as:
Sie fragten mich, ob ich Geld habe (or: hätte). *You asked me whether I had money.*

Notice.—All interrogatives assume in *Oratio Obliqua* the force of Conjunctions.

Such *Interrogative Conjunctions* are:

[*N.B.* Those **beginning with wo... must be looked upon as** oblique cases of the relative pronoun *which*.]

wann... ? *when... ?*	wie lange... ? *how long...?*	wohin... ? *whither... ?*	worunter... ? *under which... ?*
wer... ? *who... ?*	wo... ? *where. ?*	womit... ? *wherewith ... ?*	wovon... ? *of what... ?*
warum... ? *why... ?*	wobei... ? *whereat... ?*	woran... ? *whereat... ?*	wie... ? *how ?*
was... ? *what... ?*	woburch... ? *whereby... ?*	worauf... ? *upon what... ?*	or: auf welche Weise... ?
weßhalb... ? *why... ?*	woher... ? *whence... ?*	worin ? *wherein... ?*	*how ? In what manner... ?*
weßwegen... ? *why... ?*			was für ein ? was für ?
wie viel... ? *how much... ?*			*what sort of... ?*

as: Er fragte, wie lange ich dort gewesen sei. *He asked how long I had been there.*

EXAMPLES AND EXERCISES ON REFERENCE-PAGE **X**.
STATEMENTS.
(Read the Four Rules on page 78 very carefully.)

1. $\overset{1}{\text{Der junge Mann}} \overset{2}{\text{sagte}} \overset{3}{\text{mir,}} \mid \overset{1}{\text{er}} \overset{2}{\text{habe}} \overset{3}{\text{den Schüler}} \overset{4}{\text{nicht}} \overset{6}{\text{gesehen.}}$
The young man told me, he had not seen the scholar.

2. $\overset{2}{\text{Glauben}} \overset{1}{\text{Sie,}} \mid \overset{1}{\text{daß}} \overset{3}{\text{er diese Aufgabe}} \overset{4}{\text{allein}} \overset{6}{\text{geschrieben}} \overset{2}{\text{habe? (hat.)}}$
Do you believe, that he has written this exercise alone?

3. $\overset{2}{\text{Haben}} \overset{1}{\text{Sie}} \overset{6}{\text{erwähnt,}} \mid \overset{1}{\text{daß}} \overset{3}{\text{diese Soldaten}} \overset{4}{\text{in Indien}} \overset{6}{\text{gewesen}} \overset{2}{\text{sind}}$ (a fact).
*Have you mentioned, that these soldiers have **been in India**?*

Exercise.

1. It is said (**Man sagt**) (that) this young man has (is) become very rich.
2. We do not believe, **(that) the teacher will** punish those boys to-day.
3. I have already mentioned, that the ship will sail (on (am, Dat.)) next Monday.
4. Who can say, (that) these men have not fought very bravely?
5. Do you deny, that our garden is larger than yours?
6. The messenger reported that the high tower had fallen down (Conj. with **sein**).

REQUESTS OR **COMMANDS**.

1. $\overset{1}{\text{Wer}} \overset{2}{\text{hat}} \overset{3}{\text{Ihnen}} \overset{6}{\text{befohlen,}} \mid \overset{1}{\text{Sie}} \overset{2}{\text{sollen}} \overset{4}{\text{in die Stadt}} \overset{7}{\text{gehen?}} [\overset{1}{\text{daß}} \overset{}{\text{Sie}} \dots \overset{2}{\text{sollen.}}]$
Who has ordered you, to go into the town?

2. $\overset{3}{\text{Was}} \overset{2}{\text{befiehlt}} \overset{1}{\text{der Hauptmann?}} \mid \overset{1}{\text{Er}} \overset{2}{\text{befiehlt,}} \mid \overset{1}{\text{daß die Stadt}} \overset{6}{\text{zerstört}} \overset{2}{\text{werde.}}$
*What does the **captain command**? He commands, that the town be destroyed.*

3. $\overset{1}{\text{Er}} \overset{2}{\text{rief}} \overset{3}{\text{mir}} \overset{5}{\text{zu,}} \mid \overset{1}{\text{ich}} \overset{2}{\text{solle}} \overset{3}{\text{keine Äpfel}} \overset{4}{\text{mehr}} \overset{7}{\text{nehmen.}}$
He shouted to me not to take any more apples.

Exercise.

1. I told you, you should (**sollten**) remain where you were.
2. His command was, that we should allow the men to enter (**einzutreten**).
3. Will you order me to punish him for (**für**) this? (**ich solle ... strafen**).
4. He commands me (Dat.) not to lend you my book (see 3 above).
5. We shouted to them (that they should) to come here (**herkommen**) at once.

QUESTIONS.

1. $\overset{2}{\text{Wissen}} \overset{1}{\text{Sie,}} \mid \overset{4}{\text{auf welche Weise}} \overset{1}{\text{er}} \overset{3}{\text{es}} \overset{2}{\text{tat,}} \mid \overset{1}{\text{oder womit}} \overset{6}{\text{es}} \overset{3}{\text{getan wurde?}}$
Do you know, in what manner he did it, or wherewith it was done?

2. *I scarcely know where he is.* $\overset{1}{\text{Ich}} \overset{2}{\text{weiß}} \overset{4}{\text{kaum,}} \mid \overset{1}{\text{wo}} \overset{2}{\text{er ist.}}$

Exercise.

1. We asked them, where they had (were) been the whole day.
2. The scholar asked, whether the Rhine was (is) in France?
3. They knew not, how (in what manner) the boy had done **this yesterday**.
4. He knows, what (**wovon**) the teacher is speaking about now (**soeben**).

Reference-Page Y.

Interjections.

Practically speaking, interjections, or elliptical phrases used as such, are unlimited in number; **and it is not** easy to give exact equivalents of the interjections **in two languages.** Moreover, as **in English**, certain parts of a country have always certain characteristic exclamations. The following are the most common, with their approximate English equivalents:—

Ah! Ah! Ei! Oh! Aha!	*Fie!* Pfui! Schändlich!	*Help!* Hülfe! Zu Hülfe!	*'S death!* Zum Teufel!
Agreed! Topp! Es gilt!	*Forwards!* Vorwärts!	*Humph!* Hm! Hem!	*Stop!* Halt! Haft da!
Alas! Ach! Leider!	*Gently!* Leise! Sachte!	*Hurrah!* Hurrah! Juchhe!	*Take care!* Achtung!
All right! Gut! Recht!	*Get away!* Weg! Fort!	*Hush!* St! Stille!	—— Vorsicht!
Come! Frisch! Nun denn!	—— Gehen Sie mir!	*Huzza!* Heisa!	*Thank God!* Gott sei Dank!
Attention! Achtung!	*God be praised!* Gottlob!	*Indeed!* Wirklich! Nein!	*Tally ho!* Trara!
Bang! Piff, Paff!	—— Gott sei Dank!	*I say!* Holla! Hier!	*Very well!* Sehr gut!
By Jove! Gott! Himmel!	*Good bye!* Adieu!	*Long live..!* Es lebe (Nom.)!	*Well!* Nun! Wohlan!
—— Gott im Himmel!	—— Auf Wiedersehen!	*Now then!* Nun! Also!	*Well I never!* Merkwürdig!
Down! (to a dog) Leg'dich!	*Good God!* Gott!	*O!* Oh! Ah! (admiration)	*Woe!* Wehe!
—— Kusch' dich!	*Good health!* Zur Gesundheit!	—— Au! (pain)	*Ugh!* Uh! Pfui!
Faith! Bei meiner Treu!	*Hail!* Heil! Willkommen!	*O dear!* Oh weh! Ach!	*Zounds!* Donnerwetter!
—— Auf Treue!	*Hallo!* Holla! Was?!	*On!* Vorwärts!	—— Verdammt!

Impersonal Verbs.

I. True Impersonals:

  (*a*) Applying to atmospheric phenomena:

  es donnert, *it thunders;* es hagelt, *it hails;* es schneit, *it snows*   These are regularly conjugated, but of
  es blitzt,   *it lightens;* es regnet, *it rains;* es tagt, *it dawns*   course have only 3d person singular.

  (*b*) **sein,** *to be;* and **geben,** *to give,* are often used impersonally.

   (i) **es ist,** *there is;* **es sind,** *there are;* **es war,** *there was;* **es waren,** *there were,* etc. This is used with a *Nominative* after **it;** it applies to things, etc., taken in a *limited sense,* and generally with the "place where" mentioned and referring to a small limit. *N.B.*—In questions, and in the Inversion, es is omitted, as: Ist ein Knabe hier? Es waren drei Vögel in dem Häuschen.

   (ii) **es giebt,** *there is;* **es gab,** *there was,* without a plural form, is always followed by the Accusative, and applies to things, etc. taken in a *large or unlimited sense,* either with no "place where" mentioned, or referring to a very large limit. *N.B.*—es in es giebt is never omitted, as: es giebt Leute, welche . . . *There are people who* . . . Hat es keinen Krieg gegeben? *Was there no war?*

II. Other verbs used impersonally:

  (*a*) Ordinary verbs, as: es fängt an, *it begins,* etc.

  (*b*) Verbs with reflected pronoun (*not* true reflexive verbs). [See Reference-Page Q.]

   (i) With accusative of personal pronoun, as: es freut mich (dich, ihn) *I (thou, he), rejoice (it rejoices me).*

   (ii) With dative of personal pronoun, as: es gelingt mir, *it succeeds to me* = *I succeed.*

Notice the impersonal constructions: **es gieng ein Mann,** instead of **ein Mann gieng,** and in the Passive: es wird gesungen, instead of man singt.

Examples and Exercises on Reference-Page Y.

Exercise on the Interjections.

1. Forwards! Soldiers! There is the enemy! Attention! Hurrah!
2. Woe! The enemy has entered the town! (are into the town broken (ein'brechen).
3. He said: Well I never! and went to the poor horse (ging zu, Dat.).
4. Good God! you will surely (doch) not kill the unfortunate man.
5. Fie! do not do that. Faith! It would be shameful.
6. Hail! Welcome, our emperor in (Dat.) our town!
7. All people (Leute) cried: Long live our good king!
8. "Help!" cried the poor woman. God be praised! you came in time.
9. When he saw his dog, he cried to him (ihm zu): Down! Lie down!
10. 'S death! you should have (hätten . . . sollen) gone forwards.

On the Impersonal Verbs.

Examples.

1. *Do you see, how it snows!* Sehen Sie, wie es schneit!
2. *Yesterday it rained the whole day!* Gestern regnete es den ganzen Tag.
3. *It is beginning to snow now.* Es fängt jetzt an zu schneien.
4. *There was no boy in school.* Es war kein Knabe in der Schule.
5. *There have been men who said that.* Es hat Leute gegeben, die das sagten.
6. *Do you rejoice that he is ill?* Freut es Sie, daß er krank ist?
7. *No, I am very sorry.* Nein, es tut mir sehr leid.
8. *In Germany they dance much.* In Deutschland wird viel getanzt.

Exercise.

1. See, how it lightens, and do you hear how it thunders?
2. Day is dawning, the sun will rise soon.
3. Was there a bird **in your cage**? [*N.B.* es is dropped in Questions.]
4. In France they **drink much wine**. [*N.B.* es is dropped in the Inversion.] (See 8 above.)
5. There were people who did not believe that I had been (was) in America.
6. **Hurrah!** I succeeded (it succeeded to me) in catching the bird (zu fangen).
7. Some men went to that village (say: There (es) went some men into).
8. God be praised! There is (it gives, *with Accusative*) no war.
9. There were many people in the theatre (Es waren . . .).
10. We rejoice (it rejoices us) that you have succeeded (that it to you succeeded is).

L

On the Assertion and Predicate.

Special note on the exact meaning of these terms as used in this Grammar.

In order to facilitate the study of "Sequence of Words" in every German sentence, the terms "Assertion" and "Predicate" are used here in a sense somewhat departing from that which they usually have in English Grammar. The student must therefore make himself thoroughly familiar with the meaning of these two words in German Syntax.

A. The **Assertion** is always the **conjugated Verb of** the sentence, therefore in **all tenses**, formed by the aid of an auxiliary, it is this auxiliary which is called "the **Assertion**." Thus in der Knabe **spielte** gestern im Garten, the verb **spielte** is the Assertion; but in der Knabe hat gestern im Garten gespielt, the auxiliary **hat** expresses Person, Tense, Number, and Mood; and is therefore the Assertion now.

The Assertion is the only moveable part of the sentence; its ordinary place is No. 2., *i.e.* immediately after the Subject; but we see (page 83) that it can change its place, so as to be at the very beginning (*i.e.* immediately after the conjunction), or at the very end of a sentence. These are its only possible changes.

In the following sentence the *Assertion* of every clause is printed in black type :—Der Bote **kam** in mein Zimmer, | aber ich **war** ausgegangen, | denn es **war** sehr schönes Wetter; | deßhalb **hatte** er den Brief, | welchen er mir **überbrachte**, | auf meinem Tische zurückgelassen, | wo ich denselben richtig **fand**, | als ich von meinem Spaziergang **zurückkehrte** | .

B. The **Predicate,** in the sense used here, can only occur ((*c.*) below excepted) when the Verb of any sentence is one of the following :—sein, *to be;* werden, *to become;* scheinen, *to seem;* heißen, *to be called;* bleiben, *to remain;* and some Passive verbs, as: genannt werden, *to be called;* erwählt werden, *to be chosen.* The Predicate *must* always be : (*a.*) a Substantive in the Nominative ; (*b.*) an Adjective, always **invariable**; (*c.*) the separated prefix of a separable verb, used without auxiliary and in a **principal sentence**.

In the following sentence the *Predicate* of every clause is printed in black type :—Karl war letzten Abend **sehr träge** | ; er scheint überhaupt **kein** fleißiger Knabe zu sein | ; er schreibt oft seine Aufgaben einfach **ab**, | und ist daher gewöhnlich **der Letzte** in seiner Klasse | ; doch hoffen wir | , er werde nicht immer so **thöricht** bleiben | .

The above explanations should be carefully studied.

REFERENCE-PAGE Z.

Complete Rules on the Sequence of Words in a Sentence.

Subject to some modifications for the sake of emphasising a word by not placing it in its ordinary position, the following is the order of words in *every sentence*:

Remember: The Assertion (No. 2) is the *only moveable* member of any sentence.

1.	2.	3.	4.	5.	6.	7.
SUBJECT.	ASSERTION.	OBJECTS.	ADVERBIALS.	PREDICATE.	PAST PARTICIPLE.	INFINITIVES.
Noun or Pronoun, Nominative of Verb; together with their attributes, or their relative clauses.	The *conjugated* Verb; or, Auxiliary in Compound Tenses.	Nouns or Pronouns in oblique Cases; with their attributes or their relative clauses. If there be more than one Object, put Dative first; also put Pronoun before Noun; Person before Thing; shortest Pronoun first; Words governed by any Prepositions last. The reflexive Pronoun of reflexive Verbs stands also in place 3.	Put *Time* first; often before the Objects even. Put *Place* last; often after the Predicate even. The Adverb: nicht generally precedes the words which it negatives, especially other adverbs; except in noch nicht = *not yet*.	Only occurs if in connection with: werden, *to become*; scheinen, *to seem*; heißen, *to be called*; bleiben, *to remain*; and some passives, as: genannt werden, *to be called*; erwählt werden, *to be appointed*. The separated prefix of a separable verb becomes also a Predicate, and stands in place 5.	Invariable. If there are two Past Participles, that of the Auxiliary stands last.	Invariable. If there are two Infinitives, that of the Auxiliary stands last. ju is never separated from its Infinitive.

There are only three classes of Sentences in German, viz.: Principal, Relative, Subordinate. In all these the above order 1, (2), 3, 4, 5, 6, 7 holds good, with the one exception of the Assertion (No. 2).

A. This ASSERTION IS PLACED BEFORE THE SUBJECT (No. 1) in the following cases:
  (a) If the sentence is a question (or a command, expressed without sollen).
  (b) If a conjunction marked (2) on pages 74, 75, or any member of the sentence, *not* the subject (i.e. a 3, 4, 5, 6, 7 above), or a subordinate clause, precede the Principal Sentence.
  (c) If in conditional sentences the conjunction wenn is omitted.

B. The ASSERTION (No. 2) IS THROWN TO THE VERY END OF THE SENTENCE:
  (a) In *all subordinate clauses*, introduced by a conjunction marked (3) on pages 74, 75.
  (b) In *all relative clauses*, introduced always by: welcher or der; wer, was, and the oblique cases of these, to which belong: worin, worauf, wobei, womit, wodurch, wofür, woran, wozu; wie, auf welche Weise, wann, wo, warum, etc. [For complete list see page 78 at foot.]

Remember: Nos. 1, 3, 4, 5, 6, 7 are NOT influenced by the change of place of the Assertion, nor by any relative or subordinate clauses inserted in the body of the sentence.

N.B.—1. Separable Verbs *cannot* separate in relative or subordinate clauses.
  2. Subordinate clauses, when not introduced by any conjunction, have the assertion in its proper place, *i.e.* No. 2.
  3. In relative clauses introduced by the Nominative case of the relative pronoun, this latter is the subject itself.
  4. Conjunctions do not count in the sequence of words, nor do Interjections.

Examples and Exercises on Reference-Page Z.

In analysing a sentence, remember carefully:

> The *Subject* is got in answer to the question: "Who?" or "What?" (coupled with the verb). It is *always* in the *Nominative case*, and generally enlarged by article, adjective, Attributive Genitive or Relative Clause.
>
> The *Object*. (a) The *direct object* answers to the question: "Whom?" or "What?" (coupled with the verb). It is *always* in the *Accusative*, but is also generally enlarged like the subject.
>
> (b) The *indirect object* answers the question: "To whom?" "By whom?" "With whom?" etc., and is either *Genitive* or *Dative* (unless after a preposition governing accusative).
>
> The *Predicate* is got in answer to the question: "What is (becomes, is called) the subject?" It is Nominative case if a noun; and invariable if an adjective. The separated *prefix* of separable verbs, in Simple Tenses and Principal Sentences, is also a Predicate.
>
> The *Assertion* is always the *conjugated* verb or auxiliary; **never** the Infinitive, nor the Past Participle.

Example of Analysis of a Complex Sentence:

Analyse: $\overline{\text{Der arme Mann}}^{1}$ $\overline{\text{hoffte}}^{2}$, | daß $\overline{\text{Sie}}^{1}$ $\overline{\text{ihm}}^{3}$ $\overline{\text{Etwas}}^{3}$ $\overline{\text{geben}}^{7}$ $\overline{\text{würden}}^{2}$, | und $\overline{\text{er}}^{1}$ $\overline{\text{fragte}}^{2}$ $\overline{\text{mich}}^{3}$, | ob $\overline{\text{ich}}^{1}$ $\overline{\text{Ihnen}}^{3}$ $\overline{\text{das Buch}}^{3}$, | welches $\overline{\text{er}}^{1}$ $\overline{\text{mir}}^{3}$ $\overline{\text{anvertraut}}^{6}$ $\overline{\text{hatte}}^{2}$, | $\overline{\text{übergeben}}^{6}$ $\overline{\text{hätte}}^{2}$.

General Analysis.

Der arme Mann hoffte: is the 1st Principal Sentence, order according to Reference-Page Z.

daß Sie ihm Etwas geben würden: Subordinate clause, enlargement of hoffen, introduced by daß, a conjunction of 3d class (see pp. 74, 75), therefore Assertion, würden, at its end.

und er fragte mich: is the 2d Principal Sentence, joined by und, a Conjunction of 1st class, therefore no alteration in the order.

ob ich Ihnen das Buch [. . .] **übergeben hätte**: Subordinate clause, enlargement of fragen, introduced by ob, a conjunction of the 3d class, therefore Assertion, hätte, at its end.

welches er mir anvertraut hatte: a Relative clause, attributive to das Buch; has the **Assertion hatte** at its end like all relative clauses (see Reference-Page V), but does not interfere with **the order in the sentence in which it is interpolated**.

Minute Analysis.

Der arme Mann: Subject (with attribute) of the 1st Principal Sentence; hoffte: **its assertion**. Sie: Subject of 1st subordinate clause; ihm: **its indirect object**; Etwas: **its** direct object (Accusative). geben: its Infinitive; würden: **its Assertion**. er: Subject of 2d **Principal** sentence. fragte: its Assertion; mich: its direct object. ich: **Subject of the** 2d subordinate clause; Ihnen: its indirect object; das Buch, its direct **Object [welches**: relat. Pronoun, acc. Neut. **;** er: Subject of the relative clause; mir: its indirect **object; anvertraut: its Past Participle; hatte: its** Assertion]. übergeben: Past Participle of the 2d Subord. Clause; **hätte: its Assertion (Subjunctive).** (Analyse in the same way, *vivâ voce*, any sentences met with in Translation, first giving a *general analysis*, and then a *minute* one of every word.)

GENERAL EXERCISES.

Analyse the following, giving reason for position of **Assertion** *in every instance as shown on the preceding page.*

1. $\underset{a\,1}{\text{Der General}}$ $\underset{a\,2}{\text{befahl}}$ $\underset{a\,3}{\text{den Soldaten,}}$ | $\underset{b\,1}{\text{sie}}$ $\underset{b\,2}{\text{sollten}}$ $\underset{b\,3}{\text{das Dorf,}}$ | $\underset{c\,1}{\text{[welches}}$ $\underset{c\,4}{\text{auf dem Hügel stand,]}}$ $\underset{c\,2}{}$ | $\underset{b\,7}{\text{angreifen,}}$ |
$\underset{d\,1}{\text{denn}}$ $\underset{d\,2}{\text{er}}$ $\underset{}{\text{sagte,}}$ | $\underset{e\,1}{\text{das}}$ $\underset{e\,2}{\text{sei}}$ $\underset{e\,5}{\text{der Schlüssel der Stellung der Feinde,}}$ | $\underset{f\,1}{\text{die}}$ $\underset{f\,4}{\text{dahinter}}$ $\underset{f\,2}{\text{lagen.}}$ |

The general commanded the soldiers to attack the village, which stood on the hill; for he said that was the key of the position of the enemy, who were lying behind it.

2. $\underset{}{\text{Während}}$ $\underset{a\,1}{\text{die Knaben}}$ $\underset{a\,4}{\text{in dem Hofe}}$ $\underset{a\,2}{\text{spielten,}}$ | $\underset{b\,2}{\text{kam}}$ $\underset{b\,1}{\text{ein Bettler}}$ $\underset{b\,4}{\text{in das Haus}}$ | und $\underset{c\,2}{\text{stahl}}$ $\underset{c\,3}{\text{die Kleider,}}$ |
$\underset{d\,4}{\text{welche im Zimmer hingen,}}$ $\underset{d\,2}{}$ | $\underset{e\,1}{\text{ohne}}$ $\underset{e\,3}{\text{daß}}$ $\underset{}{\text{Jemand}}$ $\underset{e\,2}{\text{ihn}}$ $\underset{}{\text{beobachtete.}}$

Whilst the boys were playing in the yard, a beggar came into the house and stole the clothes, which were hanging in the room, without any one noticing him.

Translate.

1. The enemies destroyed the town, which stood by the (am) river, and escaped over the river, before (vor) the citizens, who were surprised (überrascht), could assemble (sich versammeln).

2. Since the ship has sailed, I have often thought of (an, with accusative) my friend, who is now on the sea, and I shall be glad to hear soon that he has reached London (in L. an'kommen, with *to be*) safely (glücklich).

3. I asked him, why he had done this, but he answered nothing; therefore I think he knows that he has done wrong (Unrecht tun).

4. When (als) the ship came into the harbour, we hastened (eilen, reg.) to see whether Charles had (was) arrived, but alas we found he had not come, because he was ill when the ship left London.

5. Do you know whether your friend found the book, which he had lost, or whether he bought a new [one]?

Dictionary of Words (*not on pages* 12 *or* 58 *and* 59).

For the Exercises of this Term.

about (*circa*), adv., ungefähr; preposition, um (Acc.)
to accept, an'nehmen (irreg.)
the affair, die Geschichte, —, —n
ago, vor (with Dat. *after* it)
to allow, erlauben (reg.)
alone, allein (adv.)
already, schon (adv.)
to answer, antworten (reg.)
the apple, der Apfel, —s, ⸚
to arrive, an'kommen (irreg.)
to ask, fragen (reg.)
to assemble, sich versammeln (reg.)
astonished (adj.), erstaunt
at once (adv.), sogleich
away (adv.), fort
America, *Africa* (unaltered)
the beauty, die Schönheit, —, —en
before (prep.), vor (Dat. or Acc.)
the bird, der Vogel, —s, ⸚
to blame, tadeln, rügen (reg.)
the boot, der Stiefel, —s, —
both, beide or die beiden
brave(-*ly*), tapfer
to bring, bringen (half reg.)
the cage, der Käfig, —s, —e
to call, rufen (irreg.)
the cap, die Mütze, —, —n
to catch, fangen (irreg.)
cautious, vorsichtig
certainly, sicher, gewiß
Charles, Karl, —s
the citizen, der Bürger, —s, —
clever, klug, gescheidt
to come, kommen (irreg.)
to come back, zurück'kommen
to command, befehlen (irreg.)
the command, der Befehl, —s, —e

content(-*ed*) zufrieden
costly = *dear*, teuer
the courage, der Mut, —es
to cry (= *call*), rufen, schreien (irreg.)
to dawn, tagen (impers. reg.)
the day, der Tag, —es, —e
dear = *beloved*, lieb (adj.)
—— = *costly*, teuer
to deny, verneinen (reg.)
to destroy, zerstören (reg.)
to die, sterben (irreg. with sein)
diligent, fleißig
to do (= *make*) machen (reg.), tun (irreg.)
the door, die Türe, —, —n
to drink, trinken (irreg.)
the enemy, der Feind, —es, —e
English, (adj.) englisch
to enter, ein'treten (irreg.)
——(*forcibly*) ein'brechen in (irreg.)
the exercise, die Aufgabe, —, —n
to expect, erwarten (reg.)
to fall down, nieder'fallen (irreg.)
false, falsch (never modifies)
to fear, fürchten (reg.)
to find, finden (irreg.)
to force, zwingen (irreg.)
to forget, vergessen (irreg.)
formerly, einst, früher
France, Frankreich
fresh, frisch (neu)
the friend, der Freund, —es, —e
to gain, *win*, gewinnen (irreg.)
the garden, der Garten, —s, ⸚
the general, der General, —s, —e
gentle, sanft, mild
the gentleman, der Herr, —n, —en
glad, froh (fröhlich)

the glove, der Handschuh, —es, —e
green, grün
the hand, die Hand, —, ⸚e
happy, glücklich
the harbour, der Hafen, —s, ⸚
to hasten, eilen, sich beeilen (reg.)
the health, die Gesundheit, —, —en
Henry, Heinrich
high, hoch (when declined, hoh...)
hitherto, bisher
at home, zu Hause
home (motion), nach Hause
the ice, das Eis (des Eises)
idle, träge, faul
ill, krank (unwohl)
July, der Juli
just, gerecht (adj.)
—— = *eben* = *just then* (adv.)
to kill, töten (reg.)
the lady, die Dame, —, —n
the land, das Land, —es, ⸚er
large, groß
last (adv.), zuletzt, am letzten (adj.), der Letzte (etc.)
late, spät
lazy, träge, faul
the leaf, das Blatt, —es, ⸚er
to leave, verlassen (irreg.)
to lend, leihen (irreg.)
to lie (be situated), liegen (irreg.)
to like, lieben, gern haben
little (= *small*), klein (adj.)
—— adv. = wenig
March, der März (—es)
the market, der Markt, —es, ⸚e
Mary, Marie, Maria
the messenger, der Bote, —n, —n
the mile, die Meile, —, —n

Dictionary—*Concluded*.

the minute, die Minute, —, —n
Monday, der Montag
the month, der Monat, —, —e
the neighbour, der Nachbar, —s, —n
never (not ever), nie
new, neu (frisch)
the newspaper, die Zeitung, —, —en
next, nächst (adj.)
now, jetzt, nun (adv.)
the oak, die Eiche, —, —n
o'clock, Uhr (no plural)
one (after adj.), never translated
only, nur (adv.), einzig (adj.)
to order, befehlen (irreg.) (Dat.)
own (adj.), eigen
to pay, bezahlen (reg.)
the pencil, der Bleistift, —s, —e
people, man (indeclinable)
—— die Leute (no singular)
the picture, das Gemälde, —s, —
to play, spielen (reg.)
the post, die Post, —, (—en)
the present, das Geschenk, —es, —e
the prize, der Preis, —(f)es, —(f)e
proud, stolz, hochmüthig
the quarter, das Viertel, —s, —
to reach, reichen (reg.)
to read, lesen (irreg.)
to receive, erhalten (irreg.)
—— bekommen (irreg.)
to rejoice, sich freuen (reg.)
to remain, bleiben (irreg.)
to remember, sich erinnern (reg.), with Genitive (or an and Acc.)
to report, berichten (reg.)
rich, reich, wohlhabend

the river, der Fluß, —sses, —sse
the room, das Zimmer, —s, —
to rush into, in (Acc.) stürzen (reg.)
safely, sicher, glücklich
to sail, segeln (reg.), ab'fahren (irreg.)
scarcely, kaum
the sea, das Meer, —es, —e
to see, sehen (irreg.)
to send, senden (half regular)
—— schicken (reg.)
several, mehrere
the shadow, der Schatten, —s, —
shameful, schändlich
the ship, das Schiff, —es, —e
since (preposition) seit (Dat.)
or *(adv. conjunction)* seitdem
to shout (to), zu'rufen (irreg.)
the soldier, der Soldat, —en, —en
soon, bald
to speak (of), sprechen (irreg.) (von)
to stand, stehen (very irreg.)
to succeed, gelingen (impers.)
surely, sicher, gewiß
surprised (adj.), erstaunt, überrascht
the table, der Tisch, —es, —e
to tell, sagen (with Dat.) (reg.)
the time, die Zeit, —, —en
the theatre, das Theater, —s, —
to think (of), denken (half reg.) (an)
to thunder, donnern (reg.)
towards, gegen (accus.)
the tower, der Turm, —es, —e
to try, prüfen (reg.)
ugly, häßlich (wüst)

unfortunate, unglücklich
until (prepos.), bis
—— *(conjunction)*, die, bis daß
vain, eitel
in vain, umsonst
the victory, der Sieg, —es, —e
the village, das Dorf, —es, —er
to visit, besuchen (reg.)
to wait, warten (reg.)
—— *for*, erwarten
the war, der Krieg, —es, —e
to warn, warnen (reg.)
to wash, waschen (irreg.)
the water, das Wasser, —s, (—)
the week, die Woche, —, —n
whole (wholly), ganz
why? warum?
wine, der Wein, —es, —e
with, mit (dative)
the word, das Wort, —es, —er
 (=sentences, Plural: die Worte)
to write, schreiben (irreg.)
wrong, das Unrecht, —s
I am wrong = ich habe Unrecht
[or : ich bin im Unrecht]
the year, das Jahr, —es, —e
yesterday, gestern
young, jung

NOTICE.

The Irregular Verbs (at least the roots) must be looked out on pages 49, 50, and 51.

Words given in the Reference Page immediately preceding an Exercise are as a rule not given here again.

CONVERSATIONAL SENTENCES.

A Railway Journey. Eine Reise per Eisenbahn.

1. Johann, holen Sie mir einen Wagen. — John, fetch me a cab.
2. Ja, mein Herr, ich will gleich für einen gehen. — Yes, *Sir*, *I will go for one* at *once*.
3. Um wie viel Uhr fährt Ihr Zug ab? — At what o'clock does your train leave?
4. Ich glaube, er fährt zehn Minuten nach fünf ab. — I think it leaves at ten minutes past five.
5. Es ist (die) höchste Zeit; es ist schon halb fünf. — *It is high time; it is already half-past four.*
6. Da ist der Fiaker; tragen Sie das Gepäck hinaus. — Here is the cab; carry the luggage out.
7. Es ist alles richtig; Sie können ruhig sein. — It is all right, you may be easy.
8. Adieu, meine Lieben, ich muß jetzt gehen. — Good-bye, my dears, I must go now.
9. Kinder, führt euch gut auf während meiner Abwesenheit. — Children, behave well during my absence.
10. Der Zug wartet schon. Sie haben keine Zeit zu verlieren. — The train is already waiting; you have no time to lose.
11. Haben Sie Ihr Billet gelöst? Lösen Sie es schnell. — Have you taken your ticket? Take it quickly.
12. Da pfeift die Lokomotive; adieu, auf Wiedersehen. — There, the engine *is whistling*; good-bye, au revoir.
13. Wie schnell der Zug fährt! Ja, vierzig Meilen per Stunde. — How quick the train goes! Yes, forty miles an hour.
14. Ist dies ein Rauchcoupé? Nein, mein Herr. — *Is this a smoking compartment? No, Sir.*
15. Sehen Sie das schöne Schloß dort oben? Wie heißt es? — Do you see that beautiful castle up there? What is it called?
16. Das ist Ehrenbreitstein, eine starke Festung. — That is Ehrenbreitstein, a powerful fortress.
17. Es hat eine große Besatzung, und ist sehr wichtig. — It has a large garrison, and is very important.
18. Sehen Sie diese Stromschnellen im Rhein? — Do you see these rapids in the Rhine?
19. Ja und da oben ist der Loreleifelsen. — Yes, and up there the Lurline-rock.
20. Ah! Ich weiß nicht was soll es bedeuten! u.s.w. — Ah! "I know not what it can mean," etc.
21. Da! Sehen Sie die Insel im Rhein mit dem Turm? — There; see this island in the Rhine with the tower.
22. Ja, das ist der Mäuseturm des Bischofs Hatto. — Yes, that is the mouse-tower of Bishop Hatto.
23. Wie hübsch Bingen sich von hier ausnimmt! — How beautiful Bingen looks from here!
24. Was für eine prachtvolle Brücke über den Rhein! — What a splendid bridge over the Rhine!
25. Das ist wohl der Main dort? Ja, mein Herr. — That is probably the Main there? Yes, *Sir.*
26. Es geht jetzt wieder langsamer, nicht wahr? — We are going slower again, are we not?
27. Ja, wir sind ganz nahe bei Mainz. — Yes, we are quite close to Mayence.
28. Was für starke Mauern! Ja, Mainz ist eine Festung. — What strong walls! Yes, Mayence **is a fortress.**
29. Sehen Sie die Soldaten, die da exerzieren! — Look at the soldiers who are drilling there.
30. Nun fahren wir in den Bahnhof ein. — Now we are entering the station.
31. Steigen Sie hier aus? Ja, ich gehe nur bis Mainz. — Do you get out here? Yes, *I am only going to Mayence.*
32. Sie fahren wohl weiter? Ja, ich gehe nach Mannheim. — You are probably going further? Yes, *I am going to Mannheim.*
33. Adieu, mein Herr, ich bin Ihnen sehr verbunden. — **Good-bye, Sir, I am much obliged to you.**
34. Wollen Sie eine Kutsche nehmen, oder nicht? — Will you take a cab, or not?
35. Ich ziehe vor, zu Fuß nach dem Gasthofe zu gehen. — I prefer to go on foot to the Hotel.
36. Ja, in schönem Wetter geht man lieber zu Fuß. — Yes, in fine weather one prefers to go on foot.
37. Sehen Sie, daß mein Gepäck abgegeben wird. — See that my luggage is delivered.

POEM.

(To be learnt by heart.)

Der kleine Hydriot (W. Müller).

1. Ich war ein kleiner Knabe, stand fest kaum auf dem Bein;
Da nahm mich schon mein Vater mit in das Meer hinein;
Und lehrte leicht mich schwimmen an seiner sichern Hand.
Und in die Fluten tauchen bis nieder auf den Sand.
5. Ein Silberstückchen warf er dreimal in's Meer hinab,
Und dreimal mußt' ich's holen, eh' er's zum Lohn mir gab.

Dann reicht' er mir ein Ruder, hieß in ein Boot mich geh'n;
Er selber blieb zur Seite mir unverdrossen steh'n.
Wies mir, wie man die Wogen mit scharfem Schlage bricht,
10. Wie man die Wirbel meidet und mit der Brandung ficht.
Und von dem kleinen Kahne gieng's flugs in's große Schiff;
Es trieben uns die Stürme um manches Felsenriff.
Ich saß auf hohem Maste, schaut' über Meer und Land;
Es schwebten Berg' und Türme vorüber mit dem Strand.
15. Der Vater hieß mich merken auf jedes Vogels Flug,
Auf aller Winde Wehen, auf aller Wolken Zug.
Und bogen dann die Stürme den Mast bis in die Flut,
Und spritzten dann die Wogen hoch über meinen Hut;
Dann sah der Vater prüfend mir in das Angesicht.—
20. Ich saß in meinem Korbe und rüttelte mich nicht.
Da sprach er, und die Wange ward ihm wie Blut so rot:
„Glück zu! auf deinem Maste, du kleiner Hydriot!"
Und heute gab der Vater ein Schwert mir in die Hand.
Und weihte mich zum Kämpfer für Gott und Vaterland.
25. Er maß mich mit den Blicken vom Kopf bis zu den Zeh'n;
Mir war's, als tät' sein Auge hinab in's Herz mir seh'n;
Ich hielt mein Schwert gen Himmel und schaut ihn sicher an,
Und däuchte mich zur Stunde nicht schlechter als ein Mann.

Da sprach er, und die Wange ward ihm wie Blut so rot:
30. „Glück zu! mit deinem Schwerte, du kleiner Hydriot!"

The little Boy of Hydrea.

1. *I was but a little boy,* stood scarcely firm on my feet (legs)
When my father first took me to sea with him ;
And taught me easily to swim with his safe hand,
And to dive into the waters down to the very sand.
5. *A little silver coin he thrice threw down into the sea,*
And thrice had I to fetch it up, ere he gave it me as a reward.

Then he handed me an oar, and told me to step into a boat ;
He himself remained unwearied standing by my side.
Showed me how with sharp stroke one cuts the waves,
10. *How one avoids the whirlpools and struggles with the surf.*
And from the little boat we soon went on board a large ship ;
The storms drove us around many a rocky reef.
I sat on the high mast, looked over sea and land ;
Mountains and towers floated past us with the shore.
15. *My father taught me to take notice of every bird's flight,*
Of the direction of every wind and the motion of every cloud.
And when the storms bent our mast down into the waters,
And the waves sent their spray high above my hat,
Then looked my father searchingly into my face,—
20. *I sat in my basket (cross-trees) and did not move.*
Then said he, and his cheek became as red as blood :
"All hail! upon thy mast, thou little boy of Hydrea!"
And this day put my father a sword into my hand,
And dedicated me as champion for God and Fatherland.
25. *He searched me with his glance from head to foot (toes) ;*
I felt, as if his eye looked down into my very heart ;
I lifted my sword towards heaven and firmly looked at him,
And thought myself just then no worse than a full-grown man.

Then said he, and his cheek become as red as blood :
30. *"All hail to thee, with thy sword, thou little man of Hydrea!"*

Note: Hydrea, a small island off the coast of Argolis in Morea in Greece, south-east of Athens; its inhabitants are known as brave and bold fishermen and sailors.

POEM.

(To be learnt by heart.)

Der **Erlkönig** (Göthe).

1. Wer reitet so spät durch Nacht und Wind?
   Es ist der Vater mit seinem Kind';
   Er hat den Knaben wohl in dem Arm';
   Er faßt ihn sicher, er hält ihn warm.

5. „Mein Sohn, was birgst du so bang dein Gesicht?"
   „Sieh'st, Vater, du den Erlkönig nicht?
   „Den Erlenkönig mit Kron' und Schweif?"
   „Mein Sohn, es ist ein Nebelstreif."

9. „Du liebes Kind, komm', geh' mit mir!
   „Gar schöne Spiele spiel' ich mit dir!
   „Manch' bunte Blumen sind an dem Strand';
   „Meine Mutter hat manch' gülden Gewand!"

13. „Mein Vater, mein Vater, und hörest **du nicht**
    „Was Erlenkönig mir leise verspricht?"
    „Sei ruhig, bleibe ruhig, mein Kind!
    „In dürren Blättern säuselt der Wind."

17. „Willst, feiner Knabe, du mit mir geh'n?
    „Meine Töchter sollen dich warten schön.
    „Meine Töchter führen den nächtlichen Reih'n
    „Und wiegen und tanzen und singen dich ein."

21. „Mein Vater, mein Vater, und siehst du nicht dort
    „Erlkönigs Töchter am düster'n Ort?"
    „Mein Sohn, mein Sohn, ich seh' es genau:
    „Es scheinen die alten Weiden so grau."

25. „Ich lieb' dich, mich reizt deine schöne Gestalt;
    „Und bist du nicht willig, so brauch' ich Gewalt."
    „Mein Vater, mein Vater, jetzt faßt er mich an;
    „Erlkönig hat mir ein Leid's getan!"

29. Dem Vater graufet's; er reitet geschwind;
    Er hält in den Armen das ächzende Kind;
    Erreicht den Hof mit Mühe und Not:
    In seinen Armen das Kind war tobt.

The Erl-King (Fairy-King).

1. *Who is that riding so late,* **through night and wind?**
   It is a father along with his child.
   He *has his boy snugly in his arms;*
   He grasps him securely; he holds him warm.

5. *" My son, why hidest thou so timidly thy face?"*
   " Seest thou not, father, the Fairy-king?
   " The King of the fairies, with his crown and tail?"
   " My son, 'tis but a streak of mist."

9. *" Thou dear child, come, go with me!*
   " Right lovely games shall I play with thee;
   " There are many bright flowers on the bank;
   " And my mother has many a golden **garment.**"

13. *" My father, my father, and hearest thou not*
    " What the King of the fairies promises me, whis-
    " Be still, be tranquil, my child! [*pering?"*
    "'Tis but the wind, rustling in withered leaves!"

17. *" Wilt thou, my bonny boy, go with me?*
    " My daughters shall nicely wait upon thee;
    " My daughters they lead the dance in the night;
    " They'll *rock* **thee, and** *dance thee, and sing thee*
                                              [*to sleep."*

21. *" My father, my father, and seest thou not there*
    " The Fairy-king's daughter in yon gloomy spot?"
    " My son, my son, I see it quite plainly,
    "'Tis but the old willows that seem so grey."

25. *" I love thee; thy beauteous form excites me,*
    " And, if thou art not willing, I shall use force."
    " My father, my father, now he is seizing me,
    " The Fairy-king has hurt me!"

29. *Horror falls upon the father; he rides rapidly;*
    He holds in his arms the moaning child;
    He reaches his home with trouble and difficulty:
    In his arms the child was dead.

One of the best-known and most effective pieces of recitation.
Erl-King, so called because of having his habitation among " Erlen " or Alder-trees.

FIFTH TERM

Idiomatic differences between English and German in the use of words.

THE student must now use a Dictionary for the Exercises. A few sentences from page 120 and a few lines of the Poems on pages 121 and 122 should still form an integral portion of each Lesson. The idioms also given with the Preposition, pages 98-104, should be learnt over and over again, and the Reference-Pages given hitherto should be referred to in the Translation and Composition Lessons, especially the two (pages 38 and 83) which treat of the Sequence of Words, when writing Exercises or doing Composition, which ought now to be begun.

REFERENCE-PAGE AA.

Remarks on the Noun and Article.

I. Difference between English and German **as to the use of the Article before Nouns.**

    A. The definite article *omitted in English* but *used in German*—
1. With abstract terms used in their full meaning, as: *youth*, die Jugend, etc.
2. With words representing whole species or classes, as: *man*, der Mensch, etc.
3. Before titles followed by proper names, as: *Queen Victoria*, die Königin Viktoria.
4. Before the adjective in front of proper names, if not in the Vocative, as: der arme Karl, *Poor Charles;* but: Armer Karl! *Poor Charles!* (Vocative).
5. Before names of days, metals, months, and **also meals**, as: das Gold, *gold;* das Abendessen, *supper;* der Juli, *July.*
6. Before verbals in -*ing*, as: *hunting*, die Jagd; *playing*, das Spiel.
7. In some phrases, as: *in school*, in der Schule; *in church*, in der Kirche; *at market*, auf dem Markt; *in town*, in der Stadt; also with the word *most*, as: *most men*, die meisten Menschen.

    B. *Indefinite article* in English rendered by *definite article* in German—
In such phrases as: *sixpence a pound* = Sechs Pence das (or: *per*) Pfund.

    C. Possessive adjective in English rendered by definite article in German—
1. When the ownership is undoubted, as: er hat es in der Hand, *he has it in his hand.*
2. With some reflexive verbs, as: ich wasche mir die Hände, *I wash my hands.*

    D. Article (def. or indef.) *used in English but omitted in German*—
1. With the word *all*, as: *all the boys*, alle Knaben; *all the money*, alles Geld.
2. With the word *both*, as: *both the books*, beide Bücher (or: die beiden Bücher).
3. With relatives accompanied by nouns, **as:** *the river, the beauties of which you admired,* der Fluß, dessen Schönheiten Sie bewunderten.
4. Before the words: Norden, *north;* Osten, *east;* Süden, *south;* Westen, *west;* also before Abend, *evening;* Mitternacht, *midnight;* Morgen, *morning;* if they are preceded by gegen, or nach (*towards*); as: *towards the north*, gegen Norden.
5. In the phrases: *many a, no less a, not so good a, to become a* (*soldier,* etc.), **as:** mancher Knabe, *many a boy;* he became a *soldier*, er wurde Soldat.

II. Notice that **in** German the article can *never* **stand** between an adjective and its noun, **but** *must* stand before the adjective, thus

    both the boys = die beiden Knaben; *such a man* = ein solcher Mann; *half an apple* = ein halber Apfel; *all the world* = die ganze Welt (= *the whole world*).

III. The Article in German must be repeated before each of a series of words, especially if these are of different genders, unless all the words apply to one and the same person (or thing), as:

    der König und die Königin, *the king and queen.*
    but: der König und Herr, *the king and master* (i.e. in one person).

Examples and Exercises on Reference-Page AA.

Examples.

1. *I have often told you that children should reverence old age.*
2. *Many animals, which live in very cold countries, have warm furs, which are very valuable; most of these furs are white in winter.*
3. *Dinner will be taken in the large dining-room, but we shall have tea here in this little room.*

1. Ich habe euch oft gesagt, daß die Kinder das Alter ehren sollen.
2. Viele Thiere, welche in sehr kalten Ländern leben, haben warme Pelze, die sehr werthvoll sind; die meisten dieser Pelze sind im Winter weiß.
3. Das Mittagessen wird in dem großen Speisezimmer zu sich genommen werden, aber den Thee werden wir hier in diesem Stübchen nehmen.

Translate.

1. Das Gold und das Silber sind edle Metalle, aber das Eisen ist nützlicher als alle anderen Metalle.
2. Haben Sie dieselben in der Kirche gesehen? Ich sah sie, als sie in die Kirche giengen.

3. Die Menschen sollten ihre Pflichten gegen Gott nie vergessen, denn Er hat uns Alle erschaffen, und er erhält uns.
4. Sie verdarben uns die Freude, als sie uns sagten, er werde nicht kommen weil er krank sei.

Exercise.

1. When we were in Berlin, we saw (the) prince Albert, who had (was) returned.
2. Were these cherries dear? I believe they were sevenpence a pound.
3. August and September are the best months for a tour in (the) Switzerland.
4. He had the book in his desk (Pult, m.), whilst he was looking for it in school.
5. Poor Henry! I believe (dat.) poor Charles and you.

Examples.

1. *Switzerland is bounded on the north by Germany and on the south by Italy.*
2. *All the world knows that such a man does not deserve any respect.*

1. Die Schweiz ist gegen Norden von Deutschland begrenzt und gegen Süden von Italien.
2. Die ganze Welt weiß, daß ein solcher Mann keine Achtung verdient.

Translate.

1. Wir besuchten diese Stadt, deren Gebäude Sie so schön fanden.
2. Die Angelegenheiten beider Männer waren in einem fatalen Zustande.

3. Gegen Morgen fieng es an zu regnen, und es regnete den ganzen Tag; aber gegen Abend heiterte sich das Wetter wieder recht schön auf.

Exercise.

1. He lost all the money which we gave him in town yesterday.
2. Many a good man was deceived by this fellow (Kerl) who sold these things.
3. Do you know what has become of him? (aus (dat.).) He has become a sailor.
4. Half a loaf (Laib, m.) is better than no bread;—a proverb (Sprichwort, n.).
5. "My good sword in my hand, I fear no foe," he exclaimed (ausrufen).

[See page 83, A. b.]

REFERENCE-PAGE **BB**.

Some Remarks on Gender of Nouns.

We have already given the **rules by which the Gender of many nouns can** be recognised (see Reference-Page F., page 25). In speaking of **living beings, we** may say generally that in *full-grown* beings the gender corresponds with the **sex**, whilst young *undeveloped* beings are of the **neuter gender.** Thus we have:

der Vater, *the father;* die Mutter, *the mother;* das Kind, *the child.*
der Stier, *the bull;* die Kuh, *the cow;* das Kalb, *the calf.*
der Hengst, *the stallion;* die Stute, *the mare;* das Füllen, *the colt, filly.*
der Hahn, *the cock;* die Henne, *the hen;* das Küchlein, *the chicken.*
der Eber, *the boar;* die Sau, *the sow;* das Ferkel, *the sucking-pig.*

Thus also many names indicating *species* of animals are neuter, as: das Pferd, *the horse;* das Schwein, *the pig;* das Huhn, *the fowl;* das Rind, *a head of cattle.*

In the above the sexes are expressed **by different** words; many feminines are, however, formed from the masculines—

(*a.*) By addition of *-in* and modification of root-vowel (especially in **monosyllables**), as:

der Graf, *the count;* die Gräfin, *the countess.*
der Bauer, *the peasant;* die Bäuerin, *the peasant woman.*
der Franzose, *the Frenchman;* die Französin, *the Frenchwoman.*
der Hund, *the dog;* die Hündin, *the bitch.*
der Koch, *the cook;* die Köchin, *the female cook.*
der König, *the king;* die Königin, *the queen.*

The Plural of words in *-in* is *-innen* (indeed the Singular had formerly *-inn*).

(*b.*) By **cutting off -r** of the masculine, as:

der Wittwer, *the widower;* die Wittwe, *the widow;* der Tauber, *the male pigeon;* die Taube, *the female pigeon.*

(*c.*) By adding such words as *-kuh, cow;* *-henne, hen.*

der Hirsch, *the stag;* die Hirschkuh, *the hind;* der Pfau, *the peacock;* die Pfauhenne, *the pea-hen.*

These words must be **learnt gradually** by noting them when met with in translation.

N.B.—Der Deutsche, *the German* (*gentleman*), has feminine, die Deutsche, *the German* (*woman*).

List of the most common words with two genders with different signification for each :—

der Alp, *the nightmare;* die Alp, *the Alpine meadow.*
der Band, *the volume;* das Band, *the tie, ribbon.*
der Bauer, *the peasant;* das Bauer, *the bird-cage.*
der Erbe, *the heir;* das Erbe, *the inheritance.*
die Mark, *a coin* = *one shilling;* das Mark, *the marrow.*
der See, *the lake;* die See, *the sea, ocean.*
der Schild, *the shield* (*in battle*); das Schild, *the coat of arms; sign* (*of an inn*).
der Stift, *the metal* (*etc.*) *rod;* das Stift, *a convent.*
der Thor, *the fool;* das Thor, *the gate.*
der Verdienst, *gain, wages;* das Verdienst, *the merit.*

Exercise.

[For the words in the Exercises, where not given here, a Dictionary must be used. For sequence of words, see page 83.]

1. Have you spoken to (zu. Dat.) the peasant and peasant woman, who came yesterday to our house? 2. Yes, I bought, as (wie) I said, two hens, three chickens, and one cock of (von) them. 3. What have you shot? I shot a hind, which had strayed (sich verirren, reg.) into our field. 4. This man was a fool, for he spent (vergeuten) his inheritance on (in) pleasures, which had not even (nicht einmal) the merit of being real pleasures (*of being* = zu sein, at end). 5. This French woman fought a duel with this German woman, but she was (wurde) vanquished.

REFERENCE-PAGE CC.

Some Remarks on Number in Nouns.

A. Words of same form and gender in the singular, but of different meaning, have different plurals:

das Band, *the tie, ribbon*, has die Bänder, *the ribbons;* but: die Bande, *the fetters, ties, chains* (poetical).
die Bank, *the bench, bank*, has die Bänke, *the benches;* but: die Banken, *the (money) banks*.
das Land, *the country, land*, has (usual) die Länder, *the lands;* and die Lande, *lands* (poetical).
das Wort, *the word, sentence*, has die Wörter, *disconnected words;* but: die Worte, *sentences, sayings*.

B. Nouns implying materials or metals have **no** plural. If a plural is required, it is formed with the words Arten, *kinds;* Sorten, *sorts;* as: drei Sorten Gold, *three kinds of gold*.

C. Abstract terms have no plural, if used as abstract terms, as: die Liebe, *love;* but some can be used concretely, as: die Lieben, *the loved ones*. Others have to borrow a plural, as: die Gunst, *the favour* = die Gunstbezeigung, *Plural:* die Gunstbezeigungen; such are: der Tod (*case of*) *death* = der Todesfall, *Plural:* die Todesfälle, *cases of death, deaths;* der Rat, *the advice* = der Ratschlag, *Plural:* die Ratschläge, *counsels*. *N.B.* die Räte, Plural of der Rat = *the councillor;* der Streit, *the quarrel* = die Streitigkeit, *Plural:* die Streitigkeiten, *quarrels*.

D. Nouns implying measure, number (collective), or weight, and preceded by a definite or indefinite numeral, are used in the singular though indicating plurality, if they are of the *masculine* or *neuter* gender, as: zehn Fuß lang; fünf Pfund Blei; zwanzig Grad Wärme (*ten feet long; five pounds of lead; twenty degrees of cold*). Thus also in vernacular English: *ten foot long*, etc.; **but** if they are of the *feminine* gender, they must be used in the Plural, as: sechs Ellen Tuch, *six yards of cloth*.

Used Singular in these cases (in **D.**).
der Fuß, *the foot;* der Zoll, *the inch;* das Pfund, *the pound*.
der Grad, *the degree;* der Mann, *man;* das Paar, *the brace, pair*.
das Buch, *the quire;* das Hundert, *the hundred;* das Stück, *the piece*.
das Dutzend, *the dozen;* das Tausend, *the thousand*.
der Zentner, *the hundredweight;* das Fuder, *the load*, etc.

Used Plural in these cases.
die Elle, *the yard*.
die Tonne, *the tun, ton*.
die Flasche, *the bottle*.
die Klafter, *the fathom*.
die Meile, *the mile*.

E. Some words have no singular; the most common of these are:

die Einkünfte, *the income, revenue*.
die Eltern, *the parents, father and mother*.
die Ferien, *the vacation, holidays*.
die Geschwister, *brothers and sisters*.
die Kosten = die Unkosten, *expenses*.
die Leute, *people, men* (used generally). (See *N.B.* below.)
die Trümmer, *the ruins, fragments*.
die Truppen, *the troops* = *an army*.

N.B. -leute is used for the Plural of Compounds in -mann, as: der Seemann (*sailor*), die Seeleute (if the class of men as a class is referred to).

Exercise.

1. The counsels of those councillors are not always wise.
2. There have been several quarrels between those towns.
3. We have had a severe (hart) winter, for we had often (eine Kälte von) ten degrees of cold.
4. We bought three dozen yards of that cloth when we were there.
5. These troops number (zählen) 10,000 men.

REFERENCE-PAGE DD.

Some Remarks on the Adjective.

We have already seen that adjectives **may be used**—
1. As *Attributes* in front of a noun (see Reference-Page G.), der gute König, etc.
2. As *Adverbs*, invariable, as: er schreibt gut.
3. As *Nouns* with an article, etc., and changing like the adjective attribute, der Gute, *the good man*, ein Guter, *a good man*, etc.
4. As *Predicates* (see page 82), invariable, and only with sein, werden, bleiben, heißen, genannt werden, etc.: er wird arm bleiben.

As to this *use of adjectives as* **Predicates,** notice the following carefully

The predicative adjective may be accompanied by an extension, which, unless **governed by a** preposition (see (D) below), *must* stand *in front of the adjective.* **This extension must be** either in the Accusative, the Genitive, **or the** Dative case.

A. **The Accusative** of weight, measure, age, value, **preceding the adjective, as**: er ist **fünfzehn Jahre alt**; this is used **before the following adjectives**:

alt, *old*; breit, *broad*; groß, *large*; hoch, *high*; lang, *long*; schwer, *heavy*; tief, *deep*; werth, *worth*.

B. The **Genitive** extension; **as**: **er ist seiner** Sache gewiß, *he is sure of his business.* Thus:

bewußt, *conscious of*	gewiß, *sure of*	mächtig, *master of*	*überdrüssig, *weary of*
eingedenk, *mindful of*	kundig, *acquainted with*	*müde, *tired of*	verdächtig, *suspected of*
fähig, *capable of*	*ledig, *rid of*	schuldig, *guilty of*	würdig, *worthy of*

N.B. All these, **except those marked *,** may by prefixing un ... be changed into their contraries; as: ungewiß, *uncertain of*; those marked * require nicht (as: nicht müde, *not tired of*) for their contraries.

C. **The Dative** extension, as: es ist mir angenehm, *it is agreeable to me.* Thus

ähnlich, *similar to*	dankbar, *grateful to*	lieb, *dear to*	*überlegen, *superior to*
*angeboren, *inborn in*	*feind, *strange to*	möglich, *possible to*	*verhaßt, *hateful to*
angemessen, *appropriate to*	gehorsam, *obedient to*	nötig, *necessary to*	vortheilhaft, *advantageous to*
angenehm, *agreeable to*	gleich, *equal to*	nützlich, *useful to*	willkommen, *welcome to*
bekannt, *known to*	gnädig, *gracious to*	schädlich, *hurtful to*	zuträglich, *beneficial to*
bequem, *convenient to*	günstig, *favourable to*	*treuer, *dear to*	[and a few others rarely used]
beschwerlich, *troublesome to*	*lästig, *troublesome to*	treu, *faithful to*	

N.B. All these, except those marked *, may by prefixing un ... be changed into their contraries; as: unähnlich, *dissimilar to*. Those marked * require nicht instead of un ... for their contraries.

D. The extension if governed by a *preposition* **usually follows the adjective, and must** be in the case which the preposition requires, as: er ist höflich **gegen diesen Mann**. Thus:

achtsam auf (Acc.), *heedful of*	empfänglich für (Acc.), *susceptible of*	höflich gegen (Acc.), *polite towards*
artig gegen (Acc.), *polite towards*	*eifersüchtig auf (Acc.), *jealous of*	*reich an (Acc.), *rich in*
*bange vor (Dat.), *afraid of*	*eitel auf (Acc.), *vain of*	*stolz auf (Acc.), *proud of*
bekannt mit (Dat.), *acquainted with*	ermüdet von (Dat.), *fatigued with*	überzeugt von (Dat.), *convinced of*
*beschämt über (Acc.), *ashamed of*	*froh über (Acc.), *glad of*	*verschwenderisch mit (Dat.), *prodigal with*
begierig nach (Dat.), *greedy after*	*gleichgültig gegen (Ac.), *indifferent to*	zufrieden mit (Dat.), *satisfied with*
*frei von (Dat.), *free from*	*grausam gegen (Acc.), *cruel to*	[and a few others rarely used.]

N.B. **All these,** except those marked *, may by prefixing un ... be changed into their contraries; as: unartig gegen (Acc.), *uncivil to*. Those marked * require nicht before the adjective for their contraries.

EXAMPLES AND EXERCISES ON REFERENCE-PAGE DD.

Examples.

1. The man was conscious of his guilt and tired of life; he hanged himself.
2. How high was this tree? I think it was fifty or sixty feet high.
3. I cannot believe that this news was unknown to the man who was in the house.

1. Der Mann war sich seiner Schuld bewußt, und des Lebens müde, er hat sich erhängt.
2. Wie hoch war dieser Baum? Ich glaube, er war fünfzig oder sechzig Fuß hoch.
3. Ich kann nicht glauben, daß diese Nachricht dem Manne, der in dem Hause war, unbekannt war.

Translate.

1. Er wäre des Preises würdig gewesen, wenn er die Zeichnung vollendet hätte.
2. Der Strom war an dieser Stelle jedenfalls zwanzig Fuß breit.
3. Ich fürchte, daß es uns unmöglich sein wird, dieses heute zu tun.
4. Die Nachrichten von Afrika waren dem alten Mann sehr willkommen.

Exercise.

1. Was this man suspected of theft (Diebstahl, *m.*), **or only of a mistake?** (Fehler, *m.*)
2. The sea is at this spot six fathoms (Klafter, *f.*) deep, **or more.**
3. This ought to be useful to the boy, who must write that theme (Aufsatz, *m.*).
4. **God be** (sei) gracious to us sinners (Sünder, *m.*).
5. He will be welcome to **his** friends in England, for he is worthy of their esteem.

Examples.

1. The prince was jealous of his brother; he was convinced of the truth of the news, which arrived to-day.
2. One *ought never to be vain of one's knowledge,* for *no one can know everything.*
3. Be polite towards your teachers and not indifferent to their admonitions.

1. Der Fürst war eifersüchtig auf seinen Bruder; er war von der Wahrheit der Nachricht überzeugt, die heute ankam.
2. Man sollte nie auf seine Kenntnisse eitel sein, denn Niemand kann Alles wissen.
3. Sei höflich gegen deine Lehrer und nicht gleichgültig gegen ihre Ermahnungen.

Translate.

1. Der Schüler ist unbekannt mit diesen Sachen, er kann seine Aufgabe nicht recht gelernt haben.
2. Dieser Erbe war sehr verschwenderisch mit dem Gelde, das er erbte.
3. Ich war bange (or es war mir bange) vor dem Examen in der Schule.
4. Sie sollten über die guten Zeugnisse froh sein, die Ihr Sohn aus der Schule mit nach Hause gebracht hat.

Exercise.

1. **He is** jealous of his friend, who always loved him so much (so sehr).
2. **Boys** should be polite towards their teachers, for they desire **only their good (ihr Bestes).**
3. The enemy was superior to us in this battle, which we lost.
4. Are you convinced of the truth of the news, (which) your son sent (to) you?
5. **Do not be** cruel to that horse; it feels pain (den Schmerz) as much as yourself (like you yourself).

N

Reference-Page EE.

Remarks on Prepositions.

Distinguish carefully Prepositions from adverbs and from **conjunctions**. Prepositions are followed by nouns or pronouns, and must govern an Accusative, a Genitive, or a Dative.

We give here (as an appendix to Reference-Page O., page 52) a list of the most common English prepositions in alphabetical order, with hints as to their translation into German before nouns or pronouns.

above—
- (a) indicating locality, is **über** with **dat.**, if there is no motion *towards the noun* implied, and with **acc.** in the sense of *across*, with verbs of motion, as: der Vogel schwebt über dem Haus, but: der Vogel fliegt über das Haus.
- (b) =*beyond* = über (as above); **er lebt über dem Meer; geht über das Meer.**
- (c) =*more than* = über, with accusative: **er liebt ihn über Alles** (*more than all*).

about—
- (a) =*around* = um (acc.) sie versammelten sich um ihn, *they assembled about him.*
- (b) =*through* = in (dat.) ...umher: er geht in der Stadt umher, *he goes about the town.*
- (c) =*with* = bei (dat.): ich habe kein Geld bei mir, *I have no money about me.*
- (d) =*concerning* = über (acc.) or wegen (gen.) ś ich spreche über ihn, *I talk about him.*
- (e) with nouns of number, weight, etc. = ungefähr: er hat ungefähr drei Pfund, *he has* **about** *£3.*
- (f) idiomatic: um diese Zeit, *about this time.*

at—
- (a) locality: **bei, an, in (dat.): Bei der Kirche ; an dem Haus ; in Paris.**
- (b) time: um (acc.), as: um diese Stunde = *at this hour.*
- (c) with some adjectives: *pleased at* = vergnügt über (acc.), zufrieden mit (dat.); *clever at* = geschickt in (dat.); *astonished at* = erstaunt über (acc.); *vexed at* = ärgerlich über (acc.).
- (d) with some verbs: *to rejoice at* = sich freuen über (acc.); *to aim at* = zielen nach (dat.), auf (acc.); *to laugh at* = lachen über; *to blush at* = erröten über; *to mock at* = spotten, with gen. [or über, acc.]; *to wonder at* = sich (ver)wundern über (acc.).
- (e) **idiomatic:** *at any rate* (= *at all events*) = auf jeden Fall; *at church* = in der Kirche; *at court* = bei Hofe; *at daybreak* = bei Anbruch des Tages; *at home* = zu Hause; *at play* = beim Spiel; *at school* = in der **Schule**; *at sea* = auf der See, auf dem Meer; *at table* = bei Tisch; *at the arrival of* = bei (der) Ankunft (gen.); *at the battle* = in der Schlacht; *at the beginning* = im (am) Anfang; *at the command of* = auf (den) Befehl (gen.); *at the expense* = auf Kosten; *at the house of* ... = bei (dat.); *at the same time* = zu gleicher Zeit; *at the time of* ... = zur Zeit (gen.) [and a few more].

by—
- (a) agent, always = von (dat.): er wurde von mir besiegt (*by me*).
- (b) instrument, always = durch (acc.): durch den Schuß verwundet (*by the shot*).
- (c) locality, = **bei, neben (dat.):** *it stands by the tree* = es steht bei dem Baume.
- (d) **idiomatic:** *by my honour* = bei meiner Ehre; *10 feet by 4* = zehn Fuß lang und vier breit; *by the 3d of March* = am dritten März; *by the ton* = nach der Tonne = tonnenweise; *by land* = zu Land; *by water* = zu Wasser; *by day* = bei Tag; *by night* = bei (in der) Nacht; (*take*) *by the hand* = an der Hand; *by command of* = auf Befehl (gen.); *piece by piece* = Stück auf (um) Stück; *by boat* = mit dem Schiff; *by the advice of* = auf Rat; *by Jove* = beim Jupiter! *day by day* = von Tag zu Tag, täglich [and a few more].

Examples and Exercises on Page 98.

above and about.

Examples.

1. *I am sorry to be unable to give you anything, but I have no money about me.*	1. Es tut mir leid, Ihnen Nichts geben zu können, aber ich habe kein Geld bei mir.
2. *Above this world there lives a God, who knows our inmost thoughts.*	2. Ueber dieser Welt lebt ein Gott, der unsere tiefsten Gedanken kennt.
3. *They were about this time on a journey in England and Ireland.*	3. Sie waren um diese Zeit auf Reisen in England und Irland.

Translate.

1. Wenn ihr über diese Sache reden wollt, so tut es jetzt oder nie.	3. Es ist zu schmutzig auf den Straßen, um in der Stadt herum zu wandern.
2. Die Schwalben fliegen im Herbst über's Meer nach dem Süden, und kehren im Frühling wieder zu uns zurück.	4. Man sollte immer auf seine Gesundheit Acht geben, denn die Gesundheit geht über Alles in der Welt.

Exercise.

1. Above three hundred people lost their lives during this flood (Ueberschwemmung, *f.*).
2. You ought to love (the) virtue **above** all in the world.
3. You are **about** two **miles distant** (entfernt) from the town which you see there.
4. **Has** your father spoken with the teacher about this affair?
5. He has travelled about in **America and Asia**.

at and by.

Examples.

1. *All* (the) *shops in the village are shut* (geschlossen) *at this late hour.*	1. Alle Läden im Dorfe sind um diese späte Stunde geschlossen.
2. *Do not rejoice at the misfortune of your neighbours; it is not Christian-like.*	2. Freuen Sie sich nicht über das Unglück Ihrer Nachbarn; es ist nicht christlich.
3. *At table these girls are not allowed to learn their lessons.*	3. Bei Tische dürfen diese Mädchen ihre Aufgaben nicht lernen.

Translate.

1. Sie hätten über diese Sünde erröten sollen, wenn Sie überhaupt (at all) noch über Etwas erröten können.	3. Das Schiff war dreihundert Fuß lang und zwanzig Fuß breit.
2. Er ist dieses Jahr auf Kosten seines Geschäftshauses nach Asien gereist.	4. Ich verspreche Ihnen bei meiner Ehre, Sie vor acht Uhr in Ihrem Hause zu besuchen, wenn diese Nachricht bis dann angekommen ist.

Exercise.

1. Have you aimed at that bird? I wonder at you.
2. We were at any rate at home at **seven** o'clock.
3. The house stands quite close (nahe) by the church in the village.
4. The French were beaten by the Germans in the last war.
5. We have (are) travelled about in the world by land and water.

REFERENCE-PAGE EE.—*Continued.*

for
   (a) generally für, with accusative : *for him* = für ihn.
   (b) **instead of** = anstatt (gen.) ; *he went for his son* = er gieng anstatt seines Sohnes.
   (c) with some verbs, as : *to beg for* = bitten um (acc.) ; *play for* = spielen um (acc.) ; *to care for* = sich kümmern um ; *to ask for or after* = fragen nach (dat.).
   (d) **idiomatic** : *for a time* = eine Zeit lang ; *for how long?* = auf wie lange? *for ever* = auf immer ; *for the sake of* = um (genitive) willen.
   (e) **for**, before feelings prompting an action, is = aus, as : *for fear* = aus Furcht, etc.

from
   (a) locality, origin, derivation = von or aus (dative) ; *from Germany* = von Deutschland.
   (b) **time** = seit ; *from that day* = seit jenem Tage.
   (c) with *feelings*, prompting an action = aus ; as : *from pity* = aus Mitleid.
   (d) *free from* = frei von ; *er ist nicht frei von Vorurteilen* = *he is not free from prejudices.*
   (e) with some verbs, *to abstain from* = sich enthalten (genitive) ; *to die from* = sterben an (dat.), *to suffer from* = leiden an (dat.) ; *to dismiss from* = entheben (gen. of thing, acc. of person) ; *to dissuade from* = abraten von (dat.) ; *to escape from* = entfliehen (dat.) ; *to exempt from* = entheben.
   (f) **idiomatic** : *from memory* = aus dem Gedächtnis ; *from day to day* = von Tag zu Tag ; *from town to town* = von Stadt zu Stadt ; *from time to time* = von Zeit zu Zeit.

in
   (a) generally **in** with dat. of rest and acc. of change or motion = *into.*
   (b) with *time*, always **in** with dative.
   (c) with verbs, *to believe in* = glauben an (acc.) ; *to wound in* = verwunden an (acc.) ; *to trust in* = vertrauen (dative).
   (d) with *adjectives* rare ; *rich in* = reich an (acc.) ; *fertile in* = fruchtbar an (acc.).
   (e) **idiomatic** : *in a carriage* = zu Wagen ; *in the country* = auf dem Land ; *into the country* = auf das Land ; *in German* = auf Deutsch ; *into German* = in's Deutsche ; *in a word* = mit einem Worte ; *in time* = zu rechter Zeit, zur rechten Zeit ; [*in pity*, etc., see *from*, or *of*, *pity*] ; *to take a part in* = Teil nehmen an (dat.) ; *in (this) manner* = auf (diese) Weise ; *in any case* = auf jeden Fall, jedenfalls ; *in the day-time* = bei Tag = *in the night-time* = bei Nacht or in der Nacht ; *in patience* = mit Geduld.

of is the most frequently-used preposition in English, and its rendering is very difficult ; we give it here in such a way, as to assist the English pupil in Composition.

A. *of, preceded by an adjective* in English, and *followed* by Noun or Pronoun :—

afraid of, bange vor (dat.)
ashamed of, beschämt über (acc.)
capable of, fähig (after its gen.)
careful of, achtsam auf (acc.)
conscious of, bewußt (after its gen.)
*convinced of, überzeugt von (dat.)
*covetous of, gierig nach (dat.)
*desirous of, ehrgeizig nach (dat.)
*glad of, froh über (acc.)
*good of, gut von (dat.)

*guilty of, schuldig (after its gen.)
*needful of, bedürftig (after its gen.)
*jealous of, eifersüchtig auf (acc.)
mindful of, eingedenk (after its gen.)
*prodigal of, verschwenderisch mit (dat.)
*proud of, stolz auf (acc.)
*rid of, ledig (gen.) ; frei von (dat.)
sensitive of (about), empfindlich über (acc.)

sure of, gewiß (after its gen.)
susceptible of, empfänglich für (acc.)
suspected of, verdächtig (after its gen.)
*tired of, müde (after its gen.)
*vain of, stolz auf (acc.)
worthy of, werth, würdig (after its gen.)

All those with Genitive usually must stand *after* this Genitive.

N.B.—(a) **Those of the above** *not* marked with an asterisk can take un . . . before them in German, **with the same construction,** but exactly contrary meaning, as : unschuldig (gen.), *guiltless of*, etc. ; but those marked with an asterisk must take nicht before them, if the contrary meaning is required.

N.B.—(b) After any superlative of is von (dat.), as : *the best of them*, der beste von ihnen.

Examples and Exercises on Page 100.

for and from.
Examples.

1. You ought to have pardoned (to) the poor soldier his slight offence *for* my sake, (Sir) Captain!
2. What does he care *for* war or peace? It is all the same to him.
3. The murderer, who was condemned to death, (has) escaped yesterday *from* prison with another prisoner.

1. Sie hätten dem armen Soldaten um meinetwillen sein leichtes Vergehen verzeihen sollen, Herr Hauptmann!
2. Was bekümmert er sich um Krieg oder Frieden? Es ist ihm Alles gleich.
3. Der Mörder, der zum Tode verurteilt wurde, ist gestern aus dem Gefängnisse mit einem anderen Gefangenen entflohen.

Translate.

1. Der Bettler gieng von Stadt zu Stadt und bettelte überall.
2. Wir rieten ihm ernstlich ab, nach Australien auszuwandern; jedermann riet ihm von dem Unternehmen ab.
3. Ich glaube, der Hund ist ganz frei von Untugenden (*faults*); es ist überdieß ein Preishund.
4. Junge Leute sollten sich gänzlich des Rauchens enthalten, denn diese Gewohnheit ist kostspielig und der Gesundheit sehr schädlich.

Exercise.

1. *For* what did you play? We only played *for* hazel-nuts, Sir.
2. He learnt German *for* some time at school, and was very diligent.
3. The boy did it only *from* fear of punishment, not *from* pleasure.
4. The little girl said the whole poem (*from* memory) by heart.
5. They are seen *from* time to time in the town, but not often.

in and of.
Examples.

1. We believe *in* God the Father, the Son, and the Holy Ghost.
2. One should bear one's troubles *in* patience; impatience will not make them better, and is *of* no avail.
3. You (they) ought *in* any case to have come to me first.

1. Wir glauben an Gott den Vater, den Sohn und den heiligen Geist.
2. Man sollte seine Beschwerden mit Geduld tragen. Ungeduld macht sie nicht besser und hilft Einem Nichts.
3. Sie hätten auf jeden Fall zuerst zu mir kommen sollen.

Translate.

1. Der Soldat ist in jener Schlacht am Fuß verwundet worden.
2. Wir fiengen die Diebe alle auf diese Weise in acht Tagen.
3. Er ist Ihres Vertrauens unwürdig, denn er wird sich nie bessern.
4. Dieser Mann war überdieß auch des Mordes verdächtig.

Exercise.

1. We often took drives (= spazieren fahren) *in* a carriage *in* the country.
2. Did this happen in the day-time or in the night-time?
3. Was the thief not conscious of his guilt (Schuld, *f.*)? He was innocent.
4. You must choose the smallest (*masc. acc.*) of these red balls.
5. Boys! You ought to be careful of all your books in school.

Reference-Page EE.—*Continued.*

B. of, preceded by a Verb in English, and followed by Noun or Pronoun:

accuse of, anklagen { (Acc. of Person) / (Gen. of Thing) }
assure of, versichern (same as above)
be afraid of, sich fürchten vor (Dat.)
be ashamed of, sich schämen { 1. with Gen. / 2. with über and Acc. }
be aware of, sich (Gen.) bewußt sein
become of, werden aus (Dat.)
be in *want of,* bedürfen (Gen.)
beware of, sich hüten vor (Dat.)
boast *of,* sich rühmen (Gen.)

complain of, klagen über (Acc.)
consist of, bestehen in (Dat.)
convict of, überführen { Acc. of Person / Gen. of Thing }
despair of, verzweifeln an (Dat.)
die of, sterben an (Dat.) [*an illness*]
dispose of, verfügen über (Acc.)
doubt of, zweifeln an (Dat.)
—— bezweifeln (Acc.)
get rid of, sich (Gen.) entledigen
hear of, hören von (Dat.)
make sure of, sich (Gen.) versichern

remind of, erinnern an (Acc.)
rob of, berauben { Acc. of Person / Gen. of Thing }
speak of, sprechen von (Dat.)
take care of, sorgen für (Acc.)
—— sich (Gen.) annehmen
take possession of, sich bemächtigen (Gen.)
—— Besitz nehmen von (Dat.)
think of, denken an (Acc.)
—— gedenken (with Genitive)

C. of, *not* after an adjective *or* verb, but followed by a Noun or Pronoun.

    1. *omitted* **in German,** the following Noun being in the *Nominative or Accusative.*
    (i) Before names of **towns, countries, rivers,** as : *the town of Paris,* die Stadt Paris.
    (ii) Before **materials, when not particularised,** but preceded by words indicating measure, weight, number, etc., as : *a pound of sugar =* ein Pfund Zucker. [See 3, ii. below.]
    (iii) In the days of **the month,** as : *the third of January =* der dritte Januar.
    (vi) In the following **phrases :** *what sort of . . , two kinds of . . ,* as : *What sort of man ? =* Was für ein Mann.

    2. *omitted* **in German,** the following Noun being in the *Genitive* without preposition.
    (i) **Indicating Possession,** as : *the dog of my brother =* der Hund meines Bruders.
    (ii) **In answer** to the question : *When ?* but only in indefinite time, as : *of a morning =* des Morgens.
    (iii) **In** compound Prepositions governing Genitive, as : *instead of him =* anstatt seiner.
    (iv) In the phrases : *to die of hunger =* Hungers sterben ; *be of good cheer =* gutes Mutes sein.

    3. *translated by* **von** ; with dative of the **following Noun (and its attributes).**
    (i) Before and after cardinal numbers, as : *two of my brothers =* zwei von meinen Brüdern. *a town of ten thousand inhabitants =* eine Stadt von zehntausend Einwohnern.
    (ii) **Before materials, when particularised** (especially by a whole clause), and preceded **by** words indicating **measure, weight, number,** etc., as : *a pound of the sugar which I like =* ein Pfund von dem Zucker, den ich liebe.
    (iii) After ordinal numbers, as : *the tenth of these days =* der zehnte von diesen Tagen.
    (iv) **After titles** followed by the name **of** a country, town, etc., as : *the Queen of England =* die Königin von England.
    (v) Before materials showing the nature of the preceding noun, as : *a ship of wood =* ein Schiff von Holz.
    (vi) After demonstrative or relative Pronouns, as : *this one of my boys =* dieser von meinen Knaben.

    4. Rendered by turning the noun with *of* into an adjective, **as :**
        gloves of Paris = Pariser Handschuhe ; *a ship of wood =* ein hölzernes Schiff.

    5. Rendered **by forming compound nouns, as :**

the art *of poetry,* die Dichtkunst	**the field of battle,** das Schlachtfeld	*a man of business,* ein Geschäftsmann
the *desire of pleasure,* die Vergnügungssucht	*a garland of flowers,* ein Blumenkranz	*a matter of fact,* eine Tatsache
the *drop of rain,* der Regentropfen	**the love of life,** die Lebenslust	*a sign of life,* ein Lebenszeichen

*N.B.—*The pupil must be careful not to indulge too much in any haphazard formation of such compound nouns. Let him gradually make a collection of them, as he meets with them in his reading.

Examples and Exercises on page 102.

Examples.

1. *The criminal was not only not ashamed of his deed, but boasted even of his shameful cruelty.*
2. *I must almost despair of your good-will to conclude this matter quickly.*
3. *Of what has the child died? I believe it died of the measles, or rather of their consequences.*

1. Der Verbrecher schämte sich nicht nur seiner Tat nicht, sondern rühmte sich sogar seiner schändlichen Grausamkeit.
2. Ich muß an Ihrem guten Willen, dieses Geschäft schnell zu vollenden, fast verzweifeln.
3. An was ist das Kind gestorben? Ich glaube, es starb an den Masern, oder vielmehr an deren Folgen.

Translate.

1. Wann hörten Sie zum letzten Mal von Ihrem Herrn Bruder?
2. Ich glaube fast, er hat mich und alle seine Freunde ganz vergessen, denn er hat schon seit zwei Jahren nicht mehr an uns geschrieben.
3. Was hat der Dieb ihm genommen? Er hat ihn all seines Gepäckes beraubt.
4. Er bemächtigte sich seiner Juwelen, seiner Uhr und überhaupt aller seiner Sachen; doch hat man ihn gefangen und des Verbrechens überführt.

Exercise.

1. What do you boast *of*? You have not even (nicht einmal) seen London.
2. Give me three pounds *of* tea at two shillings, and one pound at (zu, Dat.) three shillings and sixpence.
3. Have you any more (noch) *of* that tea (C, 3 iii.), which you showed me (Dat.) last week (Acc.).
4. My father died *on* the nineteenth *of* January; he was fifty-one years old.
5. Are you speaking *of* Henry, or are you thinking *of* my cousin Charles?

Of (continued).

Examples.

1. *I fear very much, that that one of your friends, whom you love most, has not remained faithful to you.*
2. *The general rode over the field of battle, upon which the dead lay thickly.*
3. *This is a matter of fact, which no one doubts, who knows him.*

1. Ich fürchte sehr, derjenige von Ihren Freunden den Sie am meisten lieben, ist (sei) Ihnen nicht treu geblieben.
2. Der General ritt über das Schlachtfeld, auf dem die Todten dicht lagen.
3. Es ist dies eine Tatsache, die Niemand bezweifelt, der ihn kennt.

Translate.

1. Die spanischen Weine sind in der ganzen Welt berühmt.
2. Diese Frau war immer gutes Mutes, obgleich sie viel Sorge um ihre Kinder gelitten hat.
3. Wir sahen die Kaiserin von Oesterreich, die in England ein Jagdschloß besaß.
4. Ohne Ihre Hülfe können wir trotz aller Anstrengungen die Sache kaum glücklich zu Ende führen.

Exercise.

1. Give me a **sign of life**, when you arrive in the town of Berlin.
2. What do you do *of* an evening? We often speak *of* our old friends in England.
3. He was the fourth *of* those unfortunate kings, who lost their lives (*singular*).
4. Was the "Victory" (*not translated*) not a wooden ship? Yes, it was (a wooden ship).
5. We lived three months in Bâle, a town in Switzerland *of* 40,000 inhabitants.

Reference-Page EE.—*Continued.*

on (*upon*)

(a) *generally with meaning of locality* = auf [Dative or Accusative (motion)].

(b) *after some verbs*: *to revenge oneself on* = sich rächen an (dat.); *to have pity on* = Mitleid haben mit (dat.); *to wait on* = bedienen (acc.); *to reflect on* = nachdenken über (acc.); *to live on* = leben von (dat.); *to feed on* = sich nähren von (dat.); *to play on an instrument* = ein Instrument spielen.

(c) **idiomatic** use: *on* (before a day of the week or the month) = am (= an dem) dat., am Montag; *on the arrival* = bei der Ankunft; *on the occasion* = bei der Gelegenheit; *on view* = ausgestellt; *on this side of* = diesseits (gen.); *on that side of* = jenseits; *on account of* = wegen (gen.), für (acc.); *on my honour* = bei meiner Ehre = auf Ehre; *on board* = an Bord; *on foot* = zu Fuß; *on horseback* = zu Pferd; **on this condition** = unter dieser Bedingung; **on** *the contrary* = im Gegenteil; *on* (a *river*) = an (einem Fluß); *on one's travels* = auf Reisen; *on* (*about*) *me* = bei mir.

to

(a) *after verbs of motion* = an (acc.), zu (dat.), nach (dat.) with towns or countries.

(b) *after adjectives*, generally not translated, but followed by dat. [see page 94, C.]. However: *polite to* = höflich gegen (acc.); *cruel to* = grausam gegen (acc.); *deaf to* = taub gegen (acc.); *indifferent to* = gleichgültig gegen (acc.); *charitable to* = barmherzig gegen (acc.).

(c) *after verbs*, generally not translated, but followed **by dative**. However: *amount to* = sich belaufen auf (acc.); *apply to* = sich richten (wenden) **an** (acc.); *to attend to* = sich abgeben mit (dat.); *consent to* = beistimmen (dat.) = sich fügen in (**acc.**); *to direct to* = adressieren an (acc.); *pay attention to* = achten or Acht geben auf (acc.); *speak to* = sprechen zu (dat.); *write to* = schreiben an (acc.).

(d) *idiomatic use*: *to church* = in die Kirche; *to the market* = auf den Markt; *to school* = in die Schule; *to a house* = in ein Haus; *to the country* (rus) = auf das Land; *to the concert* = in's Conzert; **to the townhall** = auf's Rathhaus; *to the post* = auf die Post; *to put to flight* = in die Flucht schlagen.

with

(a) generally = mit (dat.), especially speaking of the instrument or means.

(b) = *on account of* = vor (dat.), as: *to die with cold* = vor Kälte sterben.

(c) = *among, near* = bei (dat.), as: *with the English* = bei den Engländern.

(d) *after some verbs*: *to agree with*, = *to suit* = wohl bekommen (dat.) es bekommt mir wohl; *agree with* (in opinion) beistimmen (dat.) = entsprechen (dat.) = *correspond with* or *to something*, but: *correspond* = *write to* = correspondiren mit (dat.); *part with* = sich entschlagen (gen.) = scheiden von. The following have Dat. of person and Acc. of **thing**: *provide with* = liefern; *present with* = schenken; *meet with* = begegnen; *reproach with* = vorwerfen; *trust with* = anvertrauen; — *it is* **all over with him** = es geht zu Ende mit ihm; *with all my heart* = von ganzem Herzen.

N.B.—**The other** prepositions do not present much difficulty; they will be found on page 52 with their **German** equivalents. The pupil must carefully remember that prepositions must be followed by Nouns or **Pronouns**; otherwise they become adverbials. As to verbs in *-ing* after prepositions, see page 116, iv. d. iii.

Examples and Exercises on Page 104.

on and to.

Examples.

1. It is not Christian-like, to revenge oneself on one's enemies; one ought rather to have pity on the misguided ones.
2. Do think of my question! Where did you go on his arrival?
3. I will pardon you, on (the) condition, that you promise me never to do it again.

1. Es ist nicht christlich, sich an seinen Feinden zu rächen, man sollte eher mit den Verblendeten Mitleid haben.
2. Denke doch über meine Frage nach! Wohin giengst du bei seiner Ankunft?
3. Ich will Ihnen unter der Bedingung verzeihen, daß Sie mir versprechen, es nie wieder zu tun.

Translate.

1. Paris an der Seine und London an der Themse sind jetzt die größten Städte Europa's; einst war es Rom an der Tiber.
2. Der Fürst giebt sich mit Manchem ab, gegen den er, wenn er noch Privatmann wäre, gleichgültig wäre.
3. Seid nicht grausam gegen kleine Thiere; man muß nie taub sein gegen die Stimme des Schmerzes.
4. Wenn Sie nächstens an mich schreiben, so bitte ich Sie, Ihre Briefe an mich Numero dreißig, Ludwigstraße, München, Bayern, zu adressiren.

Exercise.

1. On this side of this mountain lies France, on that side Italy.
2. One often meets men on (his) journeys, whom one least expects (am wenigsten).
3. Boys, pay attention to this sentence: Be polite to your superiors (Vorgesetzten).
4. While you went to school, we were at church, and he went to his uncle.
5. This picture is on view now; it was carried to the town hall yesterday.

with and other prepositions.

Examples.

1. With the Roman emperors it was the custom to arrange great festivities for the populace, so as to gain its favour.
2. It grieves one to part with one's home, and all that one loves.

1. Bei den römischen Kaisern war es der Brauch dem Pöbel große Feste zu veranstalten, um sich denselben günstig zu stimmen.
2. Es tut weh' von seiner Heimat zu scheiden und von Allem, das man liebt.

Translate.

1. Als ich ihm begegnete, gab' ich ihm Ihr Empfehlungsschreiben, und er stimmte mit mir darin überein daß es am Besten wäre, spät im Herbst nach Rom zu gehen.
2. Die Nachrichten von verschiedenen Seiten stimmen mit dem Privatbriefe, den Sie erhalten haben, darin überein, daß er schon vor mehreren Jahren in Chicago gestorben ist.

Exercise.

1. You may trust him with your secret; he will never betray your trust.
2. We waited, but, as he did not come, we went away to school.
3. On account of the arrival of these guests, our excursion was postponed (aufschieben).
4. The king reproached his general with this negligence, and we think he was right.
5. This corresponds with my expectations (Erwartungen); he is ruined (ruiniri).

REFERENCE-PAGE **FF**.

Remarks on some of the Pronouns.

I. *Personal.*

  (*a.*) **The** genitive of Personal Pronouns is rarely used, except with verbs **and** prepositions which govern the Genitive, as: anstatt seiner, *instead of him*; ich erinnere mich **Ihrer**, *I remember you*.

  N.B. um ... willen and wegen have a peculiar alteration of r into t in the Genitive of the Personal Pronoun, um seinetwillen, *for his sake*; ihretwegen, *on her* (or *their*) *account*.

  (*b.*) sich is both dative and accusative; thus: sich (Dat.) vorwerfen, *to reproach oneself*, makes: ich werfe mir vor, du wirfst dir vor, etc.; but sich (Acc.) waschen, **to wash** *oneself*, makes: ich wasche mich, du wäschest dich, er wäscht sich, etc. Sich has often the meaning **of** einander = *one another*, as: sie lieben sich, *they love one another*.

II. *Possessive.*

  (*a*) *mine, thine,* **his***, ours,* **after to be, to become, to remain, to** *call*, are sometimes simply and invariably mein, dein, sein, unser, as: *this pen is mine* = diese Feder ist mein.

  (*b*) Such expressions as: *a* **brother of** *mine,* **both of us, all of you,** cannot be rendered literally; they are translated: einer meiner **Brüder**; wir beide; Sie alle.

  (*c*) **der (die, das)** meinige, etc.; der (die, das) **meine**, etc.; and meiner, meine, meines, can never be used before a noun; they **have** exactly the same meaning, and may be used one for the other; euphony alone decides which to use in translating *mine*, etc. (see page 66, I.).

III. *Relative.*

  (*a*) Remember that the **relative pronoun must in** German stand first in the relative clause (except it be accompanied **by a preposition**), and that the Assertion *must* be last in the clause, thus: *the town, the public buildings of which you admired so much, lies in my native country* = die Stadt, deren öffentliche Gebäude Sie so sehr bewunderten, liegt in meinem Heimatlande. Therefore such expressions as: *both of which, all of which, some of which*, cannot be literally translated; we must render: *both of which I saw*, by: welche ich beide sah; *all of which I know*, by: die ich alle kenne; *some of which he gave me*, by: von denen er mir einige gab.

  (*b*) Relative pronouns must introduce the relative clause, though in English the relative be omitted, thus: *the man I saw* must be rendered by: der Mann welchen (or den) ich sah.

  (*c*) There are two relative pronouns in German, **welcher** (etc.), and **der** (etc.); they have exactly the same meaning = *who* or *which*, and may be generally used indifferently, *but if preceded by a Personal Pronoun of the 1st or 2d person, in the Nominative,* **der** (and not welcher) must be used; in this case the personal pronoun is often, for the sake of emphasis, repeated after the relative, as: *I who went there* = ich, **der ich dahin gieng**; *we who sent you this present* = wir, die wir Ihnen dieses Geschenk schickten.

  (*d*) Remember that the interpolation of a relative sentence in any clause does not in any way alter the **sequence** of words in this latter Clause, as:

Weil der Mann, den ich Ihnen empfahl, Ihnen nicht gefiel, so **werde** ich Ihnen einen Anderen schicken. | *Because the man, whom I recommended to you, did not please you, I will send you another.*

Examples on Exercises on Page 106.
PERSONAL AND POSSESSIVE.
Examples.

1. *The messenger went for the sake of this letter to the post once more; it was only on your account, dear cousin* (f.).
2. *Do not imagine, that you will ever obtain a prize, if you do not apply yourself more to the study of German.*
3. *We lost one of our sticks on the way hither, we think.*

1. Der Bote gieng um dieses Briefes willen noch einmal auf die Post; es war nur Ihretwegen, meine liebe Base.
2. Bilde dir nicht ein, daß du je einen Preis erlangen wirst, wenn du dich des Studiums des Deutschen nicht mehr befleißest.
3. Wir verloren einen unserer Stöcke auf dem Wege hierher, glauben wir.

Translate.

1. Um eines Dankeswortes willen stürzte sich dieser junge Mann in's Wasser, um die Blume zu holen.
2. Sie wußten recht wohl, daß diese Feder nicht mein war, lieber Karl.
3. Es tut mir leid, einen meiner Handschuhe dort verloren zu haben.
4. Erinnern Sie sich noch meiner? O ja, ich kann mich Ihrer noch sehr gut erinnern.

Exercise.

1. Is this a friend *of yours?* Oh, no; it is one of my enemy's brothers.
2. The **man**, whom you saw, came to you *for my sake*. He is a messenger *of mine*.
3. We remember *him*; he went once with us to London in the train (Eisenbahn, f.).
4. We saw *both of them* at the theatre last night (gestern Abend).
5. Is this my stick? No, it is *mine*, you know you have lost *yours*.

RELATIVE.
Examples.

1. *These two men, both of whom I know well, are Americans.*
2. *We received the letter you wrote to us from Munich.*
3. *We who are Englishmen ought to learn the English language also.*

1. Diese zwei Männer, die ich beide sehr gut kenne, sind Amerikaner.
2. Wir haben den Brief erhalten, den Sie uns von München schrieben.
3. Wir, die wir Engländer sind, sollten auch die englische Sprache lernen.

Translate.

1. Wir sahen viele Knaben, von denen **wir einige** kannten, im Flusse baden; es war verboten.
2. Mein Freund schrieb mir, daß ich, der ich Lust habe, **Matrose zu** werden, mich nach Liverpool begeben sollte.
3. Die Kleider, welche Sie gestern auf der Jagd trugen und die ganz naß und schmutzig waren, sind jetzt wieder ganz trocken, und der Diener, dem ich sie gab, hat sie auch wieder gereinigt und gebürstet.

Exercise.

1. We saw the dog you bought yesterday, and we think it is beautiful.
2. Thou, who (thou) art in the house all day (= the whole day (acc.)), art not in good health.
3. This is the horse, the beauties of which you admired; but it is ill now.
4. Rome, whose armies conquered the world, was (*passive*) itself (selbst) conquered by those barbarians, whom the Romans despised as (als) barbarians.

REFERENCE-PAGE **FF**.—*Continued.*

IV. Remarks on some *Indefinite Pronouns*.

 (a) **man**, *one, people, they.* Do not confound this with ber **Mann**, *the man;* man can never change, it can only be used in the Nominative and requires its verb always in the Singular, as: *they say*, man jagt. For Genitive, Dative, and Accusative of man, we use fein, *his*, in the oblique cases, as: *one must forgive one's enemies*, man (follte) muß feinen Feinden verzeihen.

 (b) *All.* (i) Before possessive adjectives, masc. **and** neuter Singular, **all is** invariable: ber arme Mann ift all feines Gutes beraubt worden, *the poor man was robbed of all his property.*

  (ii) Before possessive adjectives in the feminine Singular and in all Plurals, alle is (except **in** poetry) changed thus: fem.: N.A. alle; G. aller; D. aller; *Plural:* N.A. alle; G. aller; D. allen, as: Alle meine Liebe, alle meine Bestrebungen find dem Baterlande geweiht, *all my love, all my endeavours are dedicated to my native land.*

  (iii) *All* in the sense of *the whole* is ber (die, das) ganze, or: ganz invariable before towns or countries, as: *all the world*, die ganze Welt; *all Germany*, ganz Deutschland.

  (iv) *All that* = alles was, where was has the force of a relative pronoun, as: Alles, was ich je besessen habe, ist verloren, *all that I ever possessed, is lost.*

  (v) *All* in the sense of *every* = jeber (jede, jedes), as: *at all hours*, zu jeder Stunde; *every day* = jeben Tag or alle Tage [cf. French: *tous les jours* = *every day*].

 (c) *Much, little*, before materials, are invariable, viel, wenig, as: *much sugar* = viel (NOT vieler) Zucker; *little gold* = wenig (NOT weniges) Gold.

 (d) *Many, few*, are declined [as well as *both* and *all*] in the Plural, thus:

N. and *A.*	viele, *many*	wenige, *few*	beide, *both*	alle, *all*	manche, *several, many*
Genitive	vieler, *of many*	weniger, *of few*	beider, *of both*	aller, *of all*	mancher, *of several*
Dative	vielen, *to many*	wenigen, *to few*	beiden, *to both*	allen, *to all*	manchen, *to several*

 As: Er glaubt wenigen Leuten = *he believes* (dat.) *few people.*

 (e) *A few*, einige, mehrere, is declined like viele; but: *a little*, ein wenig, is invariable: ich habe ein wenig Wein; Einige Knaben haben ein wenig Deutsch gelernt = *a few boys have learnt a little German.*

 (f) *Another* in the sense of "a different one" is ein anderer, eine andere, etc., declined like an adjective in the second form (see Reference-Page G), as: dieses Buch ist schmutzig, gieb mir ein anderes = *this book is dirty, give me another.*

  but: *another* in the sense of "an additional one," one more of the same kind, is noch ein, noch eine, noch eines, as: Ich habe diese Äpfel sehr gern, geben Sie mir noch einen = *I like these apples very much, give me another.*

 (g) *(Some)* more = noch (mehr) (invariable), as: *Do you like these cherries? Yes, give me some more* = Haben Sie diese Kirschen gern? Ja, bitte geben Sie mir noch mehr (or noch welche).

 (h) *No more* = keiner mehr, keine mehr, etc.; decline keiner as adj. of 2d Form: *He has no more* [*money*] = er hat keines mehr; er hat kein Geld mehr.

Examples and Exercises on Page 108.

On (a), (b), (c), (d).

Examples.

1. *'Tis indeed true*, **one must look to one's affairs oneself,** *if they are to be properly done.*
1. Es ist in der Tat wahr, **man muß seine Geschäfte selber besorgen,** wenn sie gut besorgt sein sollen.

2. *All his possessions and property the prince* **lost in** *this battle; all his hopes he buried there.*
2. All sein Gut und Besitztum verlor der Fürst in dieser Schlacht; alle seine Hoffnungen hat er da zu Grabe getragen.

3. *It is not yet the end of the world; one should never despair, hope remains still always to us.*
3. Es ist noch nicht aller Welt Ende, man muß nie verzagen, denn die Hoffnung bleibt uns ja immer noch.

Translate.

1. Es ist nicht Alles Gold, was glänzt, und doch jagen die Menschen so oft Allem nach, was von Weitem glänzt.

2. Ich fürchte vor Allem, er werde mit all seinem Wissen es nie weit bringen.

3. All sein Wissen ist nicht weit her, obschon er auf allen Universitäten studirt hat.

4. Viele gehen voll Hoffnung in die Fremde, aber Wenige kehren glücklich wieder heim: ich sage Bleib' im Land und nähr' dich redlich.

Exercise.

1. We remained ten years in America, but were unlucky in *all* our enterprises.
2. These **men** had indeed *much* luck, yet they made *little* money in two years.
3. He has forgotten *all that* he ever knew; he is now ill in body and mind.
4. One should be charitable to *one's* neighbours, for sooner or later *one may* need **charity oneself.**
5. There is *much* money in England; but **no (nicht)** *little* poverty and misery also.

On (e), (f), (g), (h).

Examples.

1. *He spoke of a few people, whom I knew formerly* **personally.**
1. Er sprach von einigen Leuten, die ich selbst früher persönlich kannte.

2. *Give me* **another** *towel; I want another; this one is* **wet and dirty.**
2. Gieb mir ein anderes Handtuch; ich brauche noch eines; dieses ist naß und schmutzig.

3. *There is no more hope; he is dead.*
3. Es ist keine Hoffnung mehr da; er ist todt.

Translate.

1. Geben Sie mir noch ein wenig Butterbrod, bitte; ich habe keines mehr, und es ist vorzüglich.

2. Haben Sie noch (mehr) von diesen Cigarren? Wenn Sie noch von dieser Sorte haben, schicken Sie mir gefälligst ein Kistchen à 25 Mark heute noch.

3. Er verlangte noch einen Apfel und dann noch einen; es scheint als ob er die Äpfel sehr gerne äße.

4. Wenige Leute sind wirklich glücklich; haben sie viel, so wünschen sie mehr; haben sie nur wenig, so sind sie mit dem Wenigen, das sie haben, nicht zufrieden.

Exercise.

1. We like these apples; please send us a dozen more to our house.
2. He has spent (ausgeben) all his money; now he has not any more (no **more**).
3. We **often** wish we had chosen another town; but we have no more choice now.
4. The king has added (hinzu'fügen) another country to his **kingdom.**
5. The merchant had a few boxes (Kisten) (of) **books**; he has learnt a *little* German now.

REFERENCE-PAGE **GG**.

On the Government of Verbs.

Verbs may be followed in German: I. by Nouns or Pronouns; II. by other Verbs in the Infinitive or Past Participle; and, III. by subordinate clauses with a verb finite in them.

I. *Verbs followed by Nouns or Pronouns.*

    A. Noun or Pronoun in the NOMINATIVE (see page 82) after these six verbs only; bleiben, *to remain;* heißen or geheißen werden, *to be called;* scheinen, *to appear;* sein, *to be;* and werden, *to become.* As: er ist ein König geblieben = *he has remained a king.*

    B. Noun or Pronoun in the ACCUSATIVE after a verb. [See also page 102, top.]

(a) After all verbs, which in German coalesce with a preposition governing accusative, as: *to answer a question* = antworten auf eine Frage; *to declare him a rascal* = ihn für einen Schurken erklären; *to consider one a fool* = Einen für einen Narren halten; *to recollect a name* = sich an einen Namen erinnern.

(b) After all transitive verbs, as: einen Apfel holen, *to fetch an apple;* i.e. all verbs which can be turned into the Passive Voice, as: der Apfel wird geholt.

(c) After the following (and a few more) the direct object (generally the *thing* which is ...d) is in the *Accusative,* and the *person* to whom the thing is ...d, is in the *Dative.* [N.B. Dative before Accusative, see p. 83.]

(approach, (sich) nähern)	impute, zu'schreiben	present (with), schenken	show, zeigen
bring, bringen	lend, leihen	recommend, empfehlen	(submit, (sich) unterwerfen)
dedicate, widmen, weihen	offer, an'bieten	refuse, ab'schlagen	spare (save), ersparen
give, geben	owe, danken, schulden	relate, erzählen	take away, weg'nehmen
grant, gewähren	pardon, verzeihen	send, schicken	tell, sagen

as: er brachte dem König einen Becher = *he brought (to) the king a cup.*

(d) After the following (and a few more) the direct object (the *person*) is in the *accusative,* and the indirect object (the *thing*) in the *genitive.* [N.B. Person before Thing, see p. 83.]

absolve from, entbinden	assure of, versichern	dismiss from, entsetzen	favour with, würdigen
accuse of, an'klagen	convict of, überführen	deprive of, entheben	rob of, berauben

    C. Noun or Pronoun in the DATIVE after a verb. [See also p. 102, *to.*]

(a) After all verbs, which coalesce in German with a preposition governing the dative, as: *to speak of* = sprechen von (dat.).

(b) After the following (and many more), with prefixes: bei, entgegen, vor, nach, zu; and: ent-, wider-).

advise, raten	command, befehlen	hurt, schaden	seem, scheinen
allow, erlauben	communicate, mit'teilen	meet, begegnen	serve, dienen
answer, antworten	escape from, entfliehen	obey, gehorchen	thank, danken
avoid, aus'weichen	flatter, schmeicheln	please, gefallen	threaten, drohen
belong to, gehören	follow, folgen	reproach, vorwerfen	trust, zu'trauen

(c) With some impersonals, as: *it is of use* = es nützt; *it happens* = es geschieht; *it occurs (to me)* = es fällt (mir) ein; *I succeed* = es gelingt mir (dir. ihm. etc.).

    D. Noun or Pronoun in the GENITIVE after a verb. [See also pp. 100 and 102.]

(a) After: *to mock* = spotten; *to need* = bedürfen; *be without* = ermangeln; *think of* = gedenken.

(a) With the *reflexive verbs:*

abstain from, sich ... enthalten	boast of, sich ... rühmen	use, sich ... bedienen
apply to, sich ... befleißen	enjoy, sich ... erfreuen	remember, sich ... erinnern
	pity, sich ... erbarmen	and a few more.

Examples and Exercises on Page 110.

On I. A. and B.
Examples.

1. We heard he had become a merchant, but they had accused him of defalcations and considered him a thief.
2. Pray, lend (to) the boy your umbrella, for it rains heavily.
3. Did he remember that event?

1. Wir haben gehört, er sei ein Kaufmann geworden, aber man habe ihn der Veruntreuung angeklagt und halte ihn für einen Dieb.
2. Bitte, leihen Sie dem Knaben Ihren Regenschirm, denn es regnet stark.
3. Erinnerte er sich an jene Begebenheit?

Translate.

1. Wer immer ein ehrlicher Mann bleiben will, muß der Versuchung aus dem Wege gehen, so viel er kann.
2. Wir erklären den Mann für einen dummen Kerl, der sich den Gesetzen des Landes, worin er lebt, widersetzt.
3. Bitte, lies diesen Brief; er ist von deinem alten Freund in St. Petersburg.
4. Die Amme erzählte den Kindern eine Geistergeschichte; doch der Vater verbot ihr, dies je wieder zu tun, denn er hielt es für ungeraten (unadvisable).

Exercise.

1. They offered him a post (Stelle, *f.*) in South Africa; but he did not go.
2. I favoured him with my confidence, but I found he betrayed it (verraten).
3. Tell the boys they ought (sollen) to bring me their exercises to-morrow.
4. That good son sent his parents every Christmas (Weihnachten, *f.*) some presents.
5. He owed it to me, that he was recommended to the principal of this school.

On I. C. and D.
Example.

1. Of what are you speaking? I speak of the clergyman who preached last Sunday.
2. It was of no use to the lawyer that he called up this witness in the lawsuit.
3. We say it serves the fellow right (it happens right to the *f.*) for he has deserved heavy punishment.

1. Von was sprechen Sie? Ich spreche von dem Geistlichen, der letzten Sonntag predigte.
2. Es nützte dem Advokaten nichts, daß er diesen Zeugen in dem Prozesse aufrief.
3. Wir sagen, es geschieht dem Kerl recht, denn er hat schwere Strafe verdient.

Translate.

1. Wie befinden Sie sich? Ich danke, ich erfreue mich recht guter Gesundheit seit einigen Monaten (dat.).
2. Obgleich dieser Fehler ihm verziehen wurde, würdigte ihn der Prinzipal der Schule doch nie wieder seines ganzen Vertrauens wie vorher.
3. Diese Art und Weise zu leben, wird nur Ihnen selbst schaden, und ich empfehle Ihnen, Ihre Lebensweise zu ändern.
4. Man sollte sich stets seiner Mitmenschen erbarmen wenn sie im Unglück sind, denn es ist möglich, daß wir ihrer, früher oder später, selbst bedürfen.

Exercise.

1. Do not accuse this boy *of the theft*, if you are not quite sure.
2. Children should (sollen) follow *the advice* of their parents and teachers.
3. You may (können) threaten *me* as much as you like (wollen); I am not afraid.
4. Permit me, my friend, to (zu) tell you, that I think you are wrong.
5. Whom did you meet? I only met two children, who were going to school.

Reference-Page GG.—Continued.

II. *Verbs followed by other Verbs.* [Infinitive or Past Participle.]

   A. The *ten* auxiliaries, and a few other verbs sometimes used like auxiliaries.

      1. ſein, *to be,*

         (*a*) with the Infinitive **Passive** in English, is rendered by zu with the Infinitive *active* in German, as: *it is to be feared* = es iſt zu fürchten. [*N.B.*—In questions and in the Inversion this es is omitted.]

         (*b*) with the Past Participle of another verb forms the Compound Tenses of the latter, as: *he has* (*is*) *gone* = er iſt gegangen.

      2. haben, *to have,*

         (*a*) with the Infinitive Active of another verb, is rendered by zu and Infinitive: *he has to do it* = er hat es zu tun.

         (*b*) with the Past Participle of another verb forms the Compound Tenses of the latter, as: *he has done it* = er hat es getan.

      3. werden, *to become,*

         (*a*) with the Infinitive, without zu, forms the Future, as: wir werden es ſehen = *we shall see it;* er wird es geſehen haben = *he will have seen it.*

         (*b*) with the Past Participle of another verb, forms its Passive voice, as: *he was* (*became*) *punished* = er wurde beſtraft. [In Compound Tenses with another verb, use worden —no ge*.]

      4. The seven auxiliaries of mood: dürfen, *to be allowed;* können, *to be able;* laſſen, *to let;* mögen, *to like;* müſſen, *to be obliged;* ſollen, *ought;* and wollen, *to be willing,* take Infinitive *without* zu after them, as: er durfte kommen, *he was allowed to come.*

   Note.—The English Infinitive **Passive** after *to allow,* laſſen, **must** be rendered by the Infinitive *Active* in German without zu, as: *I allow it to be brought* = ich laſſe es bringen.

   N.B.—The Compound tenses of these seven auxiliaries, if used with other verbs, are formed with their Infinitives and *not* their Past Participles, as: er hat kommen dürfen, *not* gedurft.

      5. Some nine verbs may be used as auxiliaries (besides the *ten* above), viz.: bleiben, *to remain;* fühlen, *to feel;* heißen, *to order;* helfen, *to help;* hören, *to hear;* ſehen, *to see;* lehren, *to teach;* lernen, *to learn;* and machen, *to make, force,* as: er bleibt ſtehen, *he remains standing.*

   N.B.—These, **however,** form their Compound Tenses with their Past Participles as all ordinary verbs do, thus: iſt er ſtehen geblieben? = *has* (*is*) *he remained standing* (*has he stopped*)?

   B. *All* other verbs require zu before the Infinitive which **may** be governed by them, **thus:** ich befahl ihm zu gehen = *I commanded him to go.*

   Remark, however, the idioms: ſpazieren gehen, *to go a walk;* ſpazieren fahren, *to take a drive;* ſpazieren reiten, *to take a ride on horseback;* ſchlafen gehen, *to go* **to bed;** betteln gehen, *to go a-begging;* and a few more with gehen, as: trinken gehen = *to go to drink,* etc.

III. *Verbs governing subordinate* **clauses.**

      (*a*) Verbs of saying, asking, etc., introducing indirect speech, either with or without daß (see page 78).

      (*b*) Verbs of wishing, fearing, doubting, are generally followed by Subjunctive **in the** subordinate clause, as: ich fürchte, er ſei tot = *I fear he is dead.*

   N.B.—Verbs connected with damit, *so that;* wenn, *if;* als ob, als wenn, *as if,* require Subjunctive in the subordinate clause; the last two always *Imperfect Subjunctive.*

Examples and Exercises on Page 112.

On II. A.

Examples.

1. *What one has to do, one ought to do soon and well; it is no use to delay it.*
1. Was man zu tun hat, soll man bald und gut tun; es nützt nichts, es aufzuschieben.
2. *When the beggar came to our door, it was to be expected that the dog would bark.*
2. Als der Bettler an unsere Türe kam, war zu erwarten, daß der Hund bellte.
3. *Peace has at last been concluded, after this long and terrible war.*
3. Es ist endlich Frieden geschlossen worden, nach diesem langen, schrecklichen Kriege.

Translate.

1. Mein Sohn hat lesen können, als er vier Jahre alt war; ich habe ihn selbst lesen gelehrt; denn er war zu schwächlich um in die öffentliche Schule zu gehen.
2. Es ist ärgerlich, daß wir an einem so schönen Tage in die Schule zu gehen haben.
3. Es ist Zeit schlafen zu gehen; Karl ist schon lange schlafen gegangen.
4. Wenn es morgen schön ist, so werden wir spazieren gehen; oder, wenn wir Geld genug haben, werden wir einen Wagen nehmen und spazieren fahren.

Exercise.

1. Our master commanded us to do this; we had to do it; it is done.
2. Was the criminal punished? Yes, he has been punished; he was imprisoned (ein'sperren).
3. I told you (Dat.), you were not allowed to go for a walk this afternoon (Acc.).
4. Where did we stop? (stehen bleiben.) We stopped (use Perfect) [on] page 132.
5. Will you help me to write this letter? it is to (an) my uncle in St. Petersburg.

On II. B., and III.

Examples.

1. *Do you wish to see this man? Yes, he invited me to visit (come to see) him; but I could not come earlier.*
1. Wünschen Sie, diesen Mann zu sehen? Ja; er hat mich eingeladen, ihn zu besuchen, aber ich konnte nicht früher kommen.
2. *Let them go a-begging, if they are hungry. He who does not work shall not eat.*
2. „Laß' sie betteln gehen, wenn sie hungrig sind." Wer nicht arbeitet, soll nicht essen.
3. *They told me you had been in Switzerland and in the Tyrol last year.*
3. Man sagte mir, Sie wären letztes Jahr in der Schweiz und im Tirol gewesen.

Translate.

1. Der Bote zweifelte, ob er die Stadt zur Zeit erreichen könnte, denn es war schon sehr spät am Tage.
2. Fürchten Sie nicht, er würde sich in große Gefahr stürzen, wenn er mit diesem Pferde auf die Jagd gienge?
3. Ich habe eine Ahnung, als ob mir etwas sehr Unangenehmes zustoßen (happen) würde.
4. Wir schrieben Ihnen, damit Sie auf der Hut sein sollten (take care) wenn er Ihnen begegnen würde; denn er ist ein Schwindler, und man darf ihm nicht trauen.

Exercise.

1. We do not fear, that you will meet with [any] thieves; but take care (see 4 above).
2. Has any one (Jemand) commanded you to go to their neighbour this evening?
3. I do this, so that you may know, that you have one friend in the old country.
4. They tell me, that you went for a walk during this rain; it was very foolish (töricht).
5. The horses go to drink, and that boy leads the first of them.

P

REFERENCE-PAGE **HH**.

On the Translation of the English Infinitive.

The English Infinitive may be used as a substantive, **or it may be** governed by a verb, an adjective, or a noun.

I. The **English Infinitive** used *substantively*:

    (*a*) As *Subject*, translate it by an infinitive with neuter article, as: *To lie is disgraceful* = das Lügen ist verabscheuungswürdig. *To sit too long* = das zu lange Sitzen.

    N.B.—The article is sometimes omitted, especially in proverbs: Beten und Arbeiten, *To pray and to work*.

    (*b*) As *Object*:

        (1) dependent on another verb, as: *he is used to work*, er ist an das Arbeiten gewöhnt.

        (2) *how to..., what to..., where to...*, after such words as *to know*, must be resolved into *subordinate clauses* introduced by wie, was, wo (wohin, etc.), as: *he knows how to write* = er weiß, wie man schreibt (or schreiben sollte).

        (3) The **English Accusative and Infinitive** after *to know, to believe, to wish,* etc., must be resolved into a subordinate clause with or without daß, *that*, as: *We knew that man to be a thief* = wir wußten, daß jener Mann ein Dieb war—or: jener Mann war ein Dieb.

II. The English Infinitive governed by a **Verb**. [For this, see page 112.]

III. The English Infinitive governed by **an adjective**. (*Remember*: Infin. at end of sentence):

    (*a*) Such adjectives as *curious*, neugierig; *difficult*, schwer; *easy*, leicht; *eager*, begierig; *possible*, möglich; *impossible*, unmöglich, require in German the Infinitive with zu: *it will be easy to do that* = es wird leicht sein, das zu tun.

    (*b*) **Adjectives preceded by** *too*, zu; and adjectives followed by *enough*, genug, require the Infinitive with um...zu, as: *He is too good to do this wicked deed* = er ist zu gut, um diese schlechte Tat zu begehen; *we are rich enough to buy that house* = wir sind reich genug, um dieses Haus zu kaufen.

IV. The *English Infinitive after some* **Nouns**, such as *the choice*, die Wahl; *the liberty*, die Freiheit; *the courage*, der Mut; *the necessity*, die Notwendigkeit; *a desire* = a mind, Lust (without article); *the duty*, die Pflicht; *the pleasure*, das Vergnügen; *the wish*, der Wunsch, must be rendered by Infinitive with zu **in** German, as:

    It will be a pleasure for me to write to you = es wird mir ein Vergnügen sein, an Sie zu schreiben; *I had a mind to go to London* = ich hatte Lust, nach London zu gehen.

Idiomatic: *He is just about to go there* = er will eben dahin gehen.

Purpose is indicated by um...zu with Infinitive, as:

    He gave me money to buy the books = er gab mir Geld, um die Bücher zu kaufen.

Examples and Exercises on Page 114.

On I. and II.

Example.

1. We scarcely know how to act in this affair; at any rate it is advisable to wait a little longer.	1. Wir wissen kaum, wie wir in dieser Angelegenheit handeln sollen; jedenfalls ist ein längeres Warten geraten.
2. Of what use is it to hunt after money and wealth?	2. Was nützt das Haschen nach Geld und Gut?
3. He hated to ride in a railway carriage; he preferred to ride on horseback.	3. Er haßte das Fahren in der Eisenbahn; er zog das Reiten zu Pferd vor.

Translate.

1. Wer das Säen (*sowing seed*) vernachlässigt, kann nicht auf reichliches Ernten (*reaping*) hoffen.	3. Man braucht sich über sein Stehlen nicht zu verwundern, denn sein Hang zum Lügen war ja wohlbekannt.
2. Das späte Zu-Bett-gehen und das späte Aufstehen am Morgen sind der Gesundheit nachteilig, wenn es zu oft geschieht.	4. Zum Faullenzen (*idling*) habe ich keine Zeit; der ganze Tag ist bei mir mit Arbeiten ausgefüllt.

Exercise.

1. **To-walk-too-rapidly or to-run-too-much** is injurious **to one's health.**
2. My dear mother always told me: "**To-pray and to-work bring blessing.**"
3. **To-read** in the dusk (Dämmerung) is injurious to one's eyes (say : *to the* eyes).
4. Do you know where to go (whither you should go) and what to say (what you should say)?
5. The king believed him to be a very capable soldier; but he proved himself **to be rash.**

On III. and IV.

Example.

1. It is scarcely possible to let Louisa have this letter before she goes away.	1. Es ist kaum möglich, Louisen diesen Brief zukommen zu lassen, vor sie fortgeht.
2. He had not the courage at all, to **stand up to** his accuser; he was too cowardly to **face** public opinion.	2. Er hatte gar nicht den Mut, vor seinen Ankläger zu treten; er war zu feige sich der öffentlichen Meinung entgegenzustellen.
3. We should like (should have a mind) to **hear him** sing once; but it cannot be to-day.	3. Wir hätten Lust, ihn einmal singen zu hören, aber es geht heute nicht.

Translate.

1. Dieser Mann war reich genug, um den Verlust nicht zu fühlen.	3. Es würde uns wirklich sehr viel Vergnügen machen, Sie mit uns zu nehmen, aber wir fürchten, Sie seien nicht stark genug, **um die Anstrengungen** auszuhalten.
2. Dieser gute Vater gab seinem Sohne Geld, um drei Monate in Rom zuzubringen, und sich daselbst mit den Werken der alten Meister bekannt zu machen.	4. Hatte er nicht Lust, Soldat zu werden? O ja, aber sein Vater erlaubte es nicht.

Exercise.

1. Will you give us the pleasure to come to (zu) us to-morrow evening?
2. The little girl was curious to see the nest, which her brother brought home (nach Hause).
3. You see, you have the choice to go to London or to (nach) Bristol.
4. We gave you this watch, in order to reward you for your diligence (Fleiß m.).
5. When the messenger arrived, we were just about to leave the town.

REFERENCE-PAGE KK.

On the Translation of the verbal in -ing.

I. The verbal in -ing used SUBSTANTIVELY, whether subject or object in a sentence, is always translated by an Infinitive without zu, but with the article, in German, unless the German idiom has a real substantive for the same idea, thus :

hunting, das Jagen or die Jagd ; *playing*, das Spielen or das Spiel.

II. The verbal in -ing in APPOSITION to a noun or adjective is rendered by an Infinitive *with* zu in German, as :

the necessity of doing this = die Notwendigkeit, dies zu tun ; *it is easy of acquiring* = es ist leicht zu lernen.

III. The verbal in -ing used as an ADJECTIVE is always translated by the Present Participle in German, and declined like an adjective in the three forms (see Reference-page G) if used before a noun, but it remains invariable if used after *to be, to become*, etc., as :

ein liebendes Kind, *a loving child* ; *I have a living dog*, ich habe einen lebenden Hund ; der Brief ist unterhaltend (invariable), *the letter is amusing* ; thus : *laughing*, lachend.

IV. The verbal in -ing used in its verbal character, *i.e.* as a VERB,—

(a) when completing the signification of another verb, as : to go on *doing* a thing, etc., is translated by Infinitive with zu, as : er hörte auf zu singen = *he stopped singing*.

(b) after *instead of* and *without*, it is translated by Infinitive with zu, as : *we went there instead of remaining at home* = wir giengen dahin, anstatt zu Hause zu bleiben.

(c) When after a noun or pronoun, with a relative force, it is translated by a relative clause in German, as : *the man bearing the weight* = der Mann, der die Last trug. . . .

N.B.—Distinguish this from the next following meaning of the verbal in -ing.

(d) In *all other cases* the verbal in -ing is resolved into a *subordinate clause*, introduced by a subordinate conjunction [generally daß, or one compounded with daß, except in iv. below].

(i.) Verbal in -ing preceded by a *possessive adjective*, as : *he heard of my doing this* = er hörte, daß ich dies tat.

(ii.) Verbal in -ing preceded by a *Genitive*, as : *his father's knowing this does not seem to disturb him* = daß sein Vater dies weiß, scheint ihn nicht zu bekümmern.

(iii.) Verbal in -ing preceded by a *preposition* (except *instead of* and *without*, and sometimes *on* or *of* [see IV. *b* above] ; with these latter the Infinitive with zu is preferable) : *he is paid for playing* = er ist dafür bezahlt, daß er spielt [*for that, that he plays*].

(iv.) Verbal in -ing not dependent on another word, indicates *reason*, or *time*.

(aa) *reason :* translate the verbal in -ing by subordinate clause introduced by da or weil, *because*, as : *he could do it, being rich* = er konnte es tun, da (weil) er reich ist.

(bb) *time :* (A) referring to a past event, use als, *when* ; thus : *arriving at the river, he hesitated to cross over* = als er am Flusse ankam, zögerte er hinüberzusetzen.

(B) referring to an action taking place at the same time as another, use indem or während, *whilst*, as : *eating his dinner, he conversed with me* = während (or indem) er zu Mittag speiste, sprach er mit mir.

(C) referring to an action completed before another action, use nachdem, *after*, thus : *having done this, he went away* = nachdem er dies getan hatte, gieng er weg.

Examples and Exercises on Page 116.

On I. II. III.

Examples.

1. *Riding is very conducive to health, if it is not continued to complete exhaustion.*
2. *Cultivating the earth is an old and honourable occupation.*
3. *Do read instructive books, instead of these stupid novels, which are so exciting.*

1. Das Reiten ist der Gesundheit sehr günstig, wenn es nicht bis zur vollständigen Ermüdung fortgesetzt wird.
2. Das Bebauen der Erde ist ein alter und ehrenwerter Beruf.
3. Lesen Sie doch belehrende Bücher, statt dieser dummen Romane, die so aufregend sind.

Translate.

1. Seinen Mantel fester an sich ziehend, trotzte er dem Sturm.
2. Der Wunsch, Sie wieder zu sehen, bewog mich heute zu kommen.
3. Das Trinken und Spielen hat schon so Viele zu Grunde gerichtet.
4. Lassen Sie doch das Wetten; man verliert zuletzt ja doch immer dabei.

Exercise.

1. He loves hunting so much, that he neglects his business often.
2. The child possesses two birds, one [a] singing [one], and [the other] a speaking **one**.
3. A shrieking (gellend) whistling (Pfiff m.) announced the arrival of the train.
4. Let us understand that there is a need of going, and we will go at once (sogleich).
5. **It** is easy to spend money; it is not so easy to earn some (welches).

On IV.

Examples.

1. *Cease playing on that violin; hearing it all day long is disagreeable.*
2. *We saw two men bringing a heavy box up-stairs.*
3. *Without seeing it, we believe it.*

1. Hören Sie auf, die Geige zu spielen; es ist unangenehm das den ganzen Tag zu hören.
2. Wir sahen zwei Männer, welche eine schwere Kiste die Treppe hinauftrugen.
3. Ohne es zu sehen, glauben wir es.

Translate.

1. Als ich den Mann sah, rief ich ihm zu, er solle mir die Zeitung sogleich herbringen.
2. Da dieses Buch Ihrem Freunde gehört, ist es Ihre Pflicht, es ihm zurückzugeben, sobald Sie es zu Ende gelesen haben.
3. Indem er mit der einen Hand einen Zweig ergriff, streckte er die andere dem Ertrinkenden (drowning one) entgegen.
4. Nachdem der Zug (train) schon angefangen hatte, sich zu bewegen, sprang der Mann in ein Coupé (compartment) und verletzte (hurt) sich am Beine.

Exercise.

1. Believing [cause] this news, I sent at once to (nach) my friend.
2. We heard of your having passed (bestehen) this examination (Examen, n.).
3. **Did you see** that woman selling (who sold) apples in the market?
4. He often read a book, smoking his cigar, whilst we wrote our letters.
5. You were speaking of his playing the piano. (thereof that he . . . **played**.)

REFERENCE-PAGE LL.

Remarks on the Past Participle.

The **Past Participle**—

(a) used as a *verb*, is invariable, as: idy habe fie gefehen. Idiomatically the Past Participle as a verb may **replace a** whole sentence, as: Gefeßt, er fei arm=*Let us suppose, he is poor*; Zugegeben,=*I grant you*, etc.; or it may imply a command, as: Aufgeftanden! *Come, get up*, etc.

(b) used as an *adjective*, the Past Participle may be—
    (i) an attribute, declined like an adjective, as: der gebildete Menfd; ein geliebter Mann.
    (ii) a predicate and **invariable**, as: er ift gebildet, *he is educated*.

(c) used as a *noun*, the Past Participle changes like an adjective, as: der Gefangene, *the prisoner (caught-one)*; ein Gelehrter, *a learned man*.

N.B.—fommen and gehen sometimes form idiomatic phrases with the Past Participle **of** laufen, fliegen, verlieren, etc., as: er fommt geflogen=*he comes flying*; **das Buch ift verloren** gegangen=*the book has (gone) been lost*.

On the idiomatic use of some Tenses.

As a rule, English and German **agree with each other in the use of the Tenses**; it must however be remembered that **the English**: *I am* —*ing*; *I was* —*ing*; *I shall be* —*ing*; *I have been* —*ing*, etc., are quite inadmissible **forms in German**. The want of these descriptive forms is **supplied** by such words as eben, gerade, etc., **as**: *I was writing*, id) fdrieb eben, id) fdrieb gerade; **and so also in the other tenses.** Emphasis, as in *I do write*; *I did go*, must in German also be **expressed** by adverbials, **as**: id) fdreibe **wirflid);** id) gieng in der Tat.

  (i) **The** *Present*, often with nod), fogleid), etc., **often stands for a near future, as**: er fieht ihn nod) heute, =*he will see him to-day*; id) gehe fogleid)=*I'll go at once*.

  (ii) **The** *Imperfect* **in** English must be rendered by the *Perfect* in German, when an action completely **past is referred** to and not in relation to another past **action, as**: *I was in Paris. How long were you there?* Id) bin in Paris gewefen. Wie lange find Sie dort gewefen? (Implying that the stay in Paris is past and over.)

    a. If, however, the time **is fixed** by reference to another past action or event, the two languages **agree in the use of the Imperfect, as**: *He was in Paris during the siege*=Er war in Paris während der Belagerung.

    b. In mentioning actions recently passed, and in colloquial sentences, the Germans prefer the **Perfect to the Imperfect, as**: *I was there yesterday*=id) bin geftern dort gewefen.

  (iii) **The** English *Perfect*, referring to an action distinctly understood as *uncompleted* at the time of speaking, must be rendered into German by the Present tense, with fd)on (*already*) or feit (*since*); as: *How long have you been in Rome?*=Wie lange find Sie fd)on in Rom? *I have been here two years*= Id) bin feit zwei Jahren hier. (Implying that he is still in Rome.)

[The other tenses present no difficulties.]

Examples and Exercises on Page 118.

On I.

Examples.

1. **Take care!** There is **a carriage coming! Let it** drive past.
2. Granted, that he is on the road to recovery, it will be a long time before he is quite well, as before.
3. **The** people have not **yet received the promised** present.

1. Aufgepaßt! da kommt ein Wagen gefahren. Laßt ihn vorüberfahren.
2. Angenommen, er sei auf dem Wege der Besserung, so wird es doch noch lange gehen, bis er ganz **gesund** ist, wie früher.
3. Die Leute haben das **versprochene** Geschenk noch **nicht erhalten.**

Translate.

1. Frisch in's Wasser gegangen! **Es ist nicht zu kalt.**
2. Verloren! **Es bleibt mir** nichts übrig, als nach Hause zu gehen und dem Spiele zu entsagen.
3. Die Gelehrten sind nicht einig, ob diese Münze von den Griechen oder den Persern abstamme.
4. Aufgesessen! (To horse!) Vorwärts! frisch in die Schlacht geritten.

Exercise.

1. These parents have lost three of their beloved children.
2. "Loved and Lost" is the title (Titel, *m.*) of a much-admired waltz (Walzer, *m.*).
3. Alas! one of my gloves has been (gone) lost at the ball; I am ashamed.
4. Don't beg always, why not work? (Use Past Participle.)
5. Granted that he is rich, he should not forget that he may (can) become poor again.

On II.

Examples.

1. Although I do not know the people, yet *I'll* see if *I* cannot help them.
2. She came *into the room as he was sitting down to* (*his*) *dinner.*
3. *We* **do** *admire the singer whom we have just been hearing.*

1. Obgleich ich die Leute nicht kenne, will ich **doch** sehen, ob ich Ihnen nicht helfen kann.
2. Sie kam in das Zimmer, als er sich eben zum Mittagessen niedergesetzt hatte.
3. Wir bewundern den Sänger in der Tat, den wir **soeben** gehört haben.

Translate.

1. Wie lange sind Sie schon in Paris? Ich bin schon seit drei Wochen hier, aber ich langweile mich.
2. Waren Sie je in St. Petersburg während des Winters? Man macht sich keine Vorstellung (*idea*) von der Kälte.
3. **Reisen Sie heute noch ab?** Ja, ich muß morgen in Hamburg sein.
4. Kann der Herr Englisch? Nein, und doch **lernt er** es schon seit zwei Jahren; er ist schon **mehr als** zwei Jahre in England und nimmt Stunden im Englischen.

Exercise.

1. Where were you? (Perf.) I was in my room (Impf.) when you arrived.
2. I do like to hear the cuckoo (Kukuk, *m.*); I am often listening to it (zuhören, dat.).
3. How long has he been learning German? He has been learning it for a whole year **(acc.)**.
4. Were you in Paris at the time of the Exhibition (Ausstellung, *f.*) of (von) 1878?
5. We should have seen you, if it had not been such a (a so) dark night.

Some Idioms and Proverbs.

To speak at random.	In den Tag hinein reden.—Dummheiten sagen.
To eat humble pie.	Zu Kreuze kriechen (lit. *crawl to the cross*).
He is ruined.	Er ist zu Grunde gerichtet; er ist ruiniert.
This man is very conceited.	Dieser Mensch ist sehr von sich eingenommen.
To try to lay aside the idea of a thing.	Versuchen, sich Etwas aus dem Sinne zu schlagen.
It is not becoming to say this.	Es schickt sich nicht, dies zu sagen.
I am sorry; I like to dance.	Es tut mir leid; ich tanze gern (*willingly*).
They condemned him.	Sie brachen den Stab über ihn.
It is customary with us.	Es ist bei uns Rechtens.—Es ist der Brauch.
You came off second-best.	Sie haben den Kürzeren gezogen.
We assist our friends.	Wir greifen unseren Freunden unter die Arme.
This uniform suits him.	Diese Uniform steht ihm gut.
To put aside childish things.	**Die Kinderschuhe vertreten.**
You did not get on well, Sir.	**Sie haben es nicht weit gebracht,** mein Herr.
He has brought his pigs to market.	**Er hat alles an den Mann gebracht.**
Every one has his hobby.	**Jeder hat sein Steckenpferd.**
He is badly off: he is very ill.	**Es steht schlecht mit ihm;** er ist sehr krank.
They live in fine style, indeed.	Sie leben auf hohem Fuße in der Tat.
He attaches importance to it.	Es ist ihm viel daran (an der Sache) gelegen.
We will pass it over.	Wir wollen Ihnen durch die Finger sehen.
Things may take a turn.	Das Blatt kann sich wenden.
That is of no importance.	Das hat Nichts zu sagen.—Es ist alles Eins.
You must put up with it.	Sie müssen sich darein **schicken.**
He was well liked here.	Er war hier wohl gelitten.
What (whom) do you take me for?	Für was (Für wen) halten Sie mich?
Be careful of your clothes, children.	Gebt Acht auf **euere Kleider, Kinder!**

Some very common **Proverbs.**

All is well that ends well.	Ende gut, Alles gut.
More haste less speed.	Eile mit Weile.
Birds of a feather flock together.	Gleich und gleich gesellt sich gern.
Practice makes perfect.	Uebung macht den Meister.
Nothing venture, nothing win.	Wer nichts wagt, **gewinnt nichts.**
Lightly come, lightly gone.	Wie gewonnen, so zerronnen.
Like father like son.	Der Apfel fällt nicht weit vom Stamme.
With the Romans do as the Romans do.	Mit den Wölfen muß man heulen.
The early bird picks up the worm.	Morgenstund' hat Gold im Mund.
To-morrow is soon enough!	„Morgen, morgen, nur nicht heute,'
(Excuse for procrastination.)	Sagen alle faulen Leute!"

POEM.

(To be learnt by heart during this Term.)

Die Drei Indianer (Lenau, 1802-50).

1. Mächtig zürnt der Himmel im Gewitter;
   Schmettert manche Rieseneich' in Splitter;
   Uebertönt des Niagara's Stimme;
   Und mit seiner Blitze Flammenruten
   Peitscht er schneller die beschäumten Fluten,
   Daß sie stürzen mit empörtem Grimme.

2. Indianer steh'n am lauten Strande,
   Lauschen nach dem wilden Wogenbrande,
   Nach des Waldes bangem Sterbgestöhne.
   Greis der Eine, mit ergrautem Haare,
   Aufrecht, überragend seine Jahre,
   Die zwei andern, seine starken Söhne.

3. Seine Söhne jetzt der Greis betrachtet;
   Und sein Blick sich dunkler jetzt umnachtet,
   Als die Wolken, die den Himmel schwärzen;
   Und sein Aug' versendet wild're Blitze,
   Als das Wetter durch die Wolkenritze;
   Und er spricht aus tief empörtem Herzen:

4. „Fluch den Weißen! Ihren letzten Spuren!
   „Jeder Welle Fluch, worauf sie fuhren,
   „Die einst, Bettler, unsern Strand erklettert!
   „Fluch dem Windhauch, dienstbar ihrem Schiffe!

   „Hundert Flüche jedem Felsenriffe,
   „Daß sie nicht hat in den Grund geschmettert!

5. „Täglich über's Meer in wilder Eile
   „Fliegen ihre Schiffe, gift'ge Pfeile;
   „Treffen unsr're Küste mit Verderben!
   „Nichts hat uns die Räuberbrut gelassen,
   „Als im Herzen tödtlich bitt'res Hassen;
   „Kommt, ihr Kinder, kommt; wir wollen sterben!"

6. Also sprach der Alte, und sie schneiden
   Ihren Nachen von den Uferweiden.
   Drauf sie nach des Stromes Mitte ringen,
   Und nun werfen sie weithin die Ruder.
   Armverschlungen, Vater, Sohn und Bruder
   Stimmen an, ihr Sterbelied zu singen.

7. Laut' ununterbroch'ne Donner krachen;
   Blitze flattern um den Todesnachen;
   Ihn umtaumeln Möven, sturmesmunter.
   Und die Männer kommen festentschlossen
   Singend schon dem Falle zugeschossen,
   Stürzen jetzt den Katarakt hinunter.

The Three Indians.

(Literal Translation.)

1. Majestically angry is the sky in its thunderstorm;
   It rends many a giant oak into fragments;
   It drowns the Niagara Falls' voice;
   And with the flaming rods of its lightning
   It whips into more rapid motion the foaming waters,
   So that they rush down in riotous fury.

2. Some Indians are standing by the noisy bank
   Listening to the wild breaking of the waves,
   And to the trembling death-groans of the forest.
   The one an old man, with hair turned grey,
   But upright, overtowering his old age,
   The two others, his strong sons.

3. And now the old man looks at his sons,
   And his glance becomes gloomy with a
   Gloom darker than the clouds which blacken the sky;
   And his eyes sends forth lightnings, fiercer
   Than the storm through the rifts in the clouds;
   And he speaks, from his deeply wrathful heart:

4. "Curses upon the White men! Upon their furthest steps!
   "Curses upon every wave, on which they rode,
   "They who once, beggars, climbed on our shore!
   "Curses upon each breath of wind wafting onward their ships!
   "A hundred curses upon each rocky reef
   "That did not wreck them utterly!

5. "Day by day across the Sea in wild haste
   "Fly their ships, empoisoned arrows,
   "Striking our shores with ruin!
   "Nothing that brood of robbers has left us
   "Save in our hearts a deadly, bitter hatred;
   "Come, my children, come; we will die!"

6. Thus spoke the old man, and they cut loose
   Their canoe from the willows of the bank.
   Then they struggle towards the centre of the stream,
   And now they throw afar their oars.
   Interlacing their arms, father, son, and brother
   Begin to sing their song of death.

7. Loudly roars the unceasing thunder;
   Lightnings flash like ribbons around the death canoe,
   Sea-gulls tumble round it, rejoicing in the storm.
   And the men are coming, firmly resolved,
   Shooting towards the Falls, and still singing,
   Now they dash down the cataract.

A piece from Schiller's "The Bell."

(To be learnt by heart.)

Literal rendering.

1. Wohltätig ist des Feuers Macht,
   Wenn sie der Mensch bezähmt, bewacht;
   Und was er bildet, was er schafft,
   Das dankt er dieser Himmelskraft.
5. Doch furchtbar wird die Himmelskraft,
   Wenn sie der Fessel sich entrafft,
   Einhertritt auf der eig'nen Spur,
   Die freie Tochter der Natur!
9. **Wehe, wenn sie losgelassen,**
   Wachsend, ohne Widerstand,
   Durch die volkbelebten Gassen
   Wälzt den ungeheuren Brand!
13. Denn die Elemente hassen
    Das Gebild der Menschenhand.
    Aus den Wolken quillt der Segen,
    Strömt der Regen;
17. **Aus der Wolke ohne Wahl**
    Zuckt der Strahl!
    Hört ihr 's wimmern hoch vom Turm?
    Das ist Sturm!
21. **Rot wie Blut**
    Ist der Himmel.
    Das ist nicht des Tages Glut!
    Welch' Getümmel
25. Straßen auf!
    Dampf wallt auf!
    Flackernd steigt die Feuersäule;
    Durch der Straße lange Zeile
29. Wächst es fort mit Windeseile.
    Kochend, wie aus Ofens Rachen
    Glüh'n die Lüfte; Balken krachen;
    Pfosten stürzen; Fenster klirren;
33. **Kinder jammern; Mütter irren;**
    Tiere wimmern unter Trümmern;
    Alles rennet, rettet, flüchtet;
    Taghell ist die Nacht gelichtet;

1. Beneficent is the strength of fire
   As long as man restrains and watches it;
   And whate'er he fashions, whate'er he creates,
   He owes to this heavenly power.
5. But awful is this heavenly power,
   When she casts off her fetters
   And strides onward in her own tracks
   The released daughter of Nature!
9. *Woe, if unrestrained,*
   Ever growing, unopposed,
   Through the populous streets
   She rolls the monstrous conflagration!
13. *For the elements do hate*
    The creations of human hands.
    Down from the clouds flows blessing,
    Pours the rain;
17. *Down from the clouds without favour*
    Flashes the lightning.
    Hear ye the wailing from the high steeple?
    That means: "Fire!"
21. *Red like blood*
    Are the heavens.
    That is not the sun's glow!
    What crowding
25. *All along the streets!*
    Steam rolls upwards!
    Flickering ascends the column of fire;
    Through the street's long row of houses
29. *Onwards it moves with the speed of the wind.*
    Red hot, as from the mouth of an oven
    The air glows; *beams are crashing;*
    Pillars falling; windows rattling;
33. *Children wailing; mothers straying;*
    Beasts are whining under ruins;
    Each one hurries, saves, rescues;
    Darkness is illumined to broad daylight.

37. Durch der Hände lange Kette, Um die Wette Fliegt der Eimer; hoch im Bogen Spritzen Quellen, Wasserwogen.	37. Through long chains of hands, In eager rivalry, Fly the fire-buckets; up in high arches, Fountains are rising, floods of water.
41. Heulend kommt der Sturm geflogen, Der die Flamme brausend sucht. Prasselnd in die dürre Frucht Fällt sie, in des Speichers Räume,	41. Howling the storm-wind comes rushing, That, roaring, seeks the flames. **Upon the dry crops, hissing** **They fall, and into the rooms** of the storehouse,
45. In der Sparren dürre Bäume; Und als wollte sie im Wehen Mit sich fort der Erde Wucht Reißen in gewalt'ger Flucht,	45. **And the** dry beams of the wood-work; And as if with their breath they wished Heavenwards to tear the whole earth's weight In one mighty rush,
49. Wächst e in des Himmels Höhen Riesengroß!—Hoffnungslos Weicht der Mensch der Götterstärke! Müßig sieht er seine Werke	49. **They grow into** the heights of heaven Giantlike.—**Bereft of hope,** **Man yields to divine force!** **Idle and yet admiring, he beholds**
53. Und bewundernd untergehen.—	53. **His works being destroyed.—**
Leergebrannt ist die Stätte, Wilder Stürme rauhes Bette. In den öden Fensterhöhlen	Burnt out is the homestead, Of wild storms now the rough bed. In the empty window-caverns
57. Wohnt das Grauen, Und des Himmels Wolken schauen Hoch hinein.—Einen Blick Nach dem Grabe seiner Habe	57. **Horror dwells,** And Heaven's clouds gaze in From on high.—One glance only Towards the grave **of his possessions**
61. Sendet noch der Mensch zurück; Greift fröhlich dann zum Wanderstabe. Was Feuerswuth ihm auch geraubt, Ein süßer Trost ist ihm geblieben:	61. Does man cast back; Then he cheerfully seizes his wanderer's staff. **Whate'er the fire's fury** may have deprived him of, **One** sweet consolation remains to him:
65. Er zählt die Häupter seiner Lieben, Und sieh'! ihm fehlt kein teures Haupt.	65. **He counts the heads of his loved ones,** And, lo, not one dear head is missing.

Die drei bedeutendsten deutschen Dichter waren:

    Göthe (Johann Wolfgang von), geboren **zu Frankfurt am Main**, den 28ten August **1749**; gestorben zu Weimar den 22ten März 1832.
    Schiller (Friedrich), geboren zu Marbach den 11ten November 1759; gestorben zu Weimar den 9ten Mai 1805.
    Lessing (Gotthold Ephraim), geboren zu **Camenz** den 22ten Januar 1729; gestorben zu Braunschweig, den 15ten Februar 1781.

Short piece for Composition.

Notice.—Do not omit to refer to the pages mentioned for reference here.

A young man had for several days been suffering[1] from[2] severe[3] toothache[4] and resolved[5] at last[6] to go to a dentist[7] and have his tooth drawn[8]. He went slowly[9] to the dentist's house but came out[10] again very soon. One of his friends seeing him coming out from the dentist's house, and observing[12] that he looked[13] quite[13] happy, said to him: "Ah! I see, you have got rid of[14] that tooth at last; you look quite happy; I congratulate[15] you!" "Oh no," answered the young man, "what makes me look so happy is, that the dentist was not at home!"

Words to above.

1. *to suffer* = leiben, irregular. See p. 50.
2. *from* = an (dat.). See p. 98, *from* (e).
3. *severe* = ſtarf. See p. 28.
4. *toothache* = Zahnweh (n.).
5. *to resolve* = ſich (acc.) entſchließen. See p. 51 (ſchließen).
6. *at last* = endlich, zuletzt.
7. *the dentist* = der Zahn'arzt, —es, —e.
8. *have drawn* = herausʻziehen laſſen. See p. 51 (irregular).
9. *slowly* = langſam (adverb).
10. *to come out (again)* = (wieder) heraus'kommen, separable verb, irregular. See kommen, p. 50.
11. *to observe* = beobachten, regular and inseparable.
12. *to look* = ausʻſehen, separable, irreg. See p. 51.
13. *quite* = ganz (adverb).
14. *to get rid of* = losʻwerden, separable (like werden) with accusative.
15. *to congratulate* = Glück wünſchen, regular, with dative.

Order of the above in German.

N.B.—Study the reasons given here very carefully. By referring to PAGE 83, the numbers above the various parts of the Sentences will be understood.

[The order of words will be found strictly adhering to the rules given on page 83.]

$\underset{1}{\text{A young man}}$ $\underset{2}{\text{had}}$ $\underset{4}{\text{several days}^a}$ from severe toothache $\underset{6}{\text{suffered}}$ — and $\underset{2}{\text{resolved}}$ $\underset{3}{\text{himself}}$ $\underset{4}{\text{at last}}$, — $\underset{4}{\text{to (zu) a dentist}}$ $\underset{7}{\text{to go}}$ — and $\underset{3}{\text{his tooth}}$ $\underset{7}{\text{drawn to have}}$.^{b} — He went slowly^c to the house of the dentist, — but $\underset{2}{\text{came}}$ $\underset{4}{\text{very}}$ $\underset{5}{\text{soon}^c}$ again out. — When^d one of his friends him out-of the house of the dentist $\underset{7}{\text{come}}^m$ $\underset{2}{\text{saw}}$,^{e} — and^d $\underset{2}{\text{observed}}$ — that $\underset{1}{\text{he}}$ $\underset{4}{\text{quite}}$ $\underset{5}{\text{happy}}$ $\underset{2}{\text{out-looked}}$,^{f} — said he^g to him: — "Ah! I see, — $\underset{1}{\text{you}}$ $\underset{2}{\text{(have)}}$ $\underset{3}{\text{are}}$ $\underset{4}{\text{your tooth}}$ $\underset{6}{\text{at last}}$ $\underset{5}{\text{got-rid-of}}$; — $\underset{1}{\text{you}}$ $\underset{2}{\text{look}}$ $\underset{3}{\text{quite}}$ happy out; I wish you^h luck!" — $\underset{3}{\text{"Oh, no,"}}$ $\underset{2}{\text{answered}}$ $\underset{1}{\text{the young man}}$, — "what me so happy out-look makes,^{i} — is, — that the dentist $\underset{4}{\text{not at home}}$ $\underset{2}{\text{was}}$.^{k}

a. Adverbials of time precede others.
b. Of two infinitives put that of the auxiliary last. [See p. 83.]
c. Of two adverbials put that of *place* last, and that of *time* first.
d. *Seeing* and *Coming* must be resolved into subordinate clauses. [See p. 116, IV. d. iv. bb.]
e. Assertion at end of subordinate clause.
f. In subordinate clause no separation can take place.
g. The principal clause *must* have a subject, and it stands after the Assertion, when a subordinate clause precedes.
h. Of two objects the Pronoun comes before the Noun.
i. In relative clauses the Assertion stands last.
k. In subordinate clauses the Assertion stands last.
l. [See p. 112, note to A. 4.]
m. [See p. 112, A. 5.]

Longer Sentences. Exercises for Analysing.

Carefully divide each long sentence into its constituent parts, considering apart each Principal, each Subordinate, and each Relative sentence, and referring to Pages 83 and 124 as to the sequence of words in each clause.

Example of analysing a longer German sentence:

^aWilhelm von Oranien gehörte zu den hagern und blassen Menschen^a, ^bwie Cäsar sie nennt^b, ^cdie des Nachts nicht schlafen und zu viel denken^c, ^dvor denen das furchtloseste aller Gemüter gewankt hat^d. ^eDie stille Ruhe eines immer gleichen Gesichts verbarg eine geschäftige, feurige Seele^e, ^fdie auch die Hülle, ^ghinter welcher sie schuf, nicht bewegte, und der List und der Liebe gleich unbetretbar war^f; ^heinen vielfachen, fruchtbaren, nie ermüdenden Geist^h, ⁱweich und bildsam genugⁱ, ^kaugenblicklich in alle Formen zu schmelzen^k; ^lbewährt genug^l, ^kin keiner sich selbst zu verlieren^k; ⁱstark genugⁱ, ^kjeden Glückswechsel zu ertragen^k.   Schiller.

(Translate the above carefully.)

[a-a] Principal Sentence; [b-b] Subordinate, therefore Assertion nennt at the end; [c-c] Compound relative clause to Menschen; Assertions schlafen and denken at the end of each component; [d-d] Relative clause to Menschen; Assertion hat at the end. ——[e-e] Principal Sentence; [f-f] Compound relative clause to Seele; Assertions bewegte and war at the end of each component; notice: the first part not disturbed in its sequence of words by the interpolated relative clause; [g-g] Relative clause to Hülle with the Assertion schuf at its own end; [h-h] direct object to the verb verbarg in [e-e]; [i-i] predicative adjectives, enlarged by Infinitive clauses [k-k]. (See page 114, iii. b, for these [k-k] clauses.)

Analyse the above sentence in detail, also as shown on Page 84 (at the foot).

Translate and analyse in the same way, both generally and minutely, the following:

i. Vielen protestantischen Predigern, die um der Religion willen Verfolgungen auszustehen hatten, ließ Katharina von Schwarzburg Schutz und Unterstützung angedeihen. Unter diesen war ein gewisser Kaspar Aquila, Pfarrer zu Saalfeld, der in jüngeren Jahren der Armee des Kaisers als Feldprediger nach den Niederlanden gefolgt war, und, weil er sich dort geweigert hatte, eine Kanonenkugel zu taufen, von den ausgelassenen Soldaten in einen Feuermörser geladen wurde, um in die Luft geschossen zu werden; ein Schicksal, dem er noch glücklich entkam, weil das Pulver nicht zünden wollte.   Schiller.

ii. Dann giengen wir in die Sixtinische Kapelle, die wir auch hell und heiter, und die Gemälde wohlerleuchtet fanden. Das „jüngste Gericht," und die mannigfaltigen Gemälde der Decke, von Michel Angelo, teilten unsere Bewunderung. Ich konnte nur sehen und anstaunen. Die innere Sicherheit und Männlichkeit des Meisters geht über allen Ausdruck. Nachdem wir Alles wieder und wieder gesehen, verließen wir dieses Heiligtum und giengen nach der St. Peterskirche.   Goethe.

Longer Sentences for Composition.

Carefully **divide** the English first into **the** separate Principal, Subordinate, and **Relative** clauses, and refer to page 83 for the sequence of words in each clause **separately**. [See also page 124, and pages 76-79.]

Example:

English.

Having heard, that your friend possessed some very *rare*[a] *specimens*[b] of *butterflies*,[c] and knowing that he *is always pleased*[d], to show his *collections*[e] to the friends of his friends, *I took the liberty*[f] of *calling*[g] upon him last Saturday, when I was in town ; I was *delighted*[h] *with* all that he showed me, and *in fact*[i] almost *envied*[k] him his treasures, some of which were *really*[l] *magnificent*[m].

Order of words in German.

As I heard had[o,n], that your friend some very rare specimens of butterflies *possessed*,[o] and *as I know*[o,n], that he always pleasure *has*[o], his collections to-the friends of-his friends to[p] *show*, so *took*[q] I to-me the liberty, him *last Saturday*[q], when I in the town was,[o] to[p] *visit* ; I was of all, which he to-me *showed*[r], delighted and in the deed, envied him almost about his treasures, of *which*[s] some really magnificent were[r].

Words to above.

[a] *rare* = felten.   [b] *the specimen* = die Art.
[c] *the butterfly* = der Schmetterling, -s, -e.
[d] *to be pleased* = Vergnügen haben.
[e] *the collection* = die Sammlung, —, —en.
[f] *to take the liberty* = sich (dat.) die Freiheit nehmen.
[g] *to call upon some one* = Jemand (acc.) besuchen.
[h] *to be delighted with* = entzückt sein, von (dat.).
[i] *in fact* = in der Tat (dat. feminine).
[k] *to envy some one something* = Jemand (acc.) um Etwas (acc.) beneiden.
[l] *really* = wirklich.
[m] *magnificent* = prachtvoll.

Notes to above.

[n] See page 116, iv. d., iv. aa. Translation of Verbal in *-ing*.
[o] Assertion last in Subordinate clauses.
[p] See page 114, iv. Translation of Infinitive after Nouns.
[q] Use accusative of definite time referred to.
[r] Assertion last in Relative clauses.
[s] The relative clause *must* begin with the relative pronoun (or its preposition), therefore *some* must follow *of which* (von denen).
[t] The Assertion in the Principal Sentence stands before the Subject, if any Subordinate clauses precede the Principal one. See page 83, A, b.

Turn first into German order of words, and then translate (with use of Dictionary).

Having arrived on the summit of the mountain, | we contemplated the view before us in mute admiration. | We were indeed scarcely prepared for such a grand spectacle, | for the mountain, | upon which we stood, | was not a very high one, | yet the landscape below us was not only lovely, but also very extensive ; | and, what lent it a special charm for us, | was the belt of snow-capped mountains, | which framed the picture in the distance. | We were delighted with what we saw | and counted ten lakes | peeping out here and there, | and four rivers, silver ribbons, | winding through the deep green of hill and vale.

SIXTH TERM

ON ETYMOLOGY AND WORD-FORMATION

WITH A SHORT

HISTORICAL OUTLINE OF THE GRADUAL GROWTH OF THE

GERMAN LANGUAGE

INTO AN INDEPENDENT IDIOM.

IN these Notes the author must acknowledge valuable aid from the excellent *Deutsche Grammatik in genetischer Zusammenstellung* of Dr. Ernst Götzinger, Professor in St. Gallen; and also from the *Etymological Dictionary* by Friedrich Kluge.

HISTORICAL OUTLINE.

The following remarks do not by any means claim to enter very deeply into the subject of German Etymology; they are merely intended to illustrate in broad outlines some very interesting facts as to the relation of German, and in fact of most of the languages now-a-days spoken in Europe, with Latin and Greek, and the descent of all these from the same ancient idiom, they may thus awaken in some students a desire of examining German words a little more closely; in any case they will enable them to answer the greater number of those questions in Etymology and Word-formation which are now set in most higher examinations in German.

There is no doubt that the study of the etymology of a modern language has a very great fascination for a student, when he is in other ways more or less acquainted with those older languages to which he is constantly referred. It is for this reason mainly that the tracing back of French words, for example, to their Latin or Greek origin has so long found great favour with students in English schools, for they are generally pretty well acquainted with at least classical Latin, and naturally recognise with pleasure ancestors of modern French words, as far as the tonic syllable is concerned, in Latin roots which they have met with previously in their study of Caesar or Cicero, Livy or Tacitus, Ovid or Vergil. But when such languages as Old High- and Low-German, Anglo-Saxon or Gothic, the acquaintance with which in other ways is naturally much rarer and less cultivated than Latin or Greek, are the main sources to which etymology points, it is little wonder that the researches should not be pursued with quite so much interest. Still the following general remarks will show that the study of German etymology brings us very often in contact both with Latin and Greek, and thus proves conclusively that the languages now spoken in Northern Europe belong to one and the same great trunk, of which the classical languages of Athens and Rome were only the earliest fixed branches.

The monuments of the literature of the oldest inhabitants of Upper India and Persia, the cuneiform characters on buildings and statues discovered there lately from time to time, point, in the light of Comparative Philology, to the important fact, that all the races which successively peopled Europe are descended originally from one and the same people, speaking one and the same language; and that in fact the ancestors of the Keltic and Teutonic and Selavonian races were the same as those of the Greeks and the Romans. The period of this identity of language is generally computed to have been some 3000 or 4000 years before our Christian era, and the locality where these ancestors lived was the South Central portion of Asia, i.e. Upper India and the plateaux between the Himalaya and the Caucasus. For want of a better name, the races which came thence have been collectively called Aryan, or Indo-Keltic, or Indo-Germanic, or Indo-European. Their original language, of which Sanscrit is held to be the nearest representative, seems to have been exceedingly capable of flexible modification and enlargement, though of course, compared with the idioms which sprung from it, very undeveloped and poor in ideas and views; indeed the objects and thoughts which required interpretation in language must have been very limited compared with later times.

The researches of philology reveal pretty much the same manner of spreading both of those nations and of those idioms as common-sense reasoning would have suggested. The broad outlines seem to be these: From Upper India parts of the original race, as it increased in numbers, overflowed towards China and the East, whilst parts travelled westward. It is these latter Japhetic races which are called Indo-European, and with which we are dealing now. They peopled Persia and Armenia, where the *Persian or Zend idiom* established itself on the banks of the Euphrates and Tigris, supplanting partly the (Semitic) Assyrian and Arabian. The overflow of this population, and also new portions from the other Asiatic plateaux, travelled more northward, and entered Europe, either through Asia Minor or by coasting the northern shores of the Black Sea, and thus our continent became peopled. As these races multiplied and separated, their idioms also became more and more changed, being exposed to different influences and meeting with different circumstances, until in the South of Europe the GREEK idiom, and later the LATIN, stood early fixed by the mighty works of great writers, and became ultimately the parents (mostly by the agency of Roman conquest) of modern French, Italian, Spanish, Portuguese, etc., whilst in the North of Europe the GOTHIC idiom established itself, and, dividing into *Scandinavian* and *Teutonic*, became ultimately the parent of modern German, English, Danish, Dutch, Swedish, etc. The KELTIC idiom in the centre of Europe, having never been spoken by a ruling and conquering nation, seems early to have been doomed to extinction, and survives now only in the *Kymric* of Wales, with which the Breton of Brittany and the extinct Cornish of Cornwall are nearly related, and the *Gaelic* of Northern Scotland, to which the Erse or Irish and the Manx of the Isle of Man are akin. As to the SCLAVONIC idiom, it remained behind in the East of Europe, where it became the parent of modern Russian, Sclavonian, Servian, and Czech in Bohemia.

The following Diagram shows these divisions:—

Indo-European Languages (Japhetic) in Europe.

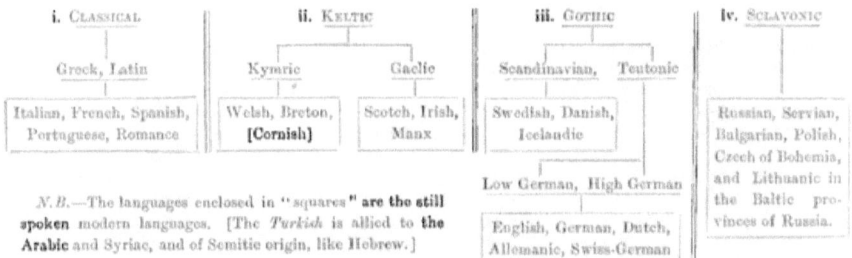

N.B.—The languages enclosed in "squares" **are the still spoken** modern languages. [The *Turkish* is allied to the **Arabic** and Syriac, and of Semitic origin, like Hebrew.]

Now these minor divisions of races and languages did not, as a rule, succeed each other chronologically, but took place mostly at about the same time ; thus the student must distinctly understand that it is not necessarily true that a German or English word is *derived* from, say, the Greek or Latin, for the sole reason that these latter languages, containing the same root in a slightly different form, were fixed at an earlier period of time. All we can say in a great

R

many instances is, that the word in a modern language is evidently related to that in the earlier idiom, and that both evidently come from the same original Indo-European root, which changed differently or assumed a different shade of meaning with the different races. Thus it would be wrong to assume that **Vater** (*father*) is *derived* from the Latin *pater*; all we can say is, that both the German and the Latin words come from the old Indo-European word *pátr* or *pitr*, which in its turn points to the root *pâ*, conveying the sense of nourishing or protecting. Still more erroneous would it be to say that the English "father" is *derived* from the German **Vater**, or *vice versa*; the two words simply point to the common origin of German and English, and it is doubtful which of the two is the older.

In examining the etymology of some modern words, the student will often notice that there is no similar word, interpreting the same idea, in the one or other of the older idioms, whilst on the other hand a root of an older idiom seems to have left no trace in the modern language. This is due mainly to the following facts: (i.) After separation, the races met each with different circumstances and objects, and formed words to interpret them, these new roots being unknown to other races; (ii.) Roots originally common to different races were gradually lost in some whilst being retained and amplified in others; (iii.) Certain roots gradually assumed distinct shades of meaning in some languages which they did not assume in others. Examples of all these are of very common occurrence.

That however all the nations now peopling Europe, as well as the old Greeks and Latins, did originally belong to one and the same race, allows of no doubt. Examine only the following striking examples by the light of the laws of Vowel and Consonant changes, of which we shall speak later on :—

1. *Words interpreting relationship.*—These were naturally much more numerous and varied in nomadic races, living together in tribes or families in patriarchal fashion, and though many such words detailing relationship are lost (as, for example, the distinction between uncle on the father's side and uncle on the mother's side [cf. Latin *patruus* and *avunculus*]), yet many remain, which evidently all point to one common **origin**. Compare, for example:

German.	English.	Dutch.	French.	Anglo-Saxon.	Gothic.	Latin.	Greek.	Sanskrit.
Mutter	mother	moeder	mère	môdor	[aithei]	mater	μήτηρ	mâtr (mā—)
Vater	father	vader	père	faeder	fadar [atta]	pater	πατήρ	patr, pitr (pā—)
Schwester	sister	zuster	sœur	sweostor	swistar	soror	[φρατήρ]	swasr

[and others which will be found in the appended Dictionary.]

2. *The numerals* (up to a hundred at least):—

zwei	two	twee	deux	twéné, twá	twai	duo	δύο	dva
zehn	ten	tien (tyn)	dix	téhan	taihun	decem	δέκα	dekn, daçan

3. *Names of parts of the human body:*—

Fuß	foot	voet	pied	fôt	fôtus	ped—	πούδ—	pód—
Zahn	tooth	tand	dent	toth (tanth)	tunthus	dent—	ὀδοντ—	dant—

4. *Names of very common domestic animals:—*

Hund	hound	hond	chien	hund	hunds	canis	κύων	çvn
Wolf	wolf	wolf	[loup]	wulf	wulfs	lupus	λύκ—	vlka

5. *Names of the most common phenomena in nature :—*

German.	English.	Dutch.	French.	Anglo-Saxon.	Gothic.	Latin.	Greek.	Sanskrit.
Tag	day	dag	(jour)	dæg	dags	dies	—	dina
Nacht	night	nacht	nuit	naht	nahts	noct—	νύκτ—	nokt—

6. *Some words interpreting common actions or qualities :—*

essen	eat	eten	[—]	etan	itan	ĕd—	ĕδ—	ĕd—
neu	new	nieuw	neuf	niwe	niujis	nov—	νέος	navas

These are only samples of many more; still it must not be supposed that the number of words which can thus be almost faultlessly traced back to their Indo-European root (as best represented by the old Sanskrit) is exceedingly large; the three reasons mentioned on page 130 will indeed account for many omissions and losses; besides, many words seem to allow of no explanation; but on the whole, the above leave little doubt that all the languages mentioned are closely related to each other, and come from the same ancient idiom.

To turn from these general remarks to the specially Indo-Germanic races, *i.e.* the Teutonic, it seems that the separation of these from the other Indo-European races, *i.e.* the Greeks, Latins, etc., took place somewhere about 2000 years before Christ, and that about the beginning of the Christian era the characteristically Teutonic transformation of vowels and consonants began to establish itself firmly. At this period, too, the Teutons and Kelts came again into contact with the conquering Romans, and the influence of the latter in a linguistic direction is very pronounced. A host of new words enriched the Gothic idiom, especially words connected with religion, politics, law, weights and measures, cooking, building, and the produce of the earth. We shall refer to this again later on. That the Gothic was a fully established idiom, rich in beauty and wealth of form, already in the fourth century after Christ, is proved by the well-known translation of the Greek Bible into Gothic by Bishop Ulfilas in that century. This Bible contains about 4000 fixed words. From that early period up to our days the development of German can be closely followed through Old and Middle High German. It culminates at last, early in the sixteenth century, in the translation of the Bible by Luther and Melanchthon, which work fixed the German language just as much as Chaucer's works fixed the English.

The earliest elements of language are: (i.) words interpreting objects and their actions or qualities (*Verb* and *Noun* with *Adjective*); (ii.) words interpreting individuality (*Personal Pronouns*) or pointing out objects, etc. (*Demonstratives*). To these were soon added words interpreting relation of time and place (*Prepositions* and *Adverbs*) and words joining or separating ideas or conceptions (*Conjunctions*). Of these none lent themselves to development except the first class; hence the stock of the other classes is limited and incapable of increase. But Verbs and Nouns with the Adjective [which is in reality also a verbal function applied to state or condition (for *great* refers to the state or condition of "being-great," etc.)] are capable of almost unlimited extension by calling in the aid of prepositions and adverbs as prefixes or suffixes, or by combining with other Verbs or Nouns; with this distinction, however, that Noun can combine with Noun or Verb, but Verb cannot combine with Verb. We can, for example, combine Haus with Garten, and get Hausgarten or Gartenhaus; but we cannot combine "to eat" and "to drink" to get a new verb "to eat-drink" or "to drink-eat."

Of these combinations we shall speak further under the heading of "Word Formation;" here we may simply mention that the capacity of German, perhaps more than any other language, is enormous in this respect. It is computed that of Nouns alone Modern German has close upon 100,000 different **forms, and of** Verbs perhaps above 50,000. **For** example, **Haus** appears in some sixty or seventy combinations, and **winden**, with its cognate **wenden** and **wandeln**, enters into the formation **of** above 900 words now.

Certainly this is true only of the latest perfection of German, still the Old Gothic idiom bore this capacity within itself. It was moreover, **as we have** seen, early enriched by a host of words through its contact with Latin (and Greek), and later by its contact with other nations in commerce or war. These are of course to be kept separate from **the truly** Teutonic roots, **and are, as** a rule, easy of recognition. With respect to Verbs belonging **to this** class of words, **all are weak** or regular, showing thus that they entered the German language after grammatical rules had been established; the only exceptions are **schreiben** from Lat. *scribere*, and **preisen from** French *prix*, Lat. *pretium dare*; **these** two entered therefore into German evidently very **early.** Altogether German obtained from foreign nations very few Verbs, compared **with** Nouns, and still fewer Adjectives. **The** principal sources of these foreign words in German were **Latin (and Greek) in the earlier** periods, and French **in more modern times.** We give here only a few examples:—

Of LATIN origin **are :**

VERBS: kochen (*to cook*), pfeifen (*to whistle*), dichten **(to compose)**, verdammen **(to condemn)**, spazieren (*to take a walk*), and a few more.

ADJECTIVES: falsch (*false*), fein (*fine*), sicher (*sure*), and very few more.

NOUNS: *Religion*. Kirche (*church*), Dom (*cathedral*), Fest (*feast*), and **a** hundred more.
Common Objects. Pferd (*horse*), Körper (*body*), Frucht (*fruit*), and a hundred more.
Plants: Kirsche (*cherry*), Birne (*pear*), Pflaume (*plum*), and many more.
Kitchen and House Utensils: Flasche (*bottle*), Schüssel (*dish*), Teller (*plate*), Büchse (*box*), Uhr (*clock*), Pfanne (*pan*), and very many more.
Building Terms: Kammer (*chamber*), Mauer (*wall*), Stube (*room*), Tisch (*table*), etc.
Law and Government: Kaiser (*emperor*), Recht (*law, right*), Advokat (*lawyer*), **etc.**
Money, Weights and Measures. Münze (*money*), Pfund (*pound*), Meile (*mile*), etc.

N.B.—Many of these may be further traced back to Greek, of course, **and many will also remind the** student of French, which is based on Latin.

Of FRENCH origin in *modern times*, and to be distinguished from those Latin roots which entered French and German at almost the same time, are many *nouns* connected with military matters, such as: Sergeant, Capitän, Offizier, General, Infanterie, etc. etc., and many *verbs*, which in German end in *iren*, as: studiren (*to study*), probiren (*to try*), poliren (*to polish*), besides many more quite recently introduced. [This *iren*, by the by, has become so much a favourite in modern German that it is added even to Teutonic roots to form new verbs, as: haus iren (*to go from house to house*) and some others, a practice which is however condemned by the best modern writers.]

In addition **to** the above sources, which are by far the most prolific, the most modern German has borrowed and incorporated some words—

From *English*, as: Jockey, Sport, Whist, Cricket, Jacht, etc.
from *Russian*, as: Droschke (*cab*), Jucht (*a kind of leather*), Knute (*whip*), etc.
from *Polish*, as: Gurke (*cucumber*), Ulan (*Ulan, light-horse soldier*), Grenze (*frontier*), etc.

From *Bohemian*, as: 𝔇𝔬𝔩𝔠𝔥 (*dagger*), 𝔎𝔲𝔱𝔰𝔠𝔥𝔢 (*cab*), 𝔓𝔢𝔱𝔰𝔠𝔥𝔞𝔣𝔱 (*seal for letters*), etc.
from *Turkish*, as: 𝔖𝔠𝔥𝔞𝔯𝔩𝔞𝔠𝔥 (*scarlet*), 𝔖𝔠𝔥𝔞𝔟𝔯𝔞𝔨𝔢 (*trappings of a horse*), etc.
from *American Indian*, as: 𝔗𝔞𝔟𝔞𝔨 (*tobacco*), ℭ𝔦𝔤𝔞𝔯𝔯𝔢 (*cigar*), etc.
from *East Indian*, as: 𝔓𝔲𝔫𝔰𝔠𝔥 (*punch*), 𝔄𝔯𝔞𝔨, 𝔑𝔲𝔪, etc.
  These words, however, are now cosmopolitan, *i.e.* adopted into all languages.

We refer the student to the short Etymological Dictionary appended for the etymology of many of the most common root-words in German, and will now proceed to a statement of the laws which have governed Vowel and Consonant changes from the earliest periods of the Indo-European languages, without a knowledge of which laws, at least in their broad outlines, etymology is impossible.

I. VOWELS.
[*See the Notice below.*]

The oldest of the vowels is *a*, of which the others are all variations, *i* and *u* being the earliest. The Indo-European idioms knew only these three, and we have still some curious remnants of this ancient "*tonic chord*," as it were, of language. Compare English *Fee-fa-fum, tit for tat, snip-snap-sn(u)orum*; and German piff=paff=puff, bim=bam=bum, and a few others. From these three original vowels sprang first of all *e* between *a* and *i*, and *o* between *a* and *u*, so that we may put the ascending scale of vowels, down thus: *u, o, a, e, i*.

A. ABLAUT (or change of sound).

The *Ablaut* and its laws form a most important chapter in the tracing back of modern words to their roots in the original Indo-European, and must be very carefully studied and distinguished from *Umlaut* or *Modification*.

Ablaut is the oldest change of vowel-sound, and it is generally impossible to give reasons for the vowel-changes which it includes. All we know is, that the oldest languages have only three vowels: ă and ĭ and ŭ. From these all other vowels and diphthongs spring:

  ă being weakened into ĭ and ŭ, and strengthened into ā and *uo*;
  ĭ being strengthened into ĕ, ē, ī, *ei* (the latter=*i* in *thine*).
  ŭ being strengthened into ŏ, ō, *iu* (eu, ü), *io* (ie), *ou* (au), (as *ou* in *thou*).

This *Ablaut* is moreover obscured by vowel-changes due to *Umlaut*, *Brechung*, etc., still we may always assume that owing to *Ablaut*,

(i.) Modern ā, ă point to *uo* in O. H. G., and to ā in Sanskrit or Indo-Germanic.
(ii.) Modern ĭ (ie), ĕ, ē, *ei* point to ī in O. H. G., and to ĭ in Sanskrit, etc.
(iii.) Modern ŏ, ō, ö, *eu*, *au* point to ŏ, *ou*, *iu* (io, ie), y in O. H. G. and to ŭ in Sanskrit, whilst modern ī (often falsely written *ie*) and ū are more doubtful, for ī may come from Indo-Germanic ā or ĭ, whilst modern ū may come from **Indo-Germanic** ā or ū. In these two cases some cognate words generally decide the question.

Notice.

It must be clearly understood, once for all, that in speaking here of
 a we refer to the broad sound of this vowel, as in *father* (never the *a* as in *lane*); in speaking of
 e we refer to the sound of *e* in *ten* (never to *e* as in *he*); in speaking of
 i we refer to the sound of *i* in *him* (never to *i* as in *mine*); also that
 u refers to the sound of *u* in *rule* (never to any other); and that
 o refers to the sound of *o* in *alone* (and no other, unless stated).

  [*Note*: — means *long*; ⌣ means *short*, in the following explanations.]

Examples of *Ablaut*.

[*N.B.*—For the meaning of G., E., M. H. G., etc., see "Abbreviations," Note on page 143.]

		E.	M. H. G.	A. S.		
(i.)	G. Dăch.	E. thătch.	M. H. G. dăch.	A. S. thăck.	Lat. tēctum (accidental *e*)	*ă* class.
(ii.)	G. Wein.	E. wine.	M. H. G. wīn.	A. S. wīn.	Got. wein; Lat. vīnum	*ī* class.
(iii.)	G. Haus.	E. house.	M. H. G. hūs.	A. S. hȳd.	Got. hūz; Lat. cūs-tos	*ū* class.
i. or iii. {	G. Blŭt.	E. blood.	M. H. G. bluot.	A. S. blōd.	Got. bloda	*ă* class.
	G. Lŭg.	E. lie.	M. H. G. lŭc.	A. S. lyge.	Got. liugn	*ŭ* class.
i. or ii. {	G. sitzen.	E. to sit.	M. H. G. sizzan.	A. S. sittan.	Lat. sedeo; Skt. sad—	*ă* class.
	G. Fri(e)de.	E. peace.	M. H. G. fride.	A. S. frithu.	Indo.-Germ. pritu-s.	*ī* class.

Notice: ie (i) if derived from *iu*, *io* as in *Knie*, always points to *ŭ* class.

Besides the above *organic Ablaut*, German admitted of a *non-organic, accidental* change of a into o, as in ſoll, von, Mond, wo, bolen, etc.; rarer is an accidental change of a into e without apparent cause, as in Adel=*nobility*, edel=*noble*; and e into i, as Berg—Gebirg. These latter two changes approach the *Umlaut*, and are more modern.

B. Umlaut

must be carefully distinguished from *Ablaut*. *It is the modification of a root-vowel due to the attraction exerted upon it by an added derivate syllable with* i (*later* e) *in the latter*. Thus angil became engil (M. G. Engel, E. angel). The *Umlaut* is of comparatively modern date, whilst the *Ablaut* is as ancient as Indo-Germanic itself; indeed, Gothic does not yet know the *Umlaut*: it was only in the seventh century after Christ that it first appeared. It affected then only *a* in the root, but soon the modification spread also to other root-vowels, as: gruoni into grüni (M. G. grün, E. green). At a later period, though the inflecting i in the derivative syllable sank into an unaccented e, or was dropped altogether, the *Umlaut* remained, as in tragen—er trägt (for trägit or träget); sconi changed into ſchön (E. *beautiful*). At a still more modern period the root-vowel became regularly modified, when derivative syllables containing i or e were added to a root, as Graf—Gräfin, Frau—Fräulein, etc.

Notice that only a, o, u, and au can be modified or suffer *Umlaut*. The change er lieſt—leſen is not an *Umlaut*, but *Brechung*, and has a much deeper and older etymological origin.

The modern mode of writing, for example, ä for ae is merely conventional, and an abbreviation for ȧ.

e as Umlaut of a often became ö, as in:

G. Hölle	E. hell.	M. H. G. helle.	O. H. G. halja.	Goth. halja.	to root vowel (i.) *ă*.
G. Zwö(lf)	E. twe(lve).	M. H. G. zwe(lif).	A. S. twe(lf).	Goth. twa(lif).	to root vowel (i.) *ă*.

N.B.—There are a few weak or regular verbs which, while retaining the original a vowel in the Imperfect Indicative, and Past Participle, have suffered what Jacob Grimm calls Rückumlaut (*Back-umlaut*) in the Infinitive, Present tenses. These are called anomalous verbs; they are the following:—brennen, kennen, nennen, rennen, ſenden, wenden, and denken.

bringen also has suffered such a *Rückumlaut* of a into i, and wiſſen of u into i (and ei). [See Grammar, page 46.]

C. Brechung,

or breaking-over, *is the change of root-vowel* i *or* u *by an* a *in the added derivative syllable; whereby* i *became* e *and* u *became* o. This change reaches much further back than the *Umlaut*, and is often as old as the *Ablaut*. Thus stilan became stelan (M. G. ſtehlen, E. *to steal*); lisan became *lesan* (M. G. lefen, E. *to read*). In the course of time this derivative a became, as we see, an e, but the *Brechung* remained. Thus also in Skt. usas=Lat. aurora=A. S. eastene= M. G. Often=E. *the East*. Similar changes by *Brechung* we find in Dorf (-*thorpe*), Ochs (*ox*), Morgen (*morning*). The influence of *Brechung* is also seen in the change of *iu* into *io* (modern *ie*), as in G. Knie, E. *knee*, O. H. G. *chniu*, Goth. *kniu*, Lat. *genu*, A. S. *cneo*.

Additional remarks on Vowel-changes.

The above three, *Ablaut*, *Umlaut*, and *Brechung*, were accompanied in more modern periods by *Schwächung*, *i.e.* weakening of a or i in derivative syllables into e, as we have seen in *gruoni* =grüne, *lisan*=lefen, etc.; and also by still more modern *Dehnung* or lengthening of short vowels into long ones by insertion of e after i and h after all vowels [and after i also] or sometimes by doubling of vowel. As to this *Dehnung* there has been a reaction within the last two decades, and Germans begin again to write more correctly: Mut for Muth (*courage*), gibt for giebt (*gives*), Tal for Thal (*valley*), Schaf for Schaaf (*sheep*), etc.

N.B.—In the examples on "Inner or Root-vowel changes," see pages 137 to 139, many instances of *Ablaut*, *Umlaut*, etc., will be found.

II. CONSONANTS.

The present system of consonants presents but little variation in the Indo-Germanic idioms except in the so-called *Lautverschiebung*, or change of consonants in the Mutes. We may, according to Jacob Grimm, distinguish three classes of consonants.

A. SPIRANTES.

Of these the most important is s. Grimm reckons among Spirantes also: (i.) h in interjections, as ha! ho! (ii.) j, which is i turned consonant, and appears before vowels only, as in jung=*young*, or is changed into h, as blühen, from blüejen, *to bloom*, etc. (iii.) w, which is u turned consonant in front of a vowel, as zwei [cf. Lat. *duo*]. The organic spirans s remains unaltered from the earliest times, but it changes often with r, as in verlieren—Verluft (*loss*), was=war (*he was*). s as spirans combines readily with other consonants, and these combinations present some interest, thus: O. H. G. *sk* becomes *sch* in M. G., as ſkriban=ſchreiben, etc.; *sl, sm, sn, sw* become in M. G. *schl, schm, schn, schw*, as ſmal=ſchmal, etc.

[This spirans s must not be confounded with the dental mute z; the latter, though now indistinguishable in writing from the former, sprang from O. H. G. *z*, a "dental."]

B. LIQUIDAE.

These are l, m, n, r, and present still less change from the earliest idioms than the Spirantes. Notice also: (i.) l often combines, as in lm, lb, lp, lg, lf, ls, rl, etc. It sometimes interchanges with r, as: Lat. *prunum*, G. Pflaume, E. *plum*; Lat. *peregrinus*, G. Pilgrim, etc.; (ii.) m and n often interchange, m replacing n before labials or dentals, as entfinden=empfinden; entfahen=empfangen; (iii.) n is perhaps the most used consonant in German, and combines readily with almost all other consonants; among these combinations ng is perhaps the most usual.

We may say l, m, n, r govern the whole inflexion of words, and play the most important part in Word-derivation or Word-formation.

C. MUTAE.

These **are the** most important of **the consonants** in Etymology, and their changes **often** furnish the **principal** light by which we trace back words to older idioms. They are divided thus, with respect to their production by the organs of speech:

	Soft.	Hard.	Aspirated.	
			Soft.	Hard.
Labials,	v, b	p	f (v)	pf
Dentals,	d	t	z (=s), th	ʒ (=ts)
Gutturals,	g (c)	k (c)	h	ch

Notes.—(i.) pf is really only one consonant.

(ii.) ch is really only one consonant, pronounced hard, guttural after a, o, and u (au); but sounded soft in all other combinations now.

Jacob Grimm was the first to point out that between the soft, the hard, **and the** aspirated mutes of each class (labials, dentals, and gutturals) a more or less regular change took place, so that a soft labial **had** a tendency to become hard; a hard **one** to become aspirated, and **an** aspirated one again **soft**, etc. **The mnemonic word** *has* **will** remind the student of these changes, beginning **with the oldest idiom**: *has* : hard, aspirate, soft ; *ash* : aspirate, soft, hard ; *sha* : soft, hard, aspirate. In these changes the Sanskrit, Greek, and Latin form the *first* period ; the Gothic, Anglo-Saxon, and **Low** German the *second* period ; and Old and Middle High German with Modern High German the *third* **period**.

Thus, tracing a mute **consonant back we shall find that**:

Modern German, (etc.)	v, b	f (v), pf	p	—	—	b	f, z (th)	t	—	—	d	g	h, ch	f (c) point to :
Anglo-Saxon (etc.)	f	p	b	—	—	s (th)	t	d	—	—	h	k (c)	g (c) and **to**:
Latin (etc.)	p	b		f	—	—	t	d	s (th)	—	—	k (c)	g (c)	h (ch)

However, these changes are but seldom found without exceptions or **leaps**; and, generally speaking, they are more recognisable in *initials* than in *final* consonants, and **also better** preserved in *dentals* than in *labials* or *gutturals*.

Examples of this change of Mutes.

3d Period : High German.			2d Period : Low German.		1st Period : Classical, etc.		
Mod. Germ.	English.	O. H. Germ.	Anglo-Saxon.	Gothic.	Latin.	Greek.	Sanskrit.
sieben	*seven	sibun	seofon	sibun	septem	ἑπτά	saptan
Feuer	fire	fiur	fýr (fuir)	fon (fun—)	(foc—)	πῦρ	[pû—]
Haupt	*hea(f)d	houbit	heafod	haubith	[caput]	[κεφαλή]	[kubh—]
drei	*three	dri	thri	threis	tres	τρεῖς	trayas
wissen	[*know](wit)	wizzan	wät—	waitan	video	ἰδεῖν	vid
Türe	*door	turi	duru	daurons	[fores]	θύρα	dur (dvara)
gestern	yester(day)	gestaron	gistran	gistra—	heri	χθές	ghyás
ich	I	ih	ic	ik	ego	ἐγώ	aham
Hund	hound	hunt	hund	hunds	[canis]	κύων	çvâ
können	(to) can	chunnan	cunnan	kunnan	gnosco	ἔ-γνων	gnâ—

[*Notice* * that English often belongs to the 2d period, *i.e.* the Low-German idioms.]

It will be seen from these examples, which are among the most perfect, that the three steps of changes of Mutes are very rarely perfect or **all** present ; still they prove the general correctness of this "Grimm's Law," as it is called. Moreover there are in *Modern German* traces of it, in the derivation of new words from older roots, as :

(i.) change of b into f before t: Schreiben—Schrift; geben—Gift, etc.
(ii.) variation of v and f, as in höfisch and hübsch; Hafer and Haber (oats).
(iii.) change of g and h into ch before i: schlagen—Schlacht; sehen—Gesicht, etc.
(iv.) hard pronunciation of final b, v, or g, as in fand, gab, Tag, formerly written, and still in some parts of Germany pronounced, fant, gav, Tak (tac).

(See also APPENDIX B.)

WORD-FORMATION.

We have already mentioned (see page 130) that the earliest (inflexible) language possessed only two word-elements, (i.) words interpreting conceptions of *objects* or *acts* or *qualities*, as: *man, to eat, to be good*, etc.; and (ii.) *Pronominal* and *pointing-words*, as: *he, that, they*, etc. By the combination of these two elements old words were inflected and new ones formed; and we must carefully distinguish between *inflection* and *word-formation*.

Examples of inflection are : (a) the t in geh-t (*he goes*) ; this t is really a remnant of the personal pronoun *hit* = *he*, so that geh-t = geh + hit (O. H. G. *gang-it*) or *go* + *he* ; thus by bodily adding a pronoun to the word for an act, this word became inflected as to *person*. (b) the -te in the Imperfect of regular verbs, as: leb-te ; this -te is really a remnant of the word *tuon, to do*, so that leb-te = leb + tat = *live* + *did, live-d* ; thus by bodily adding a verb to another verbal root the latter became inflected as to *tense*. Compare French *donner-ai* = *donner* + Pres. of *avoir*.

Examples of word-formation are: (a) the lich in glück-lich; this -lich is really the O.G. *g-lich*, E. *like*, so that by putting two independent words together a new adjective was formed. (b) the -tum in Kaiser-tum is really the old separately-used noun *tuom* = *power, authority* (E. -*dom* in king-*dom*), so that by putting together two nouns a new noun was formed.

Many of these originally independent words became in course of time mere prefixes or suffixes, incapable of being used by themselves, such as -tum.

We have here only to do with the second of the two processes mentioned above, and indeed only with that part of word-formation which is still active now-a-days; for to trace such suffixes as -er in Vater, etc., or -t in Gift from geben, would be in most cases impossible, and in all extremely difficult.

In the formation of new words three methods present themselves at once, namely : (i.) *Inner or root-vowel changes* (with obsolete derivative letters), (ii.) *Outer or derivative-syllable changes*, and (iii.) *Actual (new) Composition*.

I. INNER OR ROOT-VOWEL CHANGES.

The most prolific source of new words is to be found in the *strong* (or irregular) verbs, and we give here a few of the most important, with some words formed from each by root-vowel changes. *Notice :* the root verbs are placed in three divisions, as they belong to the Indo-Germanic *a, i*, or *u* group. [See pages 133, 134.]

8

(i) *a-Class.* [Derivatives with ä, i, ü, or e (as *Umlaut* of a. See page 134).]

binden, E. *to bind:* die Binde (*the bandage*); der Band (*the volume*); das Band (*the ribbon*); der Bund (*confederation*).
bitten, E. *to beg:* die Bitte (*the request*); beten (*to pray*); das Gebet (*the prayer*).
[M. H. G. biren] = to bear: gebären (*to bring forth*); die Geburt (*the birth*); die Bürde (*the burden*).
brechen, E. *to break:* der Verbrecher (*the criminal*); der Bruch (*the breaking*); die Brache (*ploughed fields*).
brennen, E. *to burn:* der Brand (*the conflagration*); die Brandung (*surf*); der Brunnen (*fountain*).
[*N.B.*—O. H. G. *brinnan* = the **phenomenon** when water and fire come in contact.]
dringen, *to crowd, penetrate:* der Drang (*the oppression*); das Gedränge (*the crowd*); die Drangsal, *trouble*.
fahren, *to drive:* die Fahrt (*the drive*); der Gefährte (*the companion*); die Fährte (*the ford*) = die Furt.
finden, *to find:* der Fund (*the find*); der Finder (*the finder*); der Findling (*the foundling*).
geben, *to give:* die Mit-gift (*the marriage portion*); das Gift (*the poison*); die Gabe (*the gift*).
ge-schehen, *to happen:* die Geschichte (*history*); das Geschick = das Schicksal (*fate*); die Schicht (*the layer*).
graben, *to dig:* das Grab (*the grave*); die Grube (*the hole*); der Graben (*the ditch*).
helfen, *to help*: die Hülfe (*the help*); der Helfer (*the helper*); der Gehilfe (*the helpmate*).
hehlen, *to hide*: der Held (*the hero*); die Hölle (*hell*); die Hülle (*the covering*); der Helm (*the helmet*).
kommen, *to come:* die Ankunft (*the arrival*); **die Zukunft** (*the future*); das Einkommen (*income*).
liegen, *to lie*: die Lage (*the situation*); das Lager (*the camp*); **die** Gelegenheit (*the occasion*).
mahlen, *to grind:* das Mehl (*the flour*); das Mahl (*the repast*) [originally *mal* = *fixed point or time*].
nehmen, *to take:* angenehm (*agreeable*); **die Vernunft, f.** (*reasoning*); die Zunahme, f. (*increase*).
schaffen, *to create, work:* der Schöpfer (*the creator*) [= schaft in many subst.]; das Geschäft (*business*).
schlagen, *to beat:* der Schlag (*the blow*); die Schlacht (*the battle*); schlachten (*to slaughter*).
schrecken, *to frighten:* der Schrecken (*the fright*); [die Heuschrecke, *grasshopper, doubtful?*].
sehen, *to see:* das Gesicht (*the face, sight*); der Seher (*the seer, prophet*); die Aus-sicht, etc. (*view*).
singen, *to sing:* der Gesang (*the song*); der Sänger (*the singer*); sengen (*to set fire to, burn*).
sitzen, *to sit:* der Sitz (*the seat*); der Satz (*the sentence, jump*); das Gesetz (*the law*); der Sessel, m. (*chair*).
spinnen, *to weave:* die Spinne (*the spider*); das Gespinnst (*the weft*); die Spindel (*the spindle*).
sprechen, *to speak:* das Sprichwort (*the proverb*); die Sprache (*language*); das Gespräch (*conversation*).
stechen, *to prick:* der Stich (*the prick*); der Stachel (*the sting*); das Stük (*the piece*); der Steck (*stick*).
stehen, *to stand:* der Stand ((*the standing, platform*); die Stunde (*the hour*); die Stadt (*town*).
tragen, *to carry:* der Vertrag (*truce?*); die Tracht (*the costume*); also das Getreide? (*corn*).
trinken, *to drink*: der Trunk (*the draught*); der Trank; das Getränke (*the drink*).
wachsen, *to grow*: das Gewächs (*the plant*); der Wuchs (*growth*).
wiegen, *to weigh, rock*: das Gewicht (*the weight*); die Wage (*the scales*); die Woge (*the wave*).
winden, *to turn:* die Wand (*side, wall*); die Wunde (*wound*); das **Gewand** (*dress*); der Wandel (*behaviour*).

(ii) *i-Class.* [Derivatives only with i (*ie*); ei (or e as *Schwächung* of i. See page 135).]

beißen, *to bite:* das Gebiß (*the teeth*); das Bißchen (*the little bit*); der Bissen (*the bite, morsel*).
bleiben, *to remain* (for be-liben): der Leib (*the body*); leben (*to live*); das Leben (*life*).
leiden, *to suffer:* leider (*alas*); das Glied, n. (*the member*); das Leid (*sorrow*).
reißen, *to tear:* der Riß (*the chink*); der Riß (*the tear*); der Reiz (*the charm*).
schleifen, *to grind:* der Schliff (*the polish*); die Schleppe (*the train of a garment*); schleppen (*to drag*).
schneiden, *to cut:* der Schnitt (*the cut*); der Schneider (*the tailor*).
schreiben, *to write:* die Schrift (*the writing*); der Schreiber (*the scribe*).
steigen, *to mount:* die Stiege (*the stairs*); der Steig (Steg) (*the little bridge, path*).
streichen, *to stroke*: der Strich (**the stroke**); der Streifen (*the strip*); der Strick (*the rope*).

(iii) *u-Class.* [Derivates only with u (ü) or o.] [au for ou, rare.] [ie, as Brechung of io, iu, see pp. 134, **135.**]

biegen, *to bend*: der Bogen (*the arc*); die Bucht (*the bay*); der Buckel (*the bent back, hump*).
bieten, *to offer, command:* das Gebiet (*the dominion*); der Bote (*the messenger*); das Gebot (*the order*).

fliegen, *to fly*: die Fliege (*the fly*); der Flug (*the flight*); die Flucht (*the escape*); der Flügel (**the wing**).
fließen, *to flow*: der Fluß (*the river*); der Floß (*the float*); das Fließpapier (*blotting-paper*).
genießen, *to enjoy*: der Genuß (*the enjoyment*); **der Nutzen** (*the use, advantage*); nützen (*to use*).
riechen, *to smell*: der Geruch (*the smell*); der Rauch (*the smoke*); rauchen (*to smoke*).
schieben, *to shove, push*: der Schuft (*the rascal* (*shifty*)); die Schaufel (*the spade, shovel*).
schießen, *to shoot*: der Schuß (*the shot*); das Geschoß (*the gun*); der Schütze (*the marksman*).
schließen, *to close*: das Schloß (*the lock, castle*); der Schluß (*the conclusion*); der Schlüssel (*the key*).
trügen, *to deceive*: der Betrug (*the deception*); der Betrüger (*the cheat*).
verlieren, *to loose*: der Verlust (*the loss*); der Verließ (*a prison* (**lost to** *the world's eyes*)).
ziehen, *to draw, pull*: der Zug (*the expedition*); der Herzog (**the leader (duke)**); die Zucht (*education*).

Note.—The intelligent student will **easily increase the number of such** derivatives; the above are more given only as examples, and **do not claim to form a complete list**; it would be a good practice gradually to collect derivatives and classify **them**.

II. DERIVATION OF WORDS.

A. By Suffixes.

[Very often accompanied by *Umlaut* of a, o, u, au into ä, ö, ü, äu, when the derivative syllable contains e or i.]

(a) VERBS.

1. **-en (or n)**, added to most **nouns** or adjectives: (a) to *Singulars*, as: der Pflug—pflügen (*to plough*); der Donner—donnern (*to thunder*). (b) to *Plurals*, as: die Blätter—blättern (*to turn over the leaves of a book*). (c) to *adjectives*, as: ein—einen (*to unite*); sauber—säubern (*to make clean*), etc.
2. **-eln**, added to the root of verbs, forms diminutives with *Umlaut*; the derivatives often having a contemptuous meaning, **as**: lachen—lächeln (*to smile*); tanzen—tänzeln (*to step foolishly, as in a dance*).
3. **-iren**, originally French, now sometimes added to Teutonic roots, as: halbiren (*to halve*); hausiren (**to go** *from house to house*). [-iren more usually spelt -ieren.]
4. **-ern**, rare for verbs, from nouns, as: der Schlaf—einschläfern (*to lull to sleep*). [*N.B.*—Not to be confounded with 1., where n **is** added to roots in **er**: der Eifer—eifern (*to be zealous*).]
5. **-zen**, rare; as in der Schluck—schluchzen (*to sob*); ach—ächzen (*to groan*).

(b) SUBSTANTIVES.

1. **-er**, generally **of** male persons, forms Substantives **from** (a) *Verbal roots*, **as**: schneiden—der Schneider (*tailor*); spielen—der Spieler (**player**). (b) *Substantives*, as: das Fleisch—der Fleischer (*butcher*); der Garten—der Gärtner (*gardener*). To this **class** belong also the nationalities, **as**: die Schweiz—der Schweizer (*a Swiss*); England—der Engländer (**an Englishman**). **Exceptions**: der (die) Deutsche (an adjective), der Russe, der Türke, der Franzose (etc.).
2. **-ner** belongs to **-er**, which latter was formerly only added to nouns in **-en**; by false analogy -ner was afterwards added to nouns instead of **-er** only, as: das Bild—der Bildner (*sculptor*); die Rede—der Redner (*a speaker*).
3. **-in (-inn)** forms feminines of 1. and 2., as: der Gärtner—die Gärtnerin (*gardener's wife*).
4. **-el** added **to verbal** roots forms nouns, representing the instrument used in the action, as: ziehen—der Zügel (**bridle**); gürten—der Gürtel (*girdle*); werfen—der Würfel (*a die, dice*).
5. **-sal forms nouns** from verbs relating to some influence on men's minds, as: schicken—das Schicksal (*fate*); trüben—die Trübsal (*grief, straits*).
6. **-ling** (for el+ing) has a classifying force, as: Hof—der Höfling (*courtier*); jung—der Jüngling (*young man*); thus also der Sperling (*sparrow*); der Schmetterling (*butterfly*).

7. ‑lein or ‑chen forms (neuter) diminutives, often with endearing force, as: der Vater—das Väterchen (*dear little father*); das Kind—das Kindlein (*little (dear, pretty) child*).
8. ‑ung forms (fem.) abstracts from verbs, as: handeln—die Handlung (**trade, business**); it has sometimes a collective force, as: der Wald—die Waldung (*forest-district*).
9. ‑ei forms feminine abstracts out of Person's appellations, as: der Träumer—die Träumerei (*dreaming*); der Schäfer—die Schäferei (*sheep-farm*). [*N.B.* ‑ei in die Melodei (or Melodie), etc. = ‑ie from Lat. ‑*ia*.]
10. ‑niß forms abstracts from nouns, as: der Bund—das Bündniß (*treaty*); or from adjectives, as: finster—die Finsterniß (*darkness*); it has also sometimes a meaning of locality, as: gefangen—das Gefängniß (**prison**). [Most words in ‑niß are neuter.] [‑niß now often spelt ‑nis.]
11. ‑heit (after ‑g = ‑keit) [O. H. G. die Heit = *quality, manner*] has (*a*) a collective force, as: die Christenheit (*Christendom*); (*b*) an abstract meaning, as: krank—die Krankheit (*illness*).
12. ‑tum [O. H. G. das tuom = *power, dignity*] has generally a collective force, as: das Ritter‑tum (= *body of knights*); das Priester‑tum (*priesthood*).
13. ‑schaft [O. H. G. die Schaft = *bodily form, quality*] may be added to nouns, adjectives, or participles, and has (*a*) a meaning of "connection with," relationship, as: die Bruderschaft (*brotherhood*); (*b*) an abstract force, as: wissend—die Wissenschaft (*science*).

(c) ADJECTIVES.

1. ‑en or ‑n forms adjectives from nouns implying materials, as: das Gold—golden; das Silber—silbern; die Hölzer (pl.) (*woods*)—hölzern (*wooden—of wood*).
2. ‑ern, by false analogy with above [‑er + n], as: das Eisen—eisern (*iron*).
3. ‑ig forms adjectives from almost any noun, adjective, verb, pronoun, as: der Sand—sandig (*sandy*); heute—heutig (*of our days*); fallen—fällig (*due*). [*N.B.* It often implies possession, as: mutig = having Mut (*courage*); bärtig = having a Bart (*beard*).]
4. ‑icht implies "full of," as: steinicht (*stony*); felsicht (*rocky*). [*N.B.* ‑icht is often interchanged with ‑ig, as: steinig = steinicht, etc.]
5. ‑isch applies to *persons* [whilst ‑icht generally applies to *things*]; kindisch (*childish*).
6. ‑lich [O. H. G. = g‑lich = gleich = *like, similar*] forms adjectives implying (*a*) *quality or origin*, as: königlich (*kingly*); ängstlich (*anxiously*); (*b*) *Diminutives*, often with contemptuous sense, as ärmlich (*rather poor*); süßlich (*rather sweet*).
7. ‑sam [O. H. G. samo = *the same*] implies inclination, as: schweigsam (*taciturn, inclined to keep silent*); furchtsam (*inclined to fear*); aufmerksam (*inclined to attention, attentive*).
8. ‑bar [connected with bar = *to bear, carry*] implies bearing, bringing, **affording, as:** dankbar (*thankful, bearing thanks*); ehrbar (*honourable, bringing honour*).
9. ‑haft [O. H. G. (adj.) haft = *held, prisoner*] implies having, **holding, as:** zweifelhaft (*doubtful, holding doubts*); wahrhaft (*true, having truth*), etc.

B. By Prefixes.

(a) VERBS. (Inseparable Prefixes only.)

1. ge‑ [connected with Lat. *cum*] implies *with, enduring, quiet, as in:* gefallen (*to please*); gelangen (*to arrive at*). [*N.B.* glauben, *to believe*, for ge + lauben.]
2. be‑ [O. H. G. bei] has the force (i.) of the full meaning of the conception expressed by the verb; (ii.) of forming transitive **verbs out of** neuter verbs.—be‑ can be prefixed (*a*) to *verbs*, **as:** bedenken (*to consider*); bedienen (*to serve*). (*b*) to *adjectives*, as: frei—befreien (*to free*); ruhig—beruhigen (*to quiet*). (*c*) **to nouns, as:** das Kleid—bekleiden (*to dress*); das Feuer—befeuern (*to render enthusiastic*). [*N.B.* be‑ is perhaps the most fertile prefix in German. It requires an *accusative* after it.]

3. er= [O. H. G. -ur] with sense of origin. It has the force (i.) of incipient, beginning activity ; (ii.) of emphasising the conception ; (iii.) of success through the action. er= forms verbs (a) from verbs, as: blühen—erblühen (*to bloom forth*); steigen—ersteigen (*to ascend successfully*); (b) from adjectives, as: warm—erwärmen (*to warn*).
4. ver= is the opposite of er= ; it has the force of (i.) ending, vanishing activity ; (ii.) change of condition, using up, losing.—ver= forms verbs (a) from verbs, as: spielen—verspielen (*to lose at play*) ; (b) from adjectives, as: arm—verarmen (*to become poor*) ; (c) from nouns, as: das Blut—verbluten (*to bleed to death*).
5. zer= implies entire disintegration, resolution into small particles ; it forms verbs (a) from verbs, as: reißen —zerreißen (*to tear up altogether*) ; (b) from nouns, as: das Glied—zergliedern (*to dismember*).
6. ent= [O. H. G. ant as in Antwort (*answer*), connected with Gk. ἀντί, *against*]. It has the force of (i.) implying the creation of a new condition, and (ii.) the leaving a former condition. ent= forms verbs from verbs only, as: führen—entführen (*to lead away*); schwinden—entschwinden (*to disappear, vanish*).
[*N.B.*—Before f, ent becomes em, changing f into pf, as : ent-fangen=empfangen (*to receive*) ; ent-finden=empfinden (*to feel*).]
7. miß=, with meaning of badness, as: mißfallen (*to displease*) ; mißhandeln (*to ill-treat*).

(b) SUBSTANTIVES.

1. ge= forms collectives, either of persons, as: die Gebrüder (pl.) (*brethren*) ; or of things, as : das Gebirge (*collection of mountains*); das Gestirn (*collection of stars*). Added to verbs, ge= has no special signification, as : der Gesang (*song*); das Gesicht (*face, sight*).
2. un= is the opposite of sein or chen ; it has a meaning of largeness, and often of badness or enormousness, as : der Unmensch (*monster*) ; das Unkraut (*bad weeds*).
3. miß= [O. H. G. die Misse=*the want, defect, miss*] implies error, badness, as : das Mißjahr (*a bad year*); das Mißvergnügen (*displeasure, bad enjoyment*).

(c) ADJECTIVES.

The only prefix which is used to form adjectives is un=, which is added to adjectives having a good, pleasant meaning, and which changes such adjectives into their opposites, as : weise—unweise (*unwise*) ; glücklich —unglücklich (*unhappy*).

III. COMPOSITION.

Distinguish this from II. (Derivation). By Composition we mean here the more modern putting together of words, each of which may be still used independently ; whilst in Derivation we treated of prefixes or suffixes which have now lost their independent meaning, and are no longer used by themselves.

(a) VERBS.

Verbs can combine with *prepositions or adverbs only* ; and the new forms thus obtained are called *separable verbs* ; indeed, the preposition or adverb has the accent, and clings to the root verb always, except in the Present and Imperfect tenses, and in the Imperative, and only in Principal Sentences. [See the *Grammar*, p. 54.]

There are only *six* prepositions which may give up their accent to the verb entirely, and form *inseparable verbs* with it (as do ver, zer, ge, etc.). These six prepositions are:

durch, as: durchblicken (*to look through*); durchdenken (*to think over*).
hinter, as: hintergehen (*to cheat*); hinterlassen (*to bequeath, leave behind*).
über, as: übersetzen (*to translate*); übergehen (*to omit, leave out*).
um, as: umgeben (*to surround*); umschiffen (*to sail round*).
unter, as: unterdrücken (*to oppress*); unterhalten (*to entertain*).
wider, as: widersprechen (*to contradict*); widerstehen (*to withstand, oppose*).

Of these all (except **wider**) can also **form** separable verbs, as:

durch/sehen, *to look through*; hinter...gehen, *to go behind*, etc.,

though some of these can scarcely be called compound verbs, and are rather verbs **governing prepositions**. Notice also, that when the above prepositions form inseparable verbs, these are transitive, *i.e.* require a complement, and are conjugated with haben in their Compound tenses. [See also p. 54.]

But with almost all other prepositions or adverbs, verbs can combine to form new verbs, separable, and having the **accent** on the preposition or adverb, which in fact gives its peculiar colour or signification to the **root-verb**, as:

an-fangen (*to begin*); auf-gehen (*to rise*); ab-gehen (*to depart*); wieder-kommen (*to return*), etc. etc.

N.B.—wieder- forms only *one* inseparable verb: wiederholen, *to repeat*; wider- cannot form any separable verbs at all.

(b) SUBSTANTIVES (the Substantive being the last component).

(i.) with *preposition or adverb*, as: die Ab-fahrt (*departure*); der Vorfall (*event*); der Aus-weg (*the way out, excuse*); das Ober-haupt (*the chief*), etc. etc.
(ii.) with *verb*, as: das Fahr-zeug (*the conveyance*); die Schreib-feder (*the pen*); das Wohn-haus (*dwelling-house*); die Denk-kraft (*the power of thinking*).
(iii.) with *substantive*, as: das Bilder-buch (*the picture-book*); der Blumen-tisch (*the flower-table*); das Dampf-schiff (*the steamboat*), etc. etc.
(iv.) with *adjective*, as: die Jung-frau (*the virgin*); der Freimut (*the candour*); die Neu-bildung (*the new formation*); der Eigen-sinn (*obstinacy*), etc. etc.

(c) ADJECTIVES (the Adjective being the last component).

(i.) with *preposition or adverb*, as: über-voll (*over full*); auf-recht (*upright*); außer-ordentlich (*extraordinary*); ein-drücklich (*impressive*), etc. etc.
(ii.) with *verb*, as: merk-würdig (*noteworthy*); spielfähig (*capable of play*); reise-fertig (*ready for travelling*); tanz-lustig (*fond of dancing*), etc. etc.
(iii.) with *substantive*, as: hilf-reich (*beneficent*); kunst-fertig (*accomplished in an art*); kreis-förmig (*circular*); geist-voll (*witty*); treu-los (*unfaithful*), etc. etc.
(iv.) with *adjective*, as: bleich-wangig (*pale-cheeked*); hoch-heilig (*high and holy*); groß-mütig (*generous*); braunrot (*brownish red*), etc. etc.

Notice.—In all these compounds the first component has the principal accent, but the last component takes upon itself all the functions of Gender, Number, Case, Tense, etc. The first component changes under no condition whatever. This applies equally to all Compound Verbs, Substantives, and Adjectives, and to **their Conjugation**, Declension, and Comparison.

APPENDIX A.

SHORT ETYMOLOGICAL DICTIONARY.

WE append a small Etymological Dictionary, which contains some 300 of the most important roots, with hints as to their origin. For further details the student must consult a regular, full, and complete Etymological Dictionary, such as F. Kluge's [Strasburg, K. J. Trübner], from which, indeed, many of the words here given are taken.

N.B.—The student must not forget to refer to the rules given (pp. 133 to 137) about Vowel and Consonant changes.

ABBREVIATIONS: E. = English; M. H. G. = Middle High German (about 12th century); Got. = Gothic; O. H. G. = Old High German (about 6th century); A. S. = Anglo-Saxon (before 5th century); Lat. = Latin; Gk. = Greek; O. E. = Old English; Skt. = Sanskrit; Ind. G. = Indo-Germanic; cf. = compare; m. = masculine; f. = feminine; n. = neuter; r. = regular; irr. = irregular.

Abend, m., E. evening; M. H. G. âbent; O. H. G. aband; A. S. aéfen, aefning.
Abt, m., E. abbot; M. H. G. borrowed from Lat. abbas, abbatis; A. S. abbod.
acht, E. eight; M. H. G. ahte; O. H. G. ahto; A. S. eahta; Lat. octo; Gk. ὀκτώ; Skt. astâu.
Acker, m., E. acre; O. H. G. acchar; A. S. aecer; Lat. ager; Gk. ἀγρός; Got. akrs.
Adel, m., E. noble, **nobility**; O. H. G. adal; **A.** S. aethelu (as in O. E. Ethelred, Atheling, etc.).
Adler, m., eagle [= adel-aar = noble-eagle]; **Aar, Gk.** ὄρνις, a bird (cf. Ornithology).
all, E. all; O. H. G. al; Got. alls; A. S. call; [allein = all-ein = all one = alone.]
Almosen, n., E. alms; M. H. G. almuosen; O. H. G. alamosan; A. S. aelmesse; Gk. ἐλεημοσύνη = pity, alms.
alt, E. old; A. S. eald; Got. altheis; [connected with Lat. al-o, to nourish, grow up.]
Apfel, m., E. apple; O. H. G. apful; A. S. aeppel (a word borrowed perhaps from the Finns).
Auge, n., E. eye; M. H. G. ouge; O. H. G. ouga; Got. augo; A. S. eage; Lat. oculus.
aus, E. out; O. H. G. ûz; A. S. ût; Skt. ût.

Bach, m., E. beck, brook; O. H. G. bah; A. S. becc.
bauen, r., E. to build; M. H. G. bûwen; O. H. G. bûan; Got. bauan, to dwell; [Lat. fui; Gk. φύω, to be, become.]
Beispiel, n. (E. example); M. H. G. bispil or bîspel; A. S. bispell, where spell = story, fable; cf. E. gospel = God's-spell. Spell is O. H. G. for artistic, poetic narration. bi = E. by, about; G. bei, be (as prefix).
besser, E. better [comparative of baß = good (still used in German sometimes)]; A. S. betera.
bitten, irr., E. to beg (bid); O. H. G. bitjan, bidjan; A. S. biddan. [Lat. fido; Gk. πιθ for φιθ.]
Blatt, n., E. blade, leaf; O. H. G. blat; A. S. blaed; Lat. fol-ium; Gk. φύλλον.
Blume, f., E. flower, bloom; O. H. G. bluoma; A. S. blôma; connected with Lat. flos.

143

brauen, *r.*, E. to brew ; M. H. G. briuwen ; A. S. **breowan** ; Ind. G. **brū or bhrū**. To this root belong Brod, bread, and Bier, beer ; as E. **broth** also.

Braut, *f.*, E. bride ; **O. H. G. brūt** (a specially Germanic **word**) ; A. S. bryd.—The -gam in Bräutigam, E. bridegroom, **comes from** A. S. guma ; Lat. homo = a man. [The i = r, a genitive suffix.]

brechen, *irr.*, E. **break** ; **O. H. G.** brëhhan ; Got. **brikan** ; A. S. brecan ; Lat. frango—fregi.

Brief, *m.*, E. brief, letter ; from Lat. brevis, short ; = a *short* document.

Bruder, *m.*, O. H. G. bruodar ; A. S. brothor ; Got. brothar ; Lat. frater ; Gk. φράτηρ, with political meaning.

Buch, *n.*, **E. book** ; O. H. G. buoch, buch ; Got. bōka. The Singular bōc referred to the letters engraved on trees, especially on the beech, Buche, *f.* **Cf.** Lat. fagus ; Gk. φάγός. **The Plural referred** to documents containing such letters, and then generally to documents and *books*.

Busch, *m.*, **E.** bush, from M. Lat. buscus, boscus ; M. H. G. busch, **bosch** ; **O. H. G. busk.**

Busen, *m.*, E. bosom ; **O. H. G.** buosum ; A. S. bōsm (a specially Germanic word).

Dach, *m.*, E. roof, thatch ; O. H. G. dah ; **A. S. thace** ; Got. (missing). **[Lat. togo** ; Gk. τέγος, στέγη.**]**

denken, E. to think ; O. H. G. denchen ; A. S. thencan ; Got. tha(n)kjan.

deutsch, E. German (Dutch) ; M. H. G. tiutsch [Got. thiudisco = heathenish ; cf. Gk. ἐθνικῶς] ; connected with O. H. G. diot = people ; A. S. **theod** ; Lat. tuticus. Compare E. dict. Thus deutsch really means *the people par excellence* in **early Germanic**.

Dienstag, E. Tuesday. Diens from the old Teuton god Tiu ; cf. Ζεύς (Διός) ; Lat. Jovis.

Dirne, *f.*, E. maid, servant ; **O. H. G.** diorna ; cf. Got. thiwairnō = daughter of a serf.

Dorf, *n.*, E. village (-thorpe) ; A. S. **thorp** ; Got. thaurp = land, fields.

du, E. thou ; O. H. G. dū ; A. S. **thū** ; Lat. tu ; Gk. τύ, σύ ; Skt. tvam.

dulden, E. suffer ; O. H. G. dolan ; A. S. tholian ; Lat. tolerare ; Gk. τλῆ-ναι.

dumm, E. stupid, dumb ; O. H. G. tumb ; **Got. dumbs.** [Perhaps Gk. τυφλός.]

durch, E. through ; O. H. G. duruh ; A. S. **thurh**. [Cf. E. thorough.]

Dutzend, *n.*, E. dozen (from French douzaine) ; **Lat. duodecim.**

Ehe, *f.*, E. marriage ; M. H. G. ēwe ; A. S. aow = time, eternity, law ; Lat. aevum ; Gk. αἰών.

Ei, *n.*, E. egg ; O. H. G. ei ; A. S. aêg. [Cf. Lat. ovum ; Gk. ψόν.]

Eiche, *f.*, oak ; O. H. G. eih ; A. S. āc.

Eid, *m.*, E. oath ; M. H. G. eit, eid ; A. S. āth ; Got. **aiths**. Perhaps connected with Ehe above.

ein, E. one, a ; O. H. G. ein ; A. S. ân ; Lat. **ains** ; Lat. unus (com*munis*).

Eis, *n.*, E. ice ; O. H. G. is. Perhaps connected with is, to glitter ; see next word.

Eisen, *n.*, E. iron ; M. H. G. isen ; A. S. îsern, iren ; Lat. aes = ore (Ind. G. is, to glitter).

elend, E. [miserable] ; M. H. G. ellend = living in banishment, foreign. Cf. Lat. alius, other ; Gk. ἄλλος ; E. alien [Got. alilandi = foreign, other lands].

Engel, *m.*, **E.** Angel ; O. H. G. Angil ; A. S. engel ; Lat. angelus ; Gk. ἄγγελος, a messenger.

Erde, *f.*, E. earth ; O. H. G. erda ; Got. airtha ; A. S. eortho (perhaps Lat. arvum, cultivated field).

erst, E. first ; O. H. G. ērist ; A. S. âerest, superlative of ehe = early. [Cf. Fürst = prince.]

essen, *irr.*, E. to eat ; O. H. G. ëzzan ; A. S. etan ; Got. itan. [Cf. Lat. ēsus, part. of edo ; Gk. ἔδ-ομαι].

ewig, E. eternal, for aye ; O. H. G. ēwig ; Lat. aevum ; Gk. αἰών = eternity. See Ehe.

Fahne, *f.*, E. flag, vane ; **A. S.** fana = cloth. [Perhaps Lat. pannus = piece of cloth ; Gk. πῆνος.]

fahren, *irr.*, E. drive, fare ; O. H. G. faran ; Got. farjan. **[Lat. per-itus = erfahren**, versed ; Gk. πόρος, as in Βόσπορος, a ford for oxen ; E. Bosporus ; also Gk. πορεύω, to go, lead, get on.]

falsch, E. false ; Lat. falsus [connected with fallen, to fall ; Lat. fallo ; Gk. σφάλλω]. (The -sch being the Got. ska, as adjective suffix.)

fangen, E. catch (cf. fangs of an animal) ; O. H. G. fahan ; Got. fāhan **[Lat. pango, pax ?].**

faul, E. foul, lazy ; O. H. G. fūl, root fu with derivative la, al [Lat. pūteo, pus ; Gk. πύθω].

fechten, E. to fight ; O. H. G. fëhten ; A. S. feohtan. [Cf. Lat. pugnare.]

fein, E. fine, beautiful ; M. H. G. vin, fin from Lat. finire, etc., hence fine = finished, beautiful.

𝔉eind, *m.*, E. enemy, fiend; O. H. G. fiant; A.S. feond; Goth. fijands {Lat. hostis is not related).
𝔉enster, *n.*, E. window; O. H. G. venstar from Latin fenestra introduced in early Gothic times.
finden, *irr.*, E. to find; M. H. G. vinden; O. H. G. findan; Goth. finthan [Lat. in-venio].
𝔉isch, *m.*, E. fish; O. H. G. fisk; Lat. piscis.
fliehen, *irr.*, E. flow, fleet(-ing); O. H. G. fliozzan; A. S. fleotan (compare flood, fleet) [perhaps also Gk. πλέω to sail, and even Lat. pluere, to rain, French pleuvoir].
𝔉lorin, *m.*, E. florin; late Latin from Florence in Italy, connected with flos, etc., a flower.
𝔉lut, *f.*, E. flood; O. H. G. fluot; Got. flōdus; A. S. flōd from root flō or plō (see fliehen).
fragen, *r.*, E. ask, pray; O. H. G. frāhēn. Connected with Lat. precari, to pray, beg.
𝔉rau, *f.*, E. woman; M. H. G. vrouwe; O. H. G. frouwa [frō=lord, frouwa its feminine].
𝔉reund, *m.*, E. friend; O. H. G. friunt; A. S. freond (from frijon, to love; hence also frei=free).
𝔉rucht, *f.*, E. fruit; O. H. G. fruht from Lat. fructus (c before t=t, as in French nuit).
fünf, E. five; O. H. G. funf, finf; A. S. fīf; from Lat. quinque (for pinque); Gk. πέντε.

𝔊algen, *m.*, E. gallows; O. H. G. galgo; A. S. gealga (from Got. galgan, a rod, beam). [Cf. Golgatha?]
𝔊ast, *m.*, E. guest; O. H. G. gast, gesti from old ghostis from Lat. hostis=a stranger (enemy).
geben, *irr.*, E. give; O. H. G. geban; A. S. gifan; Got. giban [from it 𝔊ift, 𝔊abe, etc.].
gehen, *irr.*, E. to go; O. H. G. gān; A. S. gan with gang. [Perhaps ge+aim, with Lat. eo, Gk. εἶμι].
gerecht, E. just, right; O. H. G. giröht from Lat. rectus, directus.
gestern, E. yester-day; O. H. G. gestaron; Got. gistra; Lat. heri for hjesi; Gk. χθές.
gleich, E. like; O. H. G. gilih; Got. galciks=[ga(ge)+] lika=a body; hence gleich=with (similar) body.
𝔊old, *n.*, E. gold; Got. gulth [connected with gelb=yellow; A. S. geolo and perhaps Gk. χλωρός].
𝔊ott, *m.*, E. God; Got. gūth. Perhaps Skt. dēva; Lat. deus; Gk. Διός?
𝔊raf, *m.*, E. Count, —grave; O. H. G. gravo, gravjo. From root grēf, to command.

haben, E. to have; O. H. G. habēn; A. S. hæbban; Got. haban; Lat. habeo.
𝔥ahn, *m.*, E. cock (hen); O. H. G. hano; A. S. hana, coce; from Lat. cano, to sing.
halb, E. half; M. H. G. halp; A. S. healf [Got. halba=on one side, hence : one half].
hart, E. hard; O. H. G. herti, harti; A. S. heard=brave; cf. Gk. κρατύς=strong for καρτύς.
𝔥aupt, *n.*, E. head; O. H. G. houbit, houpt; A. S. heafod (perhaps Lat. caput, Gk. κεφαλή?)
𝔥aut, *f.*, E. hide, skin; O. H. G. hūt; A. S. hȳd; Lat. cutis, as in scutum, a shield of hide.
𝔥eide, *m.*, E. heathen; O. H. G. heidan; A. S. hǣthen; (Lat. paganus=wild, country) Got. haithi=field.
heil, E. hale, hail! whole; A. S. hāl; Got. haila=Hail! [Lat. augurium=luck].
𝔥eld, *m.*, E. hero; O. H. G. helid; A. S. hæleth; [to Got. root: hal in hehlen, hüllen, to cover, protect].
𝔥erbst, *m.*, E. harvest, autumn; O. H. G. hervist (perhaps to Lat. carpo, to pluck, gather fruit?).
𝔥err, *m.*, E. gentleman, Sir (hero); O. H. G. herro, comparative of hēr=proud, noble; A. S. hār.
𝔥erzog, *m.*, E. duke; O. H. G. heri-zogo; A. S. heretoga=leader of army (𝔥eer).
heute, E. to-day; O. H. G. hiuta; A. S. hes-dæg=this day (cf. Lat. hodie=hoc die).
𝔥irsch, *m.*, E. hart, stag; O. H. G. hiruz, hirz; A. S. heorot (cf. Lat. cervus and Gk. κέρας=a horn).
hoch, E. high; O. H. G. hōh, hauhs; A. S. heah (connected 𝔥ügel, hill, etc.).
𝔥ölle, *f.*, E. hell; O. H. G. hella; Got. halja; A. S. hell (to root: hal in hüllen, to cover).
𝔥und, *m.*, E. dog, hound; O. H. G. hunt(d); Got. hunds (Lat. canis; Gk. κυν- from κύων).
hundert, E. hundred; Got. hunda; A. S. hund; Lat. centum; Gk. ἑκατόν).
  [*N.B.*—the *rt* in hundert belongs to Got. rathjan, **to count**, read.]

ich, E. I; M. H. G. ich; O. H. G. ih; A. S. ic; Got. ik; cf. Lat. ego; Gk. ἐγώ; Skt. aham.
𝔍nsel, *f.*, E. island, from Lat. insula. [Not to be confounded with 𝔈iland=island, from ein-land, i.e. a land by itself.]

ja, E. yes, yea; A. S. geā [cf. Gk. ἦ=indeed, really].
𝔍ahr, *n.*, E. year; O. H. G. jār; Got. jer. [Perhaps Gk. ὥρα=season, spring].
je, E. ever; M. H. G. ie; O. H. G. io, ēo; E. aye, connected with Lat. aevum, and Gk. αἰών.
jung, E. young; O. H. G. junc; A. S. geong; Got. juggs (jungs); Ind.-Ger. yuwen; Lat. juvenis.

T

Kampf, E. battle (camp); O. H. G. champf; A. S. camp (connected Lat. campus (Martius)).
Kapelle, E. chapel; from Lat. capella, dimin. of capa, a cloak, then the place where the cloak of Saint Martin was kept, then generally a sacred building (cf. E. cape).
Kar-(freitag) or **Char-** = E. Good-(Friday) from O. H. G. chara = sorrow, mourning.
kaufen, E. buy; M. H. G. koufen; O. H. G. choufōn = trade, sell or buy; A. S. cýpan, E. cheap, connected.
keck, E. bold, quick; O. H. G. chec, quec = living, quick; Lat. vivus for gwivus; Gk. βίος, life. Compare E. quick-silver; "the quick and the dead" [wick, for quick].
Kerl, E. fellow, churl; O. H. G. Karal; A. S. ceorl = serf; [cf. Karl, Charles].
Kind, n., E. child; O. H. G. chind (connected with genus; Gk. γένος, also with gens, etc.).
Kirche, f., E. church; O. H. G. chirihha; A. S. cyrice; a Greek word κυριακόν (Κύριος, the Lord).
Kirsche, f., E. cherry; O. H. G. chirsa; Lat. cerasius (adj.); Gk. κερασία, cherry-tree.
Kiste, f., E. chest; M. H. G. kiste; O. H. G. chista; A. S. cist; Lat. cista; Gk. κίστη.
klein, E. small (clean); M. H. G. kleine; A. S. clǽne. The G. borrowed from Frisian.
Kloster, E. convent, cloister, from M. Lat. claustrum (cf. claudo, to shut up).
Knabe, E. boy, knave; M. H. G. knappe; O. H. G. chnappo (perhaps to root gen; **Lat**. genus, etc.).
Knecht, E. man-servant (knight); A. S. cniht; O. H. G. chnëht (see above word).
Knie, n., E. knee; O. H. G. chniu; Got. kniu; Lat. genu; Gk. γόνυ; Ind. G. gnu, gnew.
Knopf, m., E. knob, button [A. S. cnopp], connected with Knospe, a bud.
kochen, E. to cook; O. H. G. chohhon, from Lat. coquere, French cuire.
kommen, E. to come; O. H. G. choman, queman; Lat. venio for gvenio.
König, E. king; M. H. G. künic, künc; O. H. G. chunig; A. S. cyning, from A. S. cynn = race, noble birth.
können, E. can; M. H. G. kunnan; O. H. G. chunnan; Lat. gnosco; Gk. ἔ-γνων.
Kopf, m., E. head (cup); O. H. G. choph, chuph; A. S. cuppa. [Lat. cūpa, a barrel; Gk. κεφαλή.]
Körper, m., body (corps), M. H. G. körper, körpel, borrowed from Lat. corpus—corporis.
kostspielig, E. dear, expensive, from kost = victuals, expense, and spilden (O. H. G.), to be prodigal.
Kraft, E. force (craft = force of mind); O. H. G. chraft [perhaps Gk. κράνυν, strong??].
Kreuz, n., E. cross; M. H. G. kriuz; O. H. G. chrūzi, from Lat. crucis (crux).
Kreuzer, m., E., penny, etc., a small coin with a cross on it originally, hence the name.
Krone, f., E. crown, borrowed in O. H. G. from Lat. corona; M. H. G. krōne, krōn.
Kuh, f., E. cow; M. H. G. kuo; A. S. cū; Got. kos (cf. Lat. bos; Gk. βοῦς; Skt. gaus).
Kupfer, n., E. copper; O. H. G. chupfar, from Lat. aes cyprium, from Κύπρος = Cyprus.
kurz, E. short, curt; O. H. G. skurz; A. S. sceort; from Lat. curtus.

lassen, E. to let; O. H. G. lāzzan; A. S. lǽtan; Got. lētan [cf. Lat. lassus = tired].
leben, E. to live; Got. liban; A. S. libban (cf. to leave; Leib and bleiben, to remain).
Leiche, f., E. corpse (cf. Lich-field, corpse-field); O. H. G. līh; Got. leik, lika = body. [See gleich.]
leicht, E. easy, light; M. H. G. līht; O. H. G. līhti. [Perhaps Lat. levis and Gk. ἐ-λαχύς.]
leiden, E. to suffer; M. H. G. līden, O. H. G. līdan, connected with Got. leithan, to go, i.e. leiten = go into strange lands, hence suffer. See Elend.
lernen, E. to learn; O. H. G. lërnan; A. S. lcornian; from Got. lais = I know.
lesen, E. to read; O. H. G. lēsan; Got. lisan. [Perhaps Lat. lego; Gk. λέγω, **to read**.]
letzt, E. latest, last; M. H. G. lezzist. Superlative to laz = tired (Lat. lassus).
lieb, E. dear (lief); M. H. G. liep; O. H. G. liob; **A. S.** leof; Skt. lubh = desire eagerly. Perhaps to Lat. libido, libet (**lubido, lubet**).
liegen, E. to lie down; O. H. G. licken, ligen; A. S. licgan; [Lat. lectus, a bed; Gk. λέκτρον].
Löwe, m., E. lion; M. H. G. lëwe; O. H. G. lëwo [borrowed from Lat. leo; Gk. λέων].

machen, E. to make; O. H. G. mahhōn; A. S. macian [connected with M. H. G. gemach = comfortable].
Magd, f., E. maid, servant; O. H. G. magad = virgin. [Perhaps to Ind. G. magh = be able.]
Mahl (**Mal**), E. meal (times), both from O. H. G. māl = a fixed time, a fixed point.
Mann, m., E. man; O. H. G. man; Got. manna; A. S. mon; Skt. manus; Ind. G. manū.

Marschall, *m.*, E. marshal, from O. H. G. marah = horse, mare, and schalk = servant.
Maulwurf, *m.*, E. mole, from O. H. G. molte = mould, earth, and werfen = to throw up.
Maus, *f.*, E. mouse; O. H. G. mûs; Lat. mus; Gk. μῦς; Skt. mûs (mus-ay, to take, rob).
mehr, E. more; O. H. G. Comparative merre (cf. Lat. major); Got. maiza.
Meister, *m.*, E. master; O. H. G. meistar, from Lat. magister; French maître.
Messe, *f.*, E. mass (Christ-mas); O. H. G. messa, missa, from Lat. missa est, etc. (concio), the words with which the diakonus dismissed the assembly, if no communion took place.
Mohr, *m.*, E. black(-a-moor); M. H. G. môr, from Lat. Maurus (North Africa).
Mönch, E. monk; M. H. G. münech; O. H. G. munich, from Lat. monachus, Gk. μοναχός.
Mond, *m.*, E. moon; M. H. G. mâne; O. H. G. mâno; Got. mêna; A. S. môna (Lat. mens-is; Gk. μήν).
Mühle, *f.*, E. mill; M. H. G. mül; O. H. G. mûli; A. S. myln; Lat. mola.
Münster, *n.*, E. minster; O. H. G. munustiri, borrowed from Lat. monasterium = convent.
Münze, *f.*, E. mint, coin; O. H. G. munizza; borrowed from Lat. moneta = coined money.
Mutter, *f.*, E. mother; M. H. G. muoter; A. S. môddor; Lat. mater; Gk. μήτηρ [Skt. root, mâ].

Nachbar, *m.*, E. neighbour; M. H. G. nachgebûr; O. H. G. nahgibûr [= nahe (near) and bauer = bûr]. [See bauen.]
Nacht, *f.*, E. night; O. H. G. naht; A. S. niht; Lat. noct-; Gk. νυκτ-.
Name, *m.*, E. name; O. H. G. namo; Lat. nomen; Gk. ὄ-νομα.
Nebel, *m.*, E. mist; O. H. G. nebul; Lat. nebula; Gk. νεφέλη; Skt. nabhas.
Neffe, *m.*, E. nephew; O. H. G. nevo; A. S. nefa; Lat. nepos = grandson; Gk. νέποδες = brood, little ones.
neu, E. new; M. H. G. niuwe; O. H. G. niuwi; Got. niujis; Skt. navus; Lat. novus; Gk. νέος.
neun, E. nine; O. H. G. niun; A. S. nigun; Skt. navan; Lat. novem; Gk. ἐννέα. Most likely connected with neu, new, as nine is the first or new number of the 3d tetrade (or series of four things).
nüchtern, E. fasting; O. H. G. nuohturn (perhaps Lat. nocturnus, nightly [night's fast?]).
Nuß, *f.*, E. nut; O. H. G. nuz; *not* from Lat. nux; for A. S. hnutu. [Skt. knud.]

Ohr, *n.*, E. ear; M. H. G. ôre; O. H. G. ôra; A. S. eare; Lat. auris; Gk. οὖς.
Oel, *n.*, E. oil; O. H. G. ole, ol, borrowed from Lat. oleum in the 8th century.
opfern, E. to offer, dedicate; O. H. G. opfarôn; A. S. offrian, from Lat. offerre (for ob-ferre).
Ostern, *f.*, E. Easter; O. H. G. ostarûn; from Teuton goddess Austrô, of the Dawn; East; connected with Skt. usâs, Lat. aurora (for ausos-a); Gk. ἠώς = morning, dawn.

Paar, *n.*, E. pair; O. H. G. pâr, borrowed from Lat. par = equal (E. peer).
Palast, *m.*, E. palace; M. H. G. palast, borrowed from French palais, Lat. palatium.
Papier, *n.*, E. paper, from Gk. and Lat. papyrus, a vegetable, furnishing parchment (in Egypt).
Pfalz, *f.*, E. palatinate; M. H. G. phalenze; Lat. palatium, or perhaps more correctly connected with Pfahl = palings, pales, upon which houses were built in marshes (Lat. palus).
Pfau, *m.*, E. pea-cock, -hen; O. H. G. pfawo; Lat. pavo; Gk. ταώς (perhaps onomatopoetic name).
Pferd, *n.*, E. horse; M. H. G. tpfert; borrowed from M. Lat. paraveredus, parifredus, a hybrid word from Gk. παρά and Lat. veredus = a horse. Compare E. palfrey, French palefroi.
Pfingsten, *f.*, E. pentecost, Whitsuntide; M. H. G. pfingsten, from Gk. πεντεκοστή = 50th (day), *i.e.* after Easter.
Pflaume, *f.*, E. plum; M. H. G. pflûme, from Lat. prunum (Pl. pruna).
Pfund, *n.*, E. pound; O. H. G. pfunt; A. S. pund, from Lat. pondo.
Pilgrim, Pilger, *m.*, E. pilgrim; O. H. G. piligrim, from Lat. peregrinus, French pèlerin.
Post, *f.*, E. post, from Latin posita, the place (where the horses stood).
predigen, E. preach; O. H. G. predigôn, from Lat. praedicare, to speak before others.
Priester, *m.*, E. priest; O. H. G. prêstar, from Gk. πρεσβύτερος, Lat. presbyter.
Pulver, *n.*, E. powder; M. H. G. from Lat. pulvis (-eris). dust, ashes.

Quacksalber, *m.*, E. quack-doctor. Quad from O. H. G. quacken, to boast; Salbe, salve, ointment.
Quelle, *f.*, E. fountain. New word from O. H. G. quellan; Skt. root gel, jala = water.

Rad, *n.*, (E. wheel); O. H. G. rad (a word missing in E. and Got.); Lat. rota.
Rauch, *m.*, E. smoke, reek; M. H. G. rouch; O. H. G. rouhh; Ind. Germ. root, rūk, to smoke.
Regen, *m.*, E. rain; O. H. G. rëgan (Lat. rigare, to water); cf. also to irrigate = water.
Reich, *n.*, E. empire; O. H. G. rîhhi; A. S. ríce; Got. reiki (Lat. rego = to rule, lead).
reich, E. rich, connected with above, originally = powerful, ruling.
Reue, *f.*, E. repentance (cf. to rue); O. H. G. riuwa; A. S. hreowan = to repent, be vexed, be sad.
Roß, *n.*, E. horse; O. H. G. ros; A. S. hors. [Perhaps Lat. (curso) curro.]
rot, **E. red; O.** H. G. **rōt**; Goth. rauds; A. S. reod [cf. Lat. rubido, Fk. ἐρυθρός).
Ruder, **n., E. rudder, oar**; O. H. G. ruodar; A. S. rother (Lat. re-mus, ra-tis, Gk. ἐρέτης).

Sache, *f.*, E. thing (-sake); O. H. G. sahha; A. S. sacu = quarrel, cause; Got. sakjo.
sagen, E. to say; O. H. G. sagan; A. S. sagjan, secjan.
Salz, **n.**, E. salt; O. H. G. salz; Got. salt; A. S. sealt; Lat. sal; Gk. ἅλς.
Samstag, *m.*, E. Saturday; O. H. G. sambaz-tag (-tac), from Lat. sabbati-dies) (cf. French samedi).
Sau, *f.*, E. sow; O. H. G. sû; A. S. sû (sugu); Lat. sû(s); Gk. σῦ(s) (Skt. sû = bring forth).
Schaf, *n.*, E. sheep; O. H. G. scâf; A. S. sceap (E. ewe, from Lat. ovis, not connected).
Schale, *f.*, E. scale; O. H. G. scâla = shell of fruit.
Schatz, *m.*, E. treasure; O. H. G. scaz = money, fortune; A. S. sceatt.
Scheere, *f.*, E. shears, scissors; O. H. G. scâri; A. S. sceran = to cut in two.
Schiff, *n.*, E. **skiff, vessel; O. H. G. scif, scef; A.** S. scip; cf. French é-quiper, to equip.
Schilling, *m.*, E. shilling (-ing = derivative syll.); O. Germ. skellan = to sound metallic.
Schlaf, *m.*, E. sleep; O. H. G. slâf; **Got. slêps; A.** S. **slæp.**
schlecht, E. bad; had formerly only the meaning straight, even; O. H. G. slëht; Got. slaihts, **straight.**
schließen, E. to shut; O. H. G. sliozan. (Probably, Lat. claudo-sum for s-clausum.)
Schmied, *m.*, E. smith; M. H. G. smit; O. H. G. smid; Got. smi- applies to hard wood, metals.
Schnee, *m.*, E. snow; M. H. G. snê; O. H. G. snêo; A. S. snāw; Got. snaiws. The Latin (nix) nivis, and Gk. νίφει, it snows, have lost s before the **n.**
schön, E. fine; M. H. G. schoene; O. H. G. scôni = glittering, brilliant; Got. skauns = form, originally only meaning "with a form" [cf. Lat. forma for beauty].
schreiben, E. write (cf. scribe); O. H. G. scrîban, from Lat. scribere. **[Connected with E. shrive.]**
Schule, *f.*, E. school; M. H. G. schuole; **O.** H. G. scuola, from **Lat.** scōla, schola.
Schwein, *n.*, E. swine; **M.** H. G. swîn; A. S. swîn; Got. swein [**connected with Sau, which see**].
Schwester, *f.*, E. **sister; O.** H. G. swëster; Got. swistar; A. **S. sweostor; Skt. swasr; Lat. soror.**
schwören, **E. to swear; O. H. G. sweren; Got. swaran; A. S. swerjan [cf. E. an-*swer*].**
sechs, E. **six; O. H. G. sehs;** A. S. six; Got. saihs; **Lat. sex; Gk. ἕξ; Skt. sas.**
sehen, E. **to** see; O. H. G. sehan; A. S. seohan, seon [cf. Lat. sequi = follow (with the eyes)].
sein, E. **to be;** M. H. G. sîn (from various roots, cf. Lat. sum, sunt; es, est; fio, etc.).
sich, E. oneself; O. H. G. sih; Lat. se; Gk. ἑ; Skt. sva = own.
Sieg, *m.*, E. victory; O. H. G. sigi, sigu, from Skt. root sah = to conquer. [Perhaps Gk. ἰ-σχ-ον.]
sitzen, E. to sit; O. H. G. sizzian; A. S. sittan. Cf. Lat. sedeo; Gk. ἕζομαι for σεδ-jo-.
Sklave, *m.*, E. slave, from Slavus; a Latin term, from the Slavonian war-prisoners.
Sohn, *m.*, E. son; O. H. G. sûn, sunu; Got. sunus; Skt. sûnû [sû = bring forth in Skt.].
Sold, *m.*, pay (cf. soldier), from French solde = pay, reward, wages; Lat. solidus, a coin.
Sommer, *m.*, E. summer; O. H. G. sumar; A. S. sumor [Skt. sama = year].
Sonne, *f.*, E. sun; O. H. G. sunna [cf. Lat. sol; Gk. ἥλιος; Skt. svar, sû, to shine].
Spiegel, *m.*, E. looking-glass; O. H. G. spiagal; Lat. speculum.
Staat, *m.*, state; and Stadt, E. town, from Lat. status; Ind. G. sta = stehen, to stand.
stehen, E. to stand; O. **H. G. stên, stân;** Got. standan; cf. Lat. stare; Gk. ἵ-στα-ναι.
sterben, E. to **die** (cf. starve); **O. H. G.** sterban; A. S. steorfan.
Stern, **m.,** E. star; O. H. G. stërnô; Got. stairnô; A. S. steorra; Gk. ἀ-στήρ; Lat. stella.
Straße, *f.*, **E. street; O,** H. G. strâza; A. S. stræt, from Lat. via strata = paved way.

Stube, f., E. room (cf. stove); O. H. G. stuba; A. S. stofe = room with heating contrivance (?).
Süd, m., E. South, with loss of n from O. H. G. sundan; A. S. sûth [connected with sun (?)].
süß, E. sweet; M. H. G. süeze; O. H. G. swuozi, suozi; A. S. swête; cf. Lat. suavis; Gk. ἡδύς.

Tafel, f., E. table; M. H. G. tavel; O. H. G. tavala, from Lat. tabella, tabula.
Tag, m., E. day; O. H. G. tac(g); Got. dags; A. S. daeg; Skt. dah = to burn [not Lat. dies].
Taler, m., E. dollar, a new G. **word from** Joachimstaler, a florin from the Joachimstal, valley of J.
Taufe, f., E. baptism [dip]; O. H. G. toufa; Got. daupjan; A. S. dopian (to : tief, deep).
Tausend, E. thousand; M. H. G. tusent; O. H. G. tusunt; A. S. thusend; thusundi.
Teil, m., E. share (deal); Got. dail; A. S. dael.
Teller, m., E. plate, from Italian tagliere, connected with tailler, to cut (cf. **E. tailor**).
Teufel, m., E. devil; M. H. G. tiuvel; O. H. G. tioval; Lat. diabolus (in 6th century).
Tochter, f., E. daughter; O. H. G. tohtar; A. S. dohtor; cf. Gk. θυγατήρ. (Perhaps Skt. **duh = to milk.**)
Tod, m., E. death; M. H. G. tôt; Got. dauthus; cf. E. die (root lost for G. sterben, to die).
treu, E. true; M. H. G. triuwe; A. S. treowe [cf. E. truth, troth; French trève = truce].
tun, E. to do; M. H. G. tuon; A. S. dön; cf. Lat. de-di; Gk. θε in τι-θη-μι, to put; Skt. dhâ.
Tür, f., E. door; O. H. G. turi; A. S. duru; Ind. G. dhur; **Gk. θύρα**; Lat. fores.
Tugend, f., E. virtue; **M. H. G. tugend [to verb taugen, to be worth]**.
Turm, m., E. tower, from Lat. turris; A. S. tûr, torr. (Unexplained change of r into m.)

üben, E. to practise; O. H. G. uoben [cf. Lat. opus = work; operari, to work, sacrifice].
Uhr, f., E. clock, hour; from Lat. hora, French heure (silent h).

Veilchen, n., E. violet, a diminutive; M. H. G. viel; from Lat. viola (cf. Fr. violette).
Vieh, n., E. [fee] beast; O. H. G. fehu; A. S. feoh, from Lat. pecus, cattle [cf. pecunia = money].

Wagen, m., E. carriage, wain; A. S. waegn; Ind. G. root wegh, to pull, drive; Lat. veh-iculum.
wahr, E. true; O. H. G. wâri; connected with Lat. verus [but **A. S. soth, E. sooth**].
Wasser, n., E. water; O. H. G. wazzar; A. S. waeter; Ind. G. ud = wet, in Gk. ὕδωρ, water; Lat. udus.
Weib, n., E. woman, wife; M. H. G. wîb; A. S. wîf. [Perhaps Skt. **vip = to be enthusiastic** (?)]
Wein, m., E. wine; O. H. G. wîn; A. S. wîn; Got. wein; Lat. vinum; Gk. οἶνος.
welch, E. which; O. H. G. wie-lih; Got. hwi-leika; A. S. hwylc [= wer + gleich (whe + liko)].
Welsch, E. Welsh; O. H. G. walhisc = romanic [the Keltic "foreigners," the Volcae]. [Cf. E. Wales, Cornwall; G. welsch = French or Italian; also Wallachia.]
werden, E. to become; O. H. G. werdan; Got. wairthan. Perhaps Lat. verto, to turn, change.
Westen, m., E. west; O. H. G. westan. [Cf. Lat. vesper, Gk. ἑσπέρα = evening, west.]
wild, E. wild; O. H. G. wildi = going astray (scarcely with Lat. silva or G. Wald, wood).
wissen, E. know (wit, wot); O. H. G. wizzan (cf. Got. wait = ich weiß, I know); Lat. video.
Wort, n., E. word; Got. waurd, from Ind. G. wrdho-. **(Cf. Lat. verbum.)**

zählen, E. to count, tell; M. H. G. zaln, zeln; **A. S. tellan**; Got. talzjan, **to instruct.**
zeigen, E. to show; O. H. G. zeigôn; Ind. G. root dik; cf. Lat. dico, Gk. δείκνυμι.
zwanzig, E. twenty; O. H. G. zweinzug; A. S. twentig [-tig from Got. tigu; **cf. Lat. decem**].
zwei, E. two; M. H. G. zwêne (fem. zwo, neut. zwei); A. S. fem. twô; Lat. duo; **Gk. δύο**; so that zwei, two, is really the neuter form of the word A. S. twegen; Skt. dva.
zwischen, E. be-tween; O. H. G. zwisken, between two; connected with zwei, above.

Note.—The **above** short Dictionary contains, as a rule, only root-words, and the intelligent student will easily connect a great number of derivatives with them, especially after he has studied the preceding sections **on Derivation** and Word-formation. Some words also, the derivation of which from Latin is very self-evident, or which entered straight and unchanged from Latin or Greek, such as Philologie, Astronomie, etc., Rector, Nation, etc., have been omitted.

APPENDIX B.

[*N.B.*—These Lists might be learnt with advantage very early in the Student's course.]

In order to assist the pupil in that most essential and also most difficult part in the study of any foreign language, namely, the speedy acquisition of its vocabulary, we append here the most important words which are, with slight modifications, the same in German and English. Roots only are given as a rule, but the intelligent student will find little difficulty in grouping some derivatives round each root; for example: *sleep*—Schlaf, *m.* (given): from this come schlafen, *to sleep;* einschläfern, *to send to sleep;* verschlafen (sich), *to oversleep oneself;* Schlafzimmer, *bedroom;* Schlaftrunk, *sleeping draught;* schläfrig, *sleepy,* etc. In almost all cases the etymologically related word in the one language is also the equivalent in meaning of its fellow in the other language; where this is not so, the modern meaning of the word is given in brackets, as, for example, English *town* (hedge), a walled-in or hedged-in collection of houses, and German Zaun, *a hedge.* Unchanged, or only slightly changed, Latin or Greek words are not given in the following lists; many of them are spelt the same way in German and English, as Nation (f.), April (m.), September, December, etc.; others are only different in their terminations, thus, English *-ty* = German *-tät;* as *university* = Universität, *faculty* = Fakultät, etc. English *-y* = German *-ie,* as *philosophy* = Philosophie, *geography* = Geographie, etc. English *-ics* = German *-ik,* as *politics* = Politik, *physics* = Physik, etc.

Proper names of persons, towns, or countries are not given here.

I. Words exactly alike in form and meaning in English and German.

all	all	butter	Butter, *f.*	mast	Mast, *m.*	still (quiet)	still
altar	Altar, *m.*	fall	fall-en, *irreg.*	mild	mild	stink	stink-en, *irreg.*
ball	Ball, *m.*	fast	fast-en, *reg.*	moor	Moor, *n.*	strand	Strand, *m.*
balsam	Balsam, *m.*	find	find-en, *irreg.*	name	Name, *m.*	tiger	Tiger, *m.*
band	Band, *n.*	finger	Finger, *m.*	nest	Nest, *n.*	wall	Wall, *m.*
bank	Bank, *f.*	gas	Gas, *n.*	pack	pack-en, *reg.*	wander	wander-n, *reg.*
banner	Banner, *n.*	gold	Gold, *n.*	pause	Pause, *f.*	ware	Ware, *f.*
baron	Baron, *m.*	hack	hack-en, *reg.*	post	Post, *f.*	warm	warm
begin	begin-n-en, *irreg.*	hammer	Hammer, *m.*	ring	Ring, *m.*	warn	warn-en, *reg.*
bind	bind-en, *irreg.*	hand	Hand, *f.*	rose	Rose, *f.*	wild	wild
bitter	bitter	hinder	hinder-n, *reg.*	sand	Sand, *m.*	wind	Wind, *m.*
blind	blind	horn	Horn, *n.*	send	send-en, *half reg.*	winter	Winter, *m.*
brief	Brief (= letter)	hunger	Hunger, *m.*	sink	sink-en, *irreg.*	wolf	Wolf, *m.*
bring	bring-en, *half reg.*	land	Land, *n.*	stand	Stand, *m.*	and a few others	

II. Words nearly alike.

alms	Almofen, n.	hole (cave)	Höhle, f.	pair	Paar, n.	span	Spanne, f.
bake	back·en, irreg.	hell	Hölle, f.	palm	Palme, f.	star	Stern, m.
bible	Bibel, f.	king	König, m.	paper	Papier, n.	state	Staat, m.
bundle	Bündel, n.	knot	Knoten, m.	paradise	Paradies, n.	stir (disturb)	stör·en, reg.
coal	Kohle, f.	lip	Lippe, f.	praise	preis·en, irreg.	title	Titel, m.
cell	Zelle, f.	lungs	Lunge, f.	priest	Priester, m.	true	treu (= faithful)
collar	Keller, m.	man	Mann, m.	pulse	Puls, m.	verse	Vers, m.
flame	Flamme, f.	mantle	Mantel, m.	rat	Ratte, f.	vest	Weste, f.
friend	Freund, m.	market	Markt, m.	raw	roh	well	wohl
glass	Glas, n.	naked	nackt	see	seh·en, irreg.	west	Westen, m.
grade	Grad, m.	new	neu	sole	Sohle, f.	will	Wille, m.
grass	Gras, n.	nine	neun	son	Sohn, m.	woe!	weh!
grim	grimm[·ig]	often	oft	soul	Seele, f.	wool	Wolle, f.

[These could not be classified in the following lists.]

III. Vowel Variations.

1. English *a* generally = German a, as *father*, Vater (m.); *man*, Mann, etc.; but English *a* often = German e, as in:

angel	Engel, m.	fat	fett	rain	Regen, m.
arch-	Erz-	lark	Lerche, f.	to starve (die)	sterben, irreg.
[archbishop	Erzbischof]	to lay	legen, reg.	wasp	Wespe, f.
harvest	Herbst, m.	mass	Messe, f.	way	Weg, m.

2. English *e* sometimes = German e, as *bed*, Bett (n.); *send*, senden, etc.; but,

   (i.) English *e* = German a, as in:

beck	Bach, m.	fern	Farn, m.	stem	Stamm, m.
bench	Bank, f.	guest	Gast, m.	then	dann
eel	Aal, m.	to let	lassen, irreg.	there	da (dar)
evening	Abend, m.	seed	Saat, f.	twenty	zwanzig

   (ii.) English *e* = German i (ie), as in:

fever	Fieber, n.	nether	nieder (unter)	step-	Stief-
fresh	frisch	paper	Papier, n.	[stepfather	Stiefvater]
here	hier	seven	sieben		

3. (i.) English *ea* = German a (ä), as in:

bear	Bär, m.	ear (of corn)	Ähre, f.	stead	Statt, f.
beard	Bart, m.	meagre (lean)	mager	weapon	Waffe, f.
clear	klar	meal	Mahl (·zeit)	year	Jahr, n.

   (ii.) English *ea* = German au, as in:

beam (tree)	Baum, m.	dreary	traurig	to leap (run)	laufen, irreg.
deaf	taub	heap	Haufe, m.	seam	Saum, m.
dream	Traum, m.	leaf	Laub, n.		

(iii.) English *ea* = German e (ee), as in:

to break	brechen, *irreg.*	to knead	kneten, *reg.*	to seat	setzen, *reg.*
earnest	ernst	to lean	lehnen, *reg.*	to shear	scheeren, *irreg.*
earth	Erde, *f.*	to learn	lernen, *reg.*	spear	Speer, *m.*
to eat	essen, *irreg.*	leather	Leder, *n.*	to steal	stehlen, *irreg.*
feast	Fest, *m.*	meal (flour)	Mehl, *n.*	tea	Thee, *m.*
leather	Feder, *f.*	pearl	Perle, *f.*	to tread	treten, *irreg.*
heart	Herz, *n.*	sea	See, *f.*	weather	Wetter, *n.*
hearth	Herd, *m.*				

(iv.) English *ea* = German ei, as in:

to heal	heilen, *reg.*	to reach	reichen, *reg.*	weak (soft)	weich
heath	Heide, *f.*	sheath	Scheide, *f.*	wheat	Weizen, *m.*
to mean	meinen, *reg.*	sweat	Schweiß, *m.*		

(v.) English *ea* = German o (ö), as in:

dead	todt	Easter	Ostern, *n.*	to hearken	horchen, *reg.*
death	Tod, *m.*	flea	Floh, *m.*	stream	Strom, *m.*
ear	Ohr, *n.*	great	groß	to swear	schwören, *irreg.*
east	Osten, *m.*	to hear	hören, *reg.*		

4. (i.) English *ee* = German a (ä), as in:

cheese	Käse, *m.*	sheep	Schaf, *n.*	steel	Stahl, *m.*
deed	That, *f.*	sleep	Schlaf, *m.*	street	Straße, *f.*

(ii.) English *ee* = German ei, as in:

free	frei	three	drei		

(iii.) English *ee* = German ie, as in:

beer	Bier, *n.*	deep	tief	keel	Kiel, *m.*
creep	kriechen, *irreg.*	deer [animal]	Tier, *n.*	knee	Knie, *n.*

(iv.) English *ee* = German o, as in:

fleet	Flotte, *f.*	need	Not		

(v.) English *ee* = German (ü) u, as in:

to feel	fühlen, *reg.*	heed [guard]	Hut, *f.*	to seek	suchen, *reg.*
green	grün	keen [bold]	kühn	sweet	süß

5. English *ew* = German au, as in:

to brew	brauen, *reg.*	to hew	hauen, *irreg.*	screw	Schraube, *f.*
dew	Tau, *m.*	to mew	miauen, *reg.*		

6. English *i* = often German i, as in *milk*, Milch (f.), etc.; but,

(i.) English *i* = German au, as in:

bride	Braut, *f.*	to dive	tauchen	fist	Faust, *f.*
dip (baptize)	taufen, *reg.*	to drip	traufen	to sip (sup)	saufen

(ii.) English *i* = German e, as in :

field	Feld, n.	liver	Leber, f.	slight (bad)	schlecht
to fight	fechten, *irreg.*	to milk	melken, *irreg.*	to stick	stechen, *reg.*
to give	geben, *irreg.*	quick (bold)	keck	to strive	streben, *reg.*
knight (groom)	Knecht, m.	right	Recht, n.	to think	denken, *half reg.*
to live	leben, *reg.*	six	sechs		

(iii.) English *i* = German ei, as in :

to bite	beißen, *irreg.*	to grip	greifen, *irreg.*	to smite	schmeißen, *irreg.*
to drive	treiben, *irreg.*	mile	Meile, f.	stiff	steif
ditch, dyke (pond)	Teich, m.	pipe	Pfeife, f.	swine	Schwein, n.
ice	Eis, n.	prize, price	Preis, m.	tide (time)	Zeit, f.
idle (vain, useless)	eitel	rich	reich	twig	Zweig, m.
iron	Eisen, n.	to ride	reiten, *irreg.*	white	weiß
fig	Feige, f.	ripe	reif	wide	weit
file	Feile, f.	side	Seite, f.	wife	Weib, n.
fine	fein	to shine	scheinen, *irreg.*	wise	weise
to glide	gleiten, *irreg.*				

(iv.) English *i* = German u (ü), as in :

birth	Geburt, f.	hip	Hüfte, f.	sin	Sünde, f.
cripple	Krüppel, m.	kiss	Kuß, m.	thin	dünn
to fill	füllen, *reg.*	mill	Mühle, f.	thirst	Durst, m.
flight	Flucht, f.	minster	Münster, n.	tinder	Zunder, m.
to gird	gürten, *reg.*	mint	Münze, f.		

7. (i.) English *o* = German a, as in :

cold	kalt	long	lang	to throng	sich drängen, *reg.*
to fold	falten, *reg.*	nose	Nase, f.	wold (wood)	Wald, m.
to hold	halten, *irreg.*	old	alt		

(ii.) English *o* = German e, as in :

more	mehr	snow	Schnee, m.	worth	Wert, m.
roe	Reh, n.	work	Werk, n.		

(iii.) English *o* = German ei, as in

bone	Bein, n.	holy	heilig	stone	Stein, m.
both	beide	home	Heim, n.	stroke	Streich, m.
cloth (dress)	Kleid, n.	hot	heiß	token	Zeichen, n.
ghost	Geist, m.	most	meist	two	zwei

(iv.) English *o* = German u (ü), as in :

bosom	Busen, m.	fodder	Futter, n.	over	über
box	Büchse, f.	for	für	to prove	prüfen, *reg.*
brother	Bruder, m.	ford	Furt, f.	shot	Schuß, m.
copper	Kupfer, n.	fox	Fuchs, m.	storm	Sturm, m.
to do	tun, *irreg.*	to hop	hüpfen, *reg.*	wonder	Wunder, n.
-dom as: kingdom	-tum Königtum	mother	Mutter, f.	worm	Wurm, m.

U

8. English *oa* = German ei, as in:

broad	breit	oath	Eid, *m.*	soap	Seife, *f.*
oak	Eiche, *f.*				

9. English *oo* = German u (û), as in:

blood	Blut, *n.*	cool	kühl	foot	Fuß, *m.*
bloom (flower)	Blume, *f.*	door	Türe, *f.*	good	gut
book	Buch, *n.*	flood	Flut, *f.*	hoof	Huf, *m.*
booth	Bude, *f.*	floor	Flur, *f.*	stool	Stuhl, *m.*
brood	Brut, *f.*				

10. (i.) English *ou* = German au, as in:

foul (lazy)	faul	louse	Laus, *f.*	rough	rauh
house	Haus, *n.*	mouse	Maus, *f.*	sour	sauer
loud	laut	out	aus	thousand	tausend

(ii.) English *ou* = German u, as in:

enough	genug	plough	Pflug, *m.*	through	durch
ground	Grund, *m.*	round	rund	wound	Wunde, *f.*
hound	Hund, *m.*	south	Süd(en)		

11. English *ow* = German au (u), as in:

brown	braun	cow	Kuh, *f.*	sow	Sau, *f.*
brows	Brauen	shower	Schauer, *m.*	town (hedge)	Zaun, *m.*

12. (i.) English *u* = German au, as in:

to endure	dauern, *reg.*	scum	Schaum, *m.*	up	auf
plum	Pflaume, *f.*	thumb	Daumen, *m.*		

(ii.) English *u* = German e, as in:

to burn	brennen, *half reg.*	churl (fellow)	Kerl, *m.*	to run	rennen, *half reg.*

(iii.) English *u* = German o, as in:

full	voll	summer	Sommer, *m.*	thunder	Donner, *m.*
gulf	Golf, *m.*	sun	Sonne, *f.*	tun	Tonne, *f.*
murder	Mord, *m.*	to stutter	stottern, *reg.*	turf	Torf, *m.*
spur	Sporn, *m.*				

(iv.) English *u* = German û, as in:

hut	Hütte, *f.*	must	müßen, *aux.*	to pluck	pflücken, *reg.*

IV. Consonant Variations.

[The Student is recommended to look up pp. 135-137 in the Grammar.]

1. VOWEL-CONSONANTS *y*, *i* in English = g in German, as in:

day	Tag, *m.*	rain	Regen, *m.*	wain (carriage)	Wagen, *m.*
eye	Auge, *n.*	[said	ge-fag-t]	way	Weg, *m.*
honey	Honig, *m.*	sail	Segel, *n.*	yester(-day)	gestern
to lay	leg-en, *reg.*	to say	fag-en, *reg.*	*y = j* (spirans)	
maid	Magd, *f.*	to slay (hit)	schlag-en, *irreg.*	young	jung
nail	Nagel, *m.*				

2. SPIRANS *s*, by itself, presents no variations in the two languages, but

    (*a*) English *sh* = German sch, as in:

ash(es)	Asche, *f.*	shade	Schatten, *m.*	ship	Schiff, *n.*
bishop	Bischof, *m.*	shame	Scham, *f.*	shoe	Schuh, *m.*
bush	Busch, *m.*	sharp	scharf	shot	Schuß, *m.*
fish	Fisch, *m.*	shear	scheer-en, *irreg.*	shovel	Schaufel, *f.*
flesh	Fleisch, *n.*	sheath	Scheide, *f.*	shower	Schauer, *m.*
fresh	frisch	sheep	Schaf, *n.*	to wash	wasch-en, *irreg.*
marsh	Marsch, *m.*	to shine	schein-en, *irreg.*		

    (*b*) English *sk* (*sc*) = German sch, as in:

flask	Flasche, *f.*	scarlet	Scharlach, *m.*	skiff	Schiff, *n.*
scale	Schale, *f.*	scour	scheuer-n, *reg.*	skirt	Schürze, *f.*
scarf	Schärpe, *f.*	scum	Schaum, *m.*		(= apron)

    (*c*) English *sl* = German schl, as in:

to slay (hit)	schlag-en, *irreg.*	slight (bad)	schlecht	to slumber	schlummer-n, *reg.*
to sleep	schlaf-en, *irreg.*				

        Exception: slave = Sklave [Fr. *esclave*].

    (*d*) English *sm* = German schm, as in:

small	schmal	smith	Schmied, *m.*	smut	Schmutz, *m.*
to smite (throw)	schmeiß-en, *irreg.*				

    (*e*) English *sn* = German schn, as in snow = Schnee.

3. LABIAL MUTES:

    (*a*) English *b* generally = b in German, except in:

bolster	Polster, *n.*	knob	Knopf, *m.*	table	Tafel, *f.*

        N.B.—English *mb* = German mm, as in:

chamber	Kammer, *f.*	dumb (stupid)	dumm	thumb	Daumen, *m.*
to climb	klimm-en, *irreg.*	lamb	Lamm, *n.*	to tumble	tummel-n, *reg.*
comb	Kamm	to slumber	schlummer-n, *reg.*		

(b) (i.) English p = German f (ff), as in:

ape	Affe, m.	help	Hilfe, f.	sharp	scharf
bishop	Bischof, m.	hip	Hüf-te, f.	sheep	Schaf, n.
deep	tief	to hope	hoffen, reg.	ship	Schiff, n.
to drip	triefen, irreg.	to leap (run)	laufen, irreg.	sleep	Schlaf, m.
to gape (gaze)	gaffen, reg.	open	offen	soap	Seife, f.
to grip (grasp)	greifen, irreg.	pepper	Pfeffer, m.	step	Stufe, f.
harp	Harfe, f.	ripe	reif	up	auf
heap	Haufe, m.	shape (create)	schaffen, irreg.	weapon	Waffe, f.

(ii.) English p (pp) = German pf, as in:

apple	Apfel, m.	pan	Pfanne, f.	plough	Pflug, m.
copper	Kupfer, n.	path	Pfad, m.	to pluck	pflücken, reg.
cramp	Krampf, m.	penny	Pfennig, m.	plum	Pflaume, f.
drop	Tropfen, m.	pepper	Pfeffer, m.	post (beam)	Pfosten, m.
to hop	hüpfen, reg.	pipe	Pfeife, f.	pound	Pfund, m.
hop(s)	Hopfen, m.	plant	Pflanze, f.	to stamp	stampfen, reg.
pale (paling)	Pfahl, m.	plaster	Pflaster, n.		

(c) (i.) English f = German b, as in:

calf	Kalb, n.	life	Leben, n.	staff	Stab, m.
deaf	taub	loaf	Laib, m.	thief	Dieb, m.
half	halb	self	selb(-st)	wife	Weib, n.
leaf	Laub, n.				

(ii.) English f = German p, as in:

cliff	Klippe, f.	to offer (sacrifice)	opfern, reg.	scarf	Schärpe, f.
flat	platt				

(iii.) English f = German v, as in:

father	Vater, m.	be-fore	vor	to for-get	ver-gessen, irreg.
folk	Volk, n.	(fowl (bird)	Vogel, m.]	to for-sake	ver-lassen, irreg.
four	vier	full	voll		

(d) (i.) English v = German b, as in:

dove	Taube, f.	to have	haben, aux.	to shave	schaben (rasieren), reg.
to drive	treiben, irreg.	to heave (lift)	heben, irreg.	to shove	schieben, irreg.
even	eben	knave (boy)	Knabe, m.	sieve	Sieb, n.
evening	Abend, m.	to live	leben, reg.	silver	Silber, n.
evil	übel	liver	Leber, f.	to starve (die)	sterben, irreg.
fever	Fieber, n.	navel	Nabel, m.	to strive	streben, reg.
to give	geben, irreg.	over	über	to weave	weben, irreg.
grave	Grab, n.	raven	Rabe, m.		
harvest	Herbst, m.	seven	sieben		

(ii.) English v = German f, as in:

devil	Teufel, m.	oven	Ofen, m.	shovel	Schaufel, f.
five	fü-n-f	to prove (examine)	prüfen, reg.	twelve	zwölf
haven	Hafen, m.				

4. Dental Mutes:

(a) English d = German t, as in:

beard	Bart, *m.*	dip (baptize)	taufen, *reg.*	hard	hart
to bid	bieten, *irreg.*	ditch (pond)	Teich, *m.*	idle (vain)	eitel
bladder	Blatter, *f.*	to do	tun, *irreg.*	to knead	kneten, *reg.*
blade (leaf)	Blatt, *n.*	-dom	-tum	loud	laut
blood	Blut, *n.*	door	Türe, *f.*	middle	Mitte, *f.*
bread	Brot, *n.*	dough	Teig, *m.*	need	Not, *f.*
bride	Braut, *f.*	dove	Taube, *f.*	old	alt
broad	breit	dream	Traum, *m.*	red	rot
brood	Brut, *f.*	drink	trinken, *irreg.*	to ride	reiten, *irreg.*
cold	kalt	to drip	triefen, *irreg.*	saddle	Sattel, *m.*
dale	Tal, *n.*	to drive	treiben, *irreg.*	seed	Saat, *f.*
dance	Tanz	drop	Tropfen, *m.*	seldom	selten
daughter	Tochter, *f.*	flood	Flut, *f.*	side	Seite, *f.*
day	Tag, *m.*	fodder	Futter, *n.*	shade	Schatten, *m.*
dead	tot	to fold	falten, *reg.*	spade	Spaten, *m.*
deaf	taub	ford	Furt, *f.*	stead	statt
dear	teuer	garden	Garten, *m.*	tide (time)	Zeit, *f.*
deep	tief	to gird	gürten, *reg.*	to tread	treten, *irreg.*
deer (animal)	Tier, *n.*	to glide	gleiten, *irreg.*	to wade	waten, *reg.*
devil	Teufel, *m.*	God	Gott, *m.*	wide	weit
dew	Tau, *m.*	good	gut	word	Wort, *n.*

(b) (i.) English t = German ff, ß, as in:

better	besser	kettle	Kessel, *m.*	to smite (throw)	schmeißen, *irreg.*
to bite	beißen, *irreg.*	to let	lassen, *irreg.*	spit	Spieß, *m.*
to eat	essen, *irreg.*	lot	Los, *n.*	street	Straße, *f.*
foot	Fuß, *m.*	nettle	Nessel, *f.*	sweat	Schweiß, *m.*
to forget	vergessen, *irreg.*	nut	Nuß, *f.*	sweet	süß
great	groß	out	aus	that	das, daß
to hate	hassen, *reg.*	settle (chair)	Sessel, *m.*	water	Wasser, *n.*
hot	heiß	to shoot	schießen, *irreg.*	white	weiß

(ii.) English t = German z (tz), as in:

cat	Katze, *f.*	smut (dirt)	Schmutz, *m.*	town (hedge)	Zaun, *m.*
curt	kurz	swart (black)	schwarz	twelve	zwölf
heart	Herz, *n.*	tell (count)	zählen, *reg.*	twenty	zwanzig
malt	Malz, *f., n.*	ten	zehn	twig	Zweig, *m.*
mint	Münze, *f.*	tide (time)	Zeit, *f.*	to twitter	zwitschern, *reg.*
net	Netz, *n.*	tin	Zinn, *n.*	two	zwei
plant	Pflanze, *f.*	tinder	Zunder, *m.*	wart	Warze, *f.*
salt	Salz, *n.*	to (at)	zu	wheat	Weizen, *m.*
to set	setzen, *reg.*	token	Zeichen, *n.*	to whet	wetzen, *reg.*
to sit	sitzen, *irreg.*	toll	Zoll, *m.*	wit	Witz, *m.*
skirt (apron)	Schürze, *f.*	tongue	Zunge, *f.*		

(c) (i.) English *th* = German d, as in :

bath	Bad, n.	oath	Eid, m.	thine	dein
both	beide	path	Pfad, m.	thing	Ding, n.
booth	Bude, f.	sheath	Scheide, f.	to think	denken, half reg.
brother	Bruder, m.	smith	Schmied, m.	thirst	Durst, m.
cloth	Kleid, n.	south	Süd(en), m.	this	dies(-er, -e, -es)
death	Tod, m.	that	das, daß	thorn	Dorn, m.
earth	Erde, f.	thatch	Dach, n.	thou	du
feather	Feder, f.	the	der, die, das	three	drei
heath	Heide, f.	there	da, dort	throng	Drang, m.
hearth	Herd, m.	thick	dick	through	durch
leather	Leder, n.	thief	Dieb, m.	thumb	Daumen, m.
north	Nord(en), m.	thin	dünn	thunder	Donner, m.

(ii.) English *th* = German t (tt), as in :

birth	Geburt, f.	mother	Mutter, f.	worth	Wert, m.
father	Vater, m.	weather	Wetter, n.		

5. GUTTURAL MUTES :

(a) English *ch* = German f, as in :

anchor	Anker, m.	chamber	Kammer, f.	chest	Kiste, f.
bench	Bank, f.	chapel	Kapelle, f.	chin	Kinn, n.
-chafer	Käfer, m.	cheese	Käse, m.	finch	Fink, m.
chalk (lime)	Kalk, m.				

(b) (i.) English *gh* = German ch, as in :

daughter	Tochter, f.	light	Licht, n.	sight	Sicht, f.
eight	acht	might	Macht, f.	slight (bad)	schlecht
to fight	fechten, irreg.	neighbour	Nachbar, m.	through	durch
flight	Flucht, f.	night	Nacht, f.	wight	Wicht, m.
high	hoch	right	Recht, n.	weight	Gewicht, n.
knight (groom)	Knecht, m.				

(ii.) English *gh* = German g, as in :

dough	Teig, m.	trough	Trog, m.	to weigh	wägen, reg.
plough	Pflug, m.				wiegen, irreg.

(c) English *c* (hard) = German k (ck), as in :

acre	Acker, m.	cleft	Kluft, f.	come	kommen, irreg.
calf	Kalb, n.	climb	klimmen	cook	Koch, m.
can	können, aux.	coast	Küste, f.	corn	Korn, n.
cap	Kappe, f.	cold	kalt	to cost	kosten, reg.
cat	Katze, f.	comb	Kamm, m.		

(d) English *k* (*ck*) = German ch, as in:

ark	Arche, *f.*	like	g-leich	sick	siech
beck (brook)	Bach, *m.*	to make	machen, *reg.*	sickle	Sichel, *f.*
book	Buch, *n.*	milk	Milch, *f.*	spoke (of a wheel)	Speiche, *f.*
to break	brechen, *irreg.*	monk	Mönch, *m.*		
to cook	kochen, *reg.*	oak	Eiche, *f.*	stroke	Streich, *m.*
hark!	horch!	to reek (smoke)	rauchen, *reg.*	token	Zeichen, *n.*
lark	Lerche, *f.*	to seek	suchen, *reg.*	week	Woche, *f.*

(e) English *z* = German chs, as in:

axle	Achse, *f.*	flax	Flachs, *m.*	six	sechs
box	Buchs, *m.*	fox	Fuchs, *m.*	wax	Wachs, *n.*
box	Büchse, *f.*	ox	Ochs(e), *m.*		

6. The liquids *l*, *m*, *n*, *r* present only very isolated variations in the two languages, as:

to freeze	frier-en, *irreg.*	iron	Eisen, *n.*

THE END.

www.ingramcontent.com/pod-product-compliance
Lightning Source LLC
Chambersburg PA
CBHW020258170426
43202CB00008B/425